The Fossils of the Burgess Shale

The Fossils of the Burgess Shale

Derek E. G. Briggs
Douglas H. Erwin
Frederick J. Collier

with photographs by
Chip Clark

Smithsonian Institution Press
Washington and London

To Harry B. Whittington, outstanding paleontologist, mentor, and friend

Copy Editor: Eileen D'Araujo
Production Editor: Duke Johns
Designer: Linda McKnight

Library of Congress Cataloging-in-Publication Data
Briggs, D. E. G.
The fossils of the Burgess Shale / Derek E. G. Briggs, Douglas H. Erwin, and Frederick J. Collier ; with photographs by Chip Clark.
p. cm.
Includes bibliographical references.
ISBN 1-56098-364-7
1. Invertebrates, Fossil—British Columbia—Yoho National Park—Catalogs. 2. Paleontology—Cambrian—Catalogs. 3. Paleontology—British Columbia—Yoho National Park—Catalogs. 4. Burgess Shale (B.C.)—Catalogs. 5. Fossils—Washington (D.C.)—Catalogs. 6. National Museum of Natural History (U.S.)—Catalogs. I. Erwin, Douglas H., 1958– . II. Collier, Frederick J. (Frederick Joseph), 1932– . III. Title.
QE770.B75 1994
562'.09711'68—dc20 93-44198

British Cataloguing-in-Publication Data is available

Manufactured in the United States of America
01 00 99 98 97 96 95 5 4 3 2

∞ The paper used in this publication meets the minimum requirements of the American National Standard for Performance of Paper for Printed Library Materials Z39.48-1984.

Figure 1.1. (pp ii–iii): Wapta Mountain, with Fossil Ridge running southeast from it. The Walcott Quarry is picked out by a bank of snow about halfway up the slope of exposed scree near the right edge of the photograph.

Frontispiece (p. iv): *Hallucigenia sparsa*.

Contents

Foreword

It is to Charles D. Walcott's lasting credit that he found the Burgess Shale, amassed a huge collection of these remarkable fossils, and made the outlines of his find known to paleontologists the world over. How significant his discovery was is only now beginning to be recognized, as not a local aberration to be noted in passing, but as a unique revelation of the extraordinary wealth of the Cambrian biota. How this recognition came about, what it implies for evolution, and the many problems needing further investigation are the themes of this book. Invited by the Geological Survey of Canada to lead a new study of the fossils, and stimulated by A. M. Simonetta's lively new reconstructions of arthropods, I plunged in amid the thousands of specimens of *Marrella* in Walcott's collection. It became plain that much new information on the anatomy of the fossils could be revealed by preparation and that camera lucida drawings, which forced one to look most carefully at what was revealed, were a major aid to interpretation. I was fortunate to be joined by Professor David L. Bruton and Dr. Christopher P. Hughes and to recruit two outstanding research students, Derek E. G. Briggs and Simon Conway Morris. The enthusiasm of Frederick J. Collier for our work, and his unstinting help, encouraged us all. The new photographs in this book show the extraordinary nature of the material we had to work with, and the new drawings summarize our interpretations. A more detailed picture of what the animals were like has now been built up, but is by no means complete, with respect either to Walcott's collection or to the new material garnered by the Royal Ontario Museum's parties. The need to know more about the Cambrian flora and fauna, and how it came to be preserved, offers exciting and challenging avenues for exploration by paleontologists.

HARRY B. WHITTINGTON

Preface

By preserving, with stunning clarity, soft-body parts as well as the more common skeletal record, the fossils of the Burgess Shale provide a remarkable window on the past. Today these fossils are a vital link in reconstructing the rapid unfolding of animal life during the early Cambrian Period, some 540 million years ago. Some animals of the Burgess Shale provide us with the first glimpse of groups that are common today, but others are unlike anything in modern oceans. Indeed, without this window, and similar deposits in China and elsewhere, paleontologists would have only an inkling of the otherwise-hidden history of many early soft-bodied organisms. Today the Cambrian is among the most intensively studied intervals in the history of life, with debates raging over what triggered the rapid appearance of most major groups of animals, how paleontologists should reconstruct the relationships between those taxa, and whether there was something different about the evolutionary process at that time. The animals of the Burgess Shale figure prominently in these debates.

Charles D. Walcott, then Secretary of the Smithsonian Institution, discovered the first Burgess Shale fossils, including *Marrella,* in 1909 and returned to begin excavations during the summer of 1910. Walcott continued quarrying in British Columbia with members of his family from 1910 to 1913 and again in 1917 and returned to look over the spoil piles in 1919 and 1924. He eventually brought over 65,000 specimens to the Smithsonian's National Museum of Natural History. Today the Smithsonian has the largest collection of these fossils in the world, and they serve as the basis for ongoing research by Smithsonian paleontologists and by visitors from around the world. The photographs that form the core of this book convey the visual impact of the Burgess Shale fossils. They are put in context by chapters introducing the history of work on the Burgess Shale deposits, the unusual preservation of the fossils, and the nature of the Cambrian radiation. Further information can be found in the papers listed in the comprehensive bibliography.

Fred Collier initiated this project when he was the collections manager in the Department of Paleobiology, National Museum of Natural History, subsequently recruiting Chip Clark, museum photographer (without whom this book would not have been possible), Derek Briggs, and Douglas Erwin. All the photographs are by Chip Clark except for Figures 1.1, 1.2, 1.3, 1.12, 1.13, 2.1, 2.2, 2.5, *Branchiocaris,* the *Canadaspis* before preparation, *Helmetia,* and *Perspicaris,* which are by Derek Briggs; *Sanctacaris,* taken by Simon Powell; *Fasciculus,* by Ken Harvey and Simon Conway Morris; *Thaumaptilon,* courtesy of Simon Conway Morris; and *Metaspriggina,* courtesy of A. M. Simonetta. Most of the reconstructions were drawn by Larry Isham, formerly with the Department of Paleobiology at the National Museum of Natural History. Others, by Marianne Collins, are reproduced with the kind permission of Stephen Jay Gould from his book *Wonderful Life.* Duncan Friend (Cambridge University) generously supplied his reconstruction of *Eldonia,* and J. Keith Rigby (Brigham Young University) and the Canadian Joint Committee on Paleontological Monographs gave us permission to use Rigby's reconstructions of several sponges. Simon Conway Morris drew the reconstruction of *Thaumaptilon;* other reconstructions were redrawn by Pam Baldaro. R. A. C. Goodison kindly compiled the bulk of the bibliography. Douglas Stewart generously supplied information from his Ph.D. dissertation. We are grateful to Nigel Hughes (Cincinnati Museum of Natural History) and Desmond Collins (Royal Ontario Museum) for critically reading the manuscript and to Ellis Yochelson (National Museum of Natural History) for discussions on Charles Walcott. Elisabeth Valiulis, Howard Jenerick, and Nigel Hughes helped prepare the final manuscript and collate illustrations and text. Finally, we are indebted to Peter Cannell of the Smithsonian Institution Press for his encouragement and for seeing the project through to publication.

DEREK E. G. BRIGGS
Department of Geology, University of Bristol, Bristol, England

DOUGLAS H. ERWIN
Department of Paleobiology, National Museum of Natural History, Smithsonian Institution, Washington, D.C.

FREDERICK J. COLLIER
Museum of Comparative Zoology, Harvard University, Cambridge, Massachusetts

History of Research

Out with Helena and Stuart collecting fossils from the Stephen Formation. We found a remarkable group of Phyllopod Crustaceans. Took a large number of fine samples to camp.

— CHARLES D. WALCOTT'S FIELD DIARY, AUGUST 31, 1909

The Early Years

Charles Doolittle Walcott's Burgess Shale quarry is situated at about 2,300 meters elevation on Fossil Ridge, which runs northwest–southeast from Wapta Mountain to Mount Field (Figure 1.1, pp. ii–iii) in the Canadian Rockies of southern British Columbia. To get to the Walcott Quarry (Figure 1.2), you climb the trail from the town of Field, a hike of about three hours, to the point where it passes below the quarry and the fan of man-made debris that marks it. The last few tens of meters up to the famous site is the real test, scrabbling up the steep scree after the long hike. Even in the early summer, a bank of snow often remains in the quarry, but you can sit at the front and admire the view (Figure 1.3), which is guaranteed to take away what little breath you have remaining. Dead ahead is Mount Burgess, to the right the milky green of Emerald Lake, and to the left you can pick out the Trans-Canada Highway far below, running along the edge of the braided course of the Kicking Horse River. It somehow seems appropriate that the extraordinary fossils of the Burgess Shale were found in such a spectacular setting.

Charles D. Walcott and his family spent the summer of 1909 exploring and studying Proterozoic and Cambrian rocks in the Canadian Rockies, continuing a project begun in 1907 (Figures 1.4, 1.5). Walcott, then Secretary of the Smithsonian Institution and the foremost authority on the Cambrian, was drawn to the area by the thick section of Cambrian rocks, including the famous *Ogygopsis* trilobite beds on Mount Stephen. Toward the end of the

FIGURE 1.2. The talus-filled Walcott Quarry, the back wall to the right, looking northward to Wapta Mountain.

field season, Walcott spent several days looking for fossils near Fossil Ridge. His daily field diary for August 31 (Figure 1.6) records the first mention of the soft-bodied fossils of the Burgess Shale; alongside the notes, Walcott drew sketches recognizable as *Marrella* (which he called the "lace crab"), *Waptia,* and *Naraoia.* The following day he wrote: "We continued collecting. Found a fine group of sponges on slope (in situ). Beautiful warm days." The sketches show the branching form and a detail of the sponge *Vauxia.*

Most paleontological studies are based on the remains of organisms with biomineralized skeletons. Rarely are details of soft parts preserved. By the time Walcott and his family left Fossil Ridge that September, he had realized every paleontologist's dream: the discovery of a suite of soft-bodied fossils, including a number of forms unlike anything ever seen before. Most of the material was collected from slabs on the talus slope. Walcott did find beds in place that September that yielded *Vauxia,* a sponge that occurs in abundance at a number of levels above the most prolific source of soft-bodied fossils.

FIGURE 1.3. Panoramic view westward from the Walcott Quarry. The Trans-Canada Highway can be seen on the left running along the margin of the valley of the Kicking Horse River. Mount Burgess dominates the near horizon. Emerald Lake lies in the valley below, and to the right the steep-sided valley of the Emerald Basin separates Emerald Peak from the President Range. The debris below the quarry is evident in the extreme bottom right.

FIGURE 1.4. Charles D. Walcott standing in the Phyllopod Bed quarry. Note the pick, hoe, and shovel to the right.

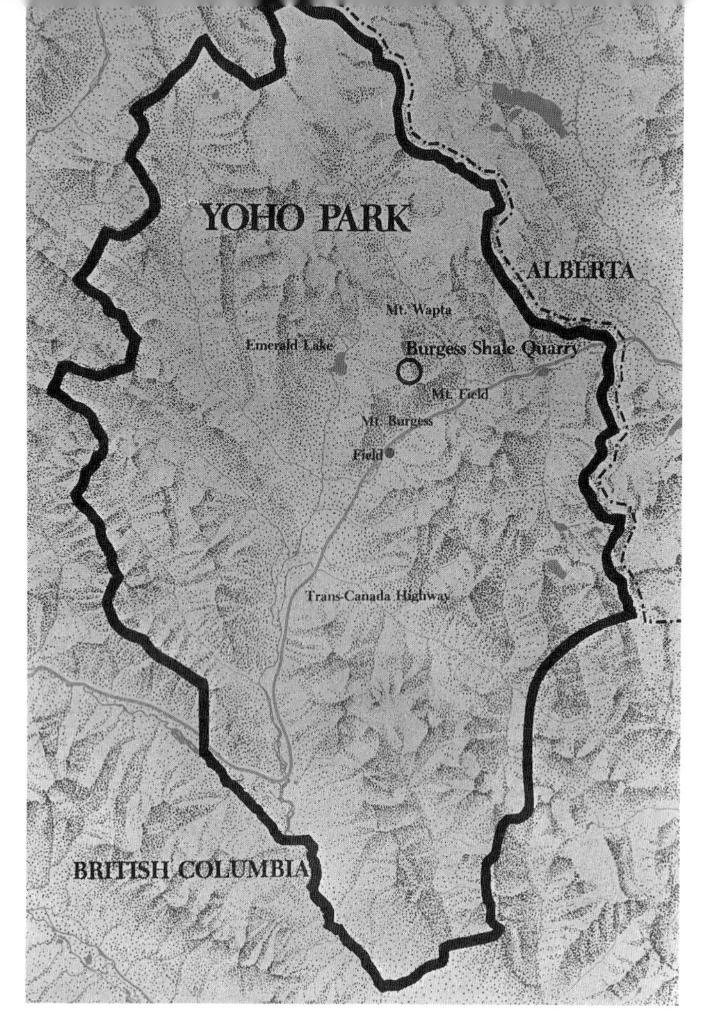

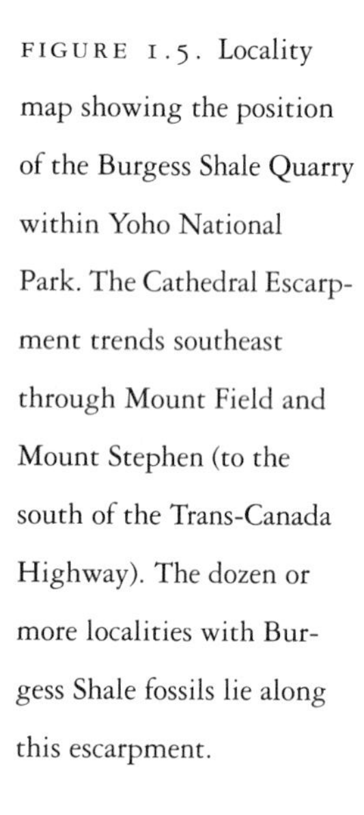

FIGURE 1.5. Locality map showing the position of the Burgess Shale Quarry within Yoho National Park. The Cathedral Escarpment trends southeast through Mount Field and Mount Stephen (to the south of the Trans-Canada Highway). The dozen or more localities with Burgess Shale fossils lie along this escarpment.

Details of the discovery of the soft-bodied fossils are somewhat confused. According to the obituary of Walcott penned by the eminent Yale paleontologist Charles Schuchert in 1927, the party was descending the trail during a snowstorm when Mrs. Walcott's horse slipped. Walcott dismounted to clear a slab of rock blocking the trail and split a piece, revealing a splendid *Marrella.* That was the last day of fieldwork, however, and snow and darkness drove Walcott off the mountain until the following summer. Walcott's field diary belies this sudden departure, however, and clearly a number of soft-bodied fossils were found during the first few days of September 1909. It appears, however, that it was not until the following year, when Walcott returned with his family to exploit the discovery, that the most prolific source of soft-bodied fossils was located. One of the intriguing puzzles surrounding the Burgess Shale is why no one discovered the fossils before Walcott. The trail through the talus was constructed in the

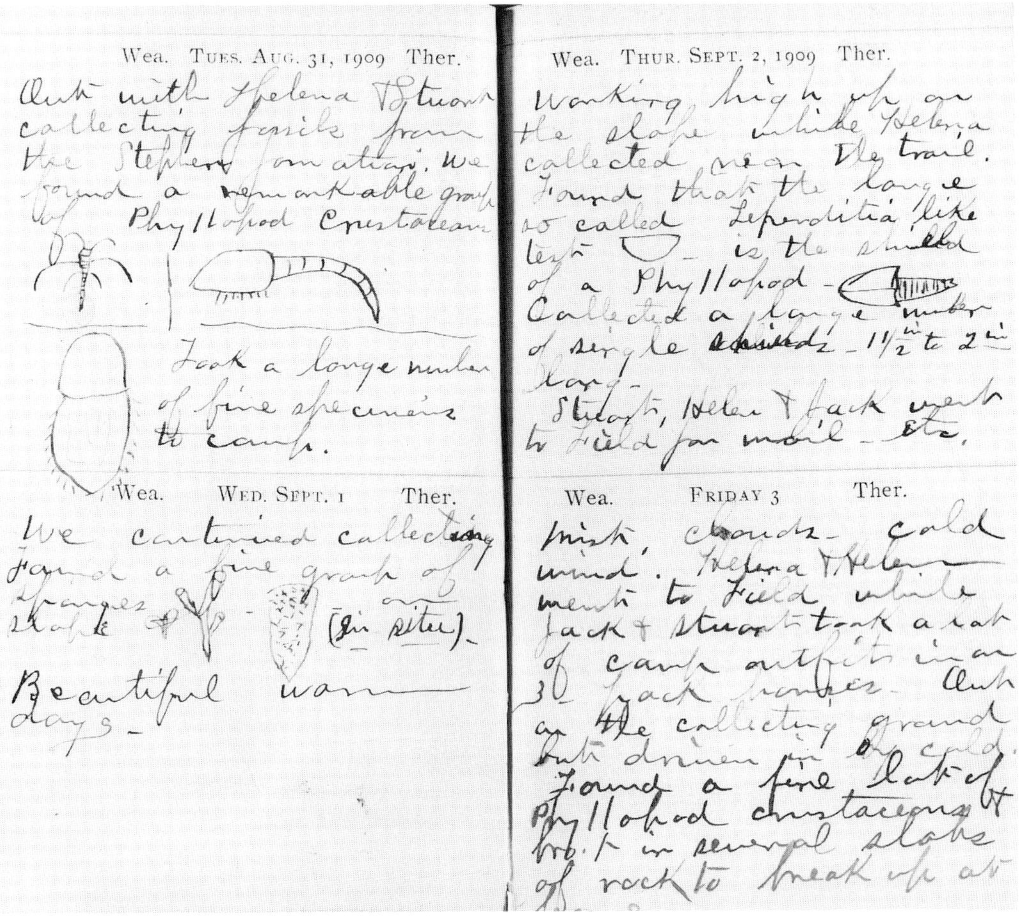

FIGURE 1.6. Walcott's field notes for August 31, 1909–September 3, 1909. The entry for August 31 has the first record of the Burgess Shale fossils and includes recognizable drawings of *Marrella, Waptia,* and *Naraoia.* The "in situ" sponges recorded on September 1 and his statement the following day that they were "working high up on the slope . . ." suggests that Walcott and his party were above the level of the Phyllopod Bed.

early 1900s and was used frequently. In contrast, the *Ogygopsis* trilobite beds on Mount Stephen were discovered by a worker helping build the Canadian-Pacific Hotel in Field and were well known by 1909.

In 1910 Walcott's party set up camp in the forested slopes below Burgess Pass, climbing 120 meters up the slope each morning to attack the shale with picks, shovels, long iron bars, and, later, small charges of explosives (Figures 1.7, 1.8). The "Lace Crab beds" (yielding *Marrella*) were found on August 9. Several other beds also contained soft-bodied fossils over a thickness of 2.3 meters, and the party spent the remainder of the summer excavating this layer, subsequently referred to as the "Phyllopod Bed." By the end of the 1911 season, Walcott recorded that the quarry was 65 feet [20 meters] long, with a floor extending 10 feet [3 meters] into the hill, and a vertical wall varying between 10 and 12 feet [3 and 3.7 meters] high. The beds were split into smaller blocks, then slid down the slope to the camp. There, Walcott's party split the samples and packed them for the trip over Burgess Pass, down

FIGURE 1.7. View of the south end of the Walcott Quarry showing the excavations in progress. Walcott is the figure in the center with his left hand on his hip.

FIGURE 1.8. The Walcott family gathered around the camp table.

to Field, and thence by rail to Washington (Figure 1.9). In the end, Walcott dispatched over 65,000 specimens to Washington.

Despite his increasing responsibilities in Washington, Walcott returned to Fossil Ridge during the summers of 1912 and 1913. Walcott also did some collecting about 20 meters higher up the mountain (at a spot later excavated by Percy Raymond of Harvard University). Besides his work as Secretary of the Smithsonian, Walcott served as President of the National Academy of Sciences, on the National Research Council of the Academy, and helped found the Carnegie Institution, the National Park Service, and the National Advisory Committee for Aeronautics (now part of NASA). Walcott publicized his work in the Canadian Rockies widely, not least with his own remarkable photographs. He took many panoramic shots of the area, including a 2.5-meter-long foldout published with his 1911 article in *National Geographic Magazine*—still the largest photograph ever to grace its pages!

This was a period of personal tragedy as well as triumph for Walcott. He lost his wife Helen during a train accident in July of 1911, but pulled himself together and left for the field a month later. He married Mary Vaux in 1914, although her father refused to attend the wedding because of doubts about Walcott's character! Two of Walcott's sons also died: his namesake, Charlie, in April of 1913 from tuberculosis and four years later his youngest son, Stuart, who was shot down over France while flying for the French Army. Walcott returned to Fossil Ridge for a summer of excavating in 1917 at the age of 67. He collected from the debris in 1919 and 1924, and continued to study the Burgess fossils until his death in 1927. His last paper was published posthumously in 1931, having been assembled by Charles Resser of the National Museum of Natural History from Walcott's extensive notes and illustrations.

The list of species recorded from the Burgess Shale on Fossil Ridge provides some indication of the importance of Walcott's contribution. About 170 species are currently recognized, and of these over 100 were originally described by Walcott himself. His classification of species into major groups, however—divisions like classes and orders at the top of the taxonomic hierarchy—has proved more controversial. Some paleontologists, particularly Stephen Jay Gould in his book *Wonderful Life: The Burgess Shale and the Nature of History,* have criticized Walcott for "shoehorning" some of the more bizarre Burgess Shale creatures into well-known groups and obscuring their evolutionary significance. Certainly Walcott classified the Burgess Shale creatures on the basis of comparisons with living forms, relying largely on the zoological treatises and monographs of the day. Ironically, this emphasis on similarities with modern creatures, at least in determining the position of Burgess Shale animals at higher levels in the classification, may prove to have been a more enlightened strategy than considering them simply as problematic forms of unknown affinity.

With new information, and new techniques and approaches, our understanding of the relationships of the Burgess Shale animals continues to improve. In Walcott's 1911 paper on the Burgess Shale annelids, for example, he included a description of a single specimen of "a slender form with only two strong setae on

FIGURE 1.9. Walcott (to right) packing specimens and camp gear for the trip over Burgess Pass and down to Field.

each very short parapodia" that he named *Canadia sparsa,* interpreting it as a bristle worm (polychaete). In 1979 a much more complete description by Simon Conway Morris was published as part of the restudy of the Burgess Shale. With about 30 specimens, in addition to the one described by Walcott in 1911, Conway Morris was able to demonstrate that the animal was not a polychaete, nor indeed any type of annelid. The morphology appeared so peculiar that he assigned *Canadia sparsa* to a new genus, *Hallucigenia,* and both the animal and its name subsequently acquired considerable notoriety as a symbol of the Burgess Shale. Further insights, prompted by discoveries in the Lower Cambrian rocks of China, have revealed that *Hallucigenia* was originally reconstructed upside down and back to front! More important, it appears to belong to a modern group, the Onychophora, or velvet worms, along with *Aysheaia,* another of the Burgess animals. Onychophorans are caterpillarlike forms with stumpy lobelike limbs that today live exclusively on land. Thus, although Walcott may have misidentified *Hallucigenia* on the basis of the sole specimen that he had collected, his attempt to ally it with a modern group does not appear so misguided after all.

Interlude

The Burgess Shale collections received surprisingly little attention between Walcott's death and the 1960s although the animals were discussed by many authors on the basis of Walcott's original accounts. Professor Percy E. Raymond of Harvard University took the Harvard Summer School out to the Canadian Rockies from 1924 into the 1930s and visited the Walcott Quarry several times. In 1930 he spent 15 days in the Walcott Quarry and also excavated a second quarry about 20 meters higher up the ridge. The Raymond Quarry has produced specimens of *Ottoia, Sidneyia, Leanchoilia,* and *Anomalocaris,* but his fossils, in the Museum of Comparative Zoology at Harvard, are far less numerous and usually not as well preserved as those at Walcott's locality. Franco Rasetti published an account of the trilobites of the Stephen Formation on Fossil Ridge in 1951 as part of a major investigation of the Middle

Cambrian stratigraphy and faunas of the Canadian Rocky Mountains. Rasetti's work on the region was based on four months of fieldwork in 1947 and 1948, during which time he made major collections of trilobites to supplement those made by Walcott. He established a number of trilobite zones through the Stephen Formation that later proved useful in determining the relationships between it and the Cathedral Formation.

Alberto Simonetta, an Italian biologist and ornithologist, visited the National Museum of Natural History as a research fellow in 1960 and began redescribing elements of the Burgess Shale fauna, particularly the arthropods, which he published in four major papers between 1962 and 1970 (with a summary in 1975). Simonetta's work was important because it demonstrated how much new information a restudy of Walcott's collections could yield. Equally, it showed that it was very difficult to accommodate the Burgess Shale forms in the major taxonomic groups recognized today, thereby heralding the debates that were to follow about the evolutionary significance of these Cambrian animals.

Walcott noted that most of the best-preserved fossils came from only a few thin layers within the "Phyllopod Bed." The vast majority of Walcott's specimens at the National Museum of Natural History are labeled 35k, indicating that they came from these layers, but with no indication of the exact level at which they were found. A small number are labeled 35k/10 or 35k/1, indicating the higher level that later became known as the Raymond Quarry. This lack of precise locality information is a feature of both Walcott's and Raymond's material. It makes it difficult to reconstruct community assemblages and analyze patterns of preservation in the Burgess Shale because animals that accumulated during many separate deposition events are combined in the collections.

The Cambridge Project

Much of the impetus for a restudy of the Burgess Shale fauna came from Harry Whittington, an international authority on trilobites, whose office at the Museum of Comparative Zoology at Harvard University was home to Percy Raymond's collection (and is now occupied by Stephen Jay Gould). Whittington approached the Geological Survey of Canada (GSC) with the suggestion that a Burgess Shale project should be initiated. His idea was timely, not only because of the importance of the fauna for understanding Cambrian evolution, but also for the much more prosaic reason that the GSC was engaged at that time in mapping the geology of the Rocky Mountains of British Columbia and Alberta. Thus an investigation of the Burgess Shale formed a natural part of a wider review of the Cambrian stratigraphy of the area. A team led by James Aitken and William Fritz of the Survey together with Whittington (Figure 1.10) excavated the Walcott and Raymond quarries in 1966 and 1967. A primary objective was to record the precise levels in the section where the fossils occurred, but it was also hoped that a collection of the famous Burgess Shale

FIGURE 1.10. Harry Whittington splitting rock in the Walcott Quarry during 1966 or 1967. The white circle on the wall behind Whittington's head marks the datum from which all stratigraphic measurements were taken.

fossils might be obtained for Canada. (At that time the only major collections were in the United States, at the Smithsonian and at Harvard, a situation now redressed by the Royal Ontario Museum collecting expeditions.)

The specimens collected by the GSC number less than 20% of the total amassed by Walcott, and they include few new taxa. However, some specimens have provided vital new evidence of the morphology of particular animals (these include, for example, a specimen showing the large segmented limbs of the head of one of the species of *Anomalocaris* in place). More important, careful documentation of the distribution of trilobites through the Stephen Formation allowed Fritz to show that a change in faunas in the thick shales below the Walcott Quarry also occurred in the much thinner shales high on top of the adjacent Cathedral dolomite. This confirmed that the Burgess Shale sediments were deposited just off the steep front of an enormous limestone cliff that was initially over 100 meters high. Later, Ian McIlreath, while a graduate student with Jim Aitken in Calgary, showed that this same cliff, the Cathedral Escarpment, could be traced for 20 kilometers southeast from the Burgess Shale quarry.

The GSC team concentrated their excavation at the northern end of the Walcott Quarry because the amount of debris left by Walcott and Raymond at the southern end made the outcrop inaccessible. They split some 700 cubic meters of rock and confirmed that the best-preserved soft-bodied fossils occur within about 2.3 meters of the base of the Walcott Quarry. The GSC also made a much smaller excavation at the level of the Raymond Quarry. In 1966, with the excavation stage of the Burgess Shale project under way, Whittington moved from Cambridge, Massachusetts, to take up the Woodwardian Chair at the University of Cambridge, England. The project moved with him.

After the GSC excavations were completed, Whittington embarked on a restudy of the fossils, beginning with the most common, the arthropod *Marrella.* He investigated not only the new GSC collection but also the existing holdings at the Smithsonian and at Harvard (much of Walcott's material had been collected after he had published his preliminary descriptions and had not been prepared or studied in detail). A small number of the arthropods were to be described by Whittington's colleagues, David Bruton at the University of Oslo and Christopher Hughes at Cambridge. It soon became clear, however, that the task was much larger than Whittington had at first envisaged, and in 1972 he took on two graduate students, Derek Briggs to work on arthropods and Simon Conway Morris to study worms.

Under Whittington's leadership, the Cambridge group set new standards for the description of the Burgess Shale fossils. The shale often splits unevenly through the specimens, leaving some of the animal on one slab, the part, and the remainder on the opposing one, the counterpart. Whittington realized that the evidence of part and counterpart could be combined in reconstructing the anatomy of these animals. Careful preparation with a modified dental drill allowed sediment to be removed where it concealed areas of the specimens. More significantly, it proved possible to "dissect" individual specimens, removing layers of the soft parts to reveal details beneath. The carapace of *Canadaspis,* for example, could be removed to uncover the appendages beneath (Illustrations 100, 101) and each limb in turn "dissected" away to reveal the outline of the one below. Where no sediment separates two layers of a fossil (at the base of the limbs where they attach to the trunk, for example), they tend to have fused together during flattening and diagenesis. This makes it difficult, if not impossible, to separate them.

An important aspect of reinvestigating the fossils was illustrating the evidence for new interpretations. High-quality photographs were taken, often in several different illuminations to reveal different features; the contrast between the specimen and the shale surrounding it was enhanced by using ultraviolet light. Photographs were complemented by explanatory drawings, sometimes including the evidence of both part and counterpart. Burgess Shale specimens in different attitudes to the bedding are comparable to photographs of the animal taken from a variety of directions. The animals were not flattened in the way that a shrimp carcass would be if we were to squeeze it between two sheets of glass. When the animals were buried, some decay occurred, sufficient to cause at least the collapse of internal spaces in the carcass, resulting in an almost two-dimensional specimen. Subsequent dewatering and compaction changed the mud into the hard shale in which the fossils are preserved. Distortion was minimal and the relative dimensions of the organism are retained. Realization of this process has allowed the animals to be restored in three dimensions. In some cases it proved useful to prepare a rough three-dimensional model and photograph it from various angles to compare with the fossil specimens. The new reconstructions superseded the few prepared by Walcott (published mainly in the posthumous 1931 paper assembled by Resser), by Raymond, and those made by Simonetta, who was not permitted to "dissect" the specimens. Now computerized image analysis should allow three-dimensional graphic restorations to be produced from photographs of a suite of specimens preserved in different orientations.

The initial focus of the Cambridge project was the preparation of accurate descriptions of the Burgess Shale animals, illustrated in sufficient detail to allow others to assess the evidence for themselves. Subsequently, attention shifted to analyses of the relationships and evolutionary significance of the fauna, with particular reference to the early radiation of the metazoans—the Cambrian explosion. The most striking initial result was the realization that few of the Burgess Shale animals fell within our definition of modern groups. A large number, the so-called Problematica, could not even be accommodated easily in any living phylum. Clearly, something strange had happened in the Cambrian.

The work on the Burgess Shale fauna gained increasing attention among paleontologists as the results of the research carried out by the Cambridge group appeared in print. It was not until 1989, however, when Stephen Jay Gould's book *Wonderful Life* appeared, that the fossils became widely known among the community at large. Gould emphasized the special and peculiar appearance of many of the Cambrian animals, the Problematica, which he epitomized in the memorable phrase "weird wonders." He also argued that chance or contingency played a major role in determining which body plans became extinct and which survived and radiated to populate the earth. But Gould's brilliant account of Walcott's discovery, and of the progress of research and development of our understanding of the evolutionary significance of the Burgess Shale fossils, has done far more than make the story accessible to a wider public. It has also served as an important stimulus to further research on the Cambrian radiation.

More Localities, More Animals

The latest phase of research on the Burgess Shale was begun in 1975 when Desmond Collins, Curator of Invertebrate Palaeontology at the Royal Ontario Museum (ROM) in Toronto, Canada, was granted permission to collect from the loose material on Fossil Ridge. That summer, his ROM team worked systematically through the talus piles below the Walcott and Raymond quarries and the discarded material in the vicinity of Walcott's camp. They

FIGURE 1.11. Desmond Collins (left) and Derek Briggs in the field near the Walcott Quarry, 1981.

found many fine specimens, including rare forms (especially *Tuzoia*) that indicated the possible presence of fossil-bearing horizons on Fossil Ridge in addition to the Walcott and Raymond quarries. Having gained the confidence of the Parks Canada rangers, Collins returned during the summers of 1981 and 1982 to search for additional localities, particularly in the Stephen Formation along the line of the Cathedral Escarpment.

During the first summer, Collins was joined by Derek Briggs, Simon Conway Morris, and James Eckert (Figure 1.11); Briggs returned the following year to join a larger party from the ROM. This reconnaissance work led to some of the most significant discoveries since Walcott's day. The ROM parties demonstrated that the deposits of soft-bodied fossils are far more extensive than previously recognized. At the north end of the Walcott Quarry the fossiliferous deposits are truncated by an abrupt change from the shales of the Stephen Formation to the massive dolomites of the Cathedral Formation; to the south the deposits are disrupted and compressed. Most paleontologists assumed that the Walcott and Raymond quarries were the total extent of the soft-bodied preservation; when Walcott ceased excavations in 1917, he believed that he had recovered most of the preserved fossils. To everyone's surprise, however, Collins and his colleagues uncovered more than a dozen new localities extending over 20 kilometers to the southeast along the Cathedral Escarpment, including outcrops on Mount Field, Mount Stephen, Mount Odaray, Park Mountain, and Curtis Peak, as well as high above the Walcott Quarry on Fossil Ridge itself. Some of these new localities are at about the same stratigraphic level as the Walcott and Raymond quarries, but most are higher or lower, and several yield different assemblages of fossils, probably reflecting different environments.

Several new localities on Mount Stephen, across the Kicking Horse Valley from Fossil Ridge, proved highly productive, yielding over 1,000 specimens. Many specimens of *Ottoia, Leanchoilia,* and other animals characteristic of the Raymond Quarry were found on the north shoulder of Mount Stephen. A locality about 1,500 meters farther southwest (Figures 1.12, 1.13) yielded the

FIGURE 1.12. Des Collins (left) and David Rudkin of the Royal Ontario Museum excavating the new locality on the west side of Mount Stephen that yielded *Sanctacaris,* the first chelicerate (July 1982).

biggest surprises during excavations in 1983, including a new arthropod that Collins nicknamed Santa Claws (Illustrations 131, 132). Santa Claws has five sets of spiny limbs ("claws") forming a sort of prey-capturing basket near the mouth, as well as a rather different sixth limb farther back on the head. When they finally described this arthropod, Briggs and Collins latinized Santa Claws to give *Sanctacaris* (saintly crab!). It proved to be one of the earliest chelicerate arthropods, the group that gave rise to the eurypterids (sea scorpions), horseshoe crabs, and spiders.

FIGURE 1.13. View looking down on the Royal Ontario Museum party excavating the new locality on the west side of Mount Stephen, with the Kicking Horse River below (July 1982).

In 1981, UNESCO designated the Burgess Shale locality a World Heritage site, joining (at that time) 85 other sites ranging from the Grand Canyon to Chartres Cathedral. Research by the ROM group continued from 1988 through 1993. During 1988 they excavated a new locality discovered in 1984 on the upper level at Fossil Ridge, and party members continued to explore both the Ridge and Mount Stephen during 1989. In that year Collins began to employ professional fossil collectors, because they split much larger volumes of rock than the geology and paleontology graduate students who had earlier served on the project. Collins has continued to use two or three experienced collectors, several of whom have subsequently entered university programs in paleontology. During 1990, Collins excavated the *Ehmaniella burgessensis* Zone some 65 meters stratigraphically above Walcott's original quarry on Fossil Ridge. The Raymond Quarry was reopened during 1991, 1992, and 1993. A magnificent new specimen of *Anomalocaris* was recovered during the first year.

The work of the ROM field parties has opened new vistas into the world of the Cambrian, revealing that Burgess Shale–type animals are not confined to Fossil Ridge but occur in a variety of other localities in the region. This development has been compounded by subsequent discoveries in other parts of the world, including younger (Middle Cambrian) examples from Utah and older (Lower Cambrian) examples from Chengjiang in Yunnan Province, China; Sirius Passet in northern Greenland; and the Emu Bay Shale on Kangaroo Island, South Australia. Many of the Burgess Shale animals are not unusual or unique to British Columbia; it appears that they were typical of the Cambrian seas. Successes in discovery and collection have far outpaced the enormous task of description, interpretation, and illustration required to make this new treasure trove of data on Cambrian fossils available to the scientific community. By continuing to accumulate remarkable specimens for future scientific research, Collins and others are storing up vital pieces that will in due course find their place in the jigsaw puzzle of the history of life.

Further Reading

Walcott described his work on the Burgess Shale in the Smithsonian Miscellaneous Collections (1912c, 1913, 1914, 1918a, 1922, 1923b, 1924b, 1925, 1926), and the history of research is discussed in Collier (1983), Collins (1986b), Gould (1989), and Whittington (1971a, 1985b).

Geologic Setting and Preservation of the Fossils

In one of these favorable places the most delicate of organisms, like the jelly fish, have been exquisitely preserved and we have crustaceans of many varieties.

— WALCOTT, JUNE 1911, *NATIONAL GEOGRAPHIC MAGAZINE*, P. 511

The Setting of the Walcott Quarry

The "jelly fish" Walcott reported turned out to be the jaw of the giant Cambrian predator *Anomalocaris,* but the preservation of the Burgess Shale remains no less remarkable, and even now it is only imperfectly understood. The Burgess Shale is the informal term that Walcott used to refer to the fossil-bearing unit. It is now also applied more widely to describe the type of fossil assemblage that is found in the Walcott Quarry. Similar occurrences elsewhere (in China and Greenland, for example) are called Burgess Shale–type faunas. The dark, horizontally bedded shales in the Walcott Quarry belong to a major unit called the Stephen Formation; just over 150 meters is exposed in the section on Fossil Ridge. The best vantage point from which to view the geological setting of the Burgess Shale on Fossil Ridge (Figure 2.1) is from a helicopter. From the air, it is clear that just a few meters to the north of the quarry the Stephen Formation disappears, abutting directly against the massive light-colored dolomites of the Cathedral Formation, named after the spectacular pinnacles of Cathedral Crags. The contact between these two units is almost vertical—indeed Walcott interpreted it as a structural break, a normal fault. However, when the geology is viewed on the face of Mount Field (Figure 2.2), it is evident that overlying the dolomites of the Cathedral Formation is a thin unit of shale that continues uninterrupted across the line of this supposed fault (Figure 2.3). The overlying limestones of the Eldon Formation are likewise unaffected by the abrupt change between the Stephen Formation shales and the

FIGURE 2.1. The scree-covered slope of Fossil Ridge. The Walcott Quarry is picked out by a bank of snow. Not far to the left the contact between the dark-colored shales of the Stephen Formation and the light-colored dolomites of the Cathedral Formation is evident.

FIGURE 2.2. The southeast face of Mount Field photographed from Mount Stephen, across the valley of the Kicking Horse River. The edge of the Cathedral Escarpment is a pronounced feature on the mountain. The contact between the Cathedral and Stephen formations is indicated, as is the boundary with the overlying Eldon Formation.

Cathedral Formation dolomites near the Walcott Quarry. Thus it appears that the contact is not a later tectonic fault (such a fracture would have disrupted the entire sequence), but was a feature of the Cambrian seabed. The shales of the Stephen Formation (including, of course, the Burgess Shale itself) must have been deposited in front of an enormous submarine cliff. This cliff was interpreted by James Aitken and Ian McIlreath as the front of a massive reef built by lime-precipitating algae. Behind it, a carbonate platform developed; beyond it, deeper-water basinal shales were deposited. Initially, the reef built up more rapidly than sedimentation filled the basin. Later, however, the growth of the reef slowed and the basin gradually filled up.

Recently, however, Douglas Stewart put forward a new interpretation of the Cathedral Escarpment that involves erosion rather than the deposition of carbonate. Newly documented exposures of the escarpment provide convincing evidence that the cliff face is the product of large-scale collapse of the platform margin. During much of the deposition of the Cathedral limestones, the reef fringing the carbonate platform grew and migrated farther out into the basin. Finally a 200-meter-thick section of the outer platform be-

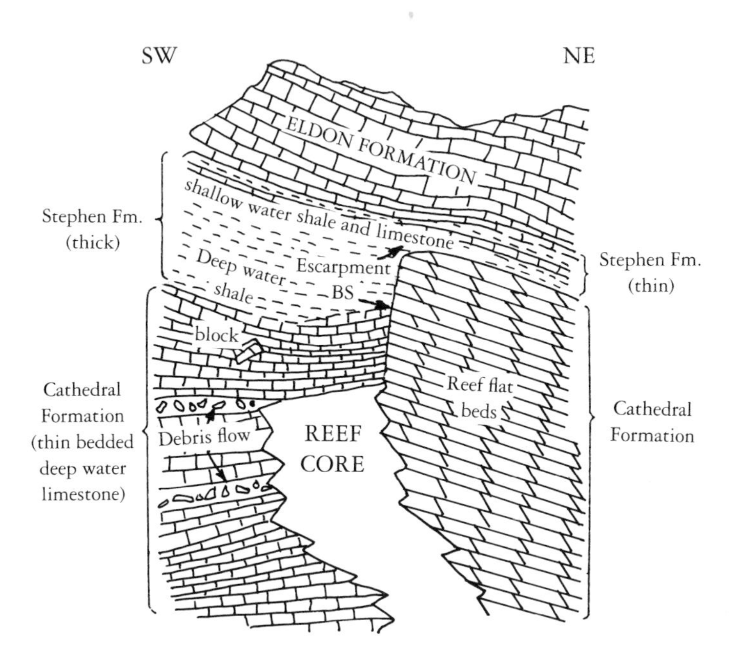

FIGURE 2.3. Explanatory diagram showing the main lithological units exposed on the southeast face of Mount Field. The Escarpment runs northwest through the mountain to crop out at the Burgess Quarry on Fossil Ridge. Soft-bodied fossils were also discovered adjacent to the Escarpment here on Mount Field by the Royal Ontario Museum party in 1981. The Cathedral Formation consists of different units or facies. The "mega-truncation" surface that forms the Escarpment cut through the thin-bedded limestones of the carbonate platform. To the southwest, below the cliff that was formed, muddy limestones, giving way in time to the shales of the Stephen Formation, were deposited in deeper water. Note that the near vertical line of the Escarpment does not continue upward through the thin shales and the thick limestones of the Eldon Formation above as would be expected if it were a tectonic fault. The stratigraphic nomenclature of some of the units within the Cathedral Formation is under revision by W. D. Stewart. [From Figure 3.2 of Whittington (1985b), which was adapted, in turn, from Figure 3 of Aitken and McIlreath (1984).]

came detached and collapsed, probably sliding several kilometers or even tens of kilometers downslope into the basin. The resulting "megatruncation" surface formed the Cathedral Escarpment. It is steep at the top where it formed the cliff, and it curved into an almost horizontal attitude to form the floor of the basin.

Similar megatruncation surfaces are evident elsewhere cutting the overlying Eldon and Pika formations. Such large-scale gravity-slide scars are also known in younger sequences elsewhere in the world, and on modern carbonate platform margins. Clearly their scale is such that they are usually difficult to detect by normal geological field mapping. In the modern oceans they are evident on the seismic profiles studied by geophysicists.

After the formation of the submarine cliff (the Cathedral Escarpment), carbonate sediment continued to accumulate on the platform. Initially, some of this material, including blocks of talus, was transported into the basin; this phase ended with the deposition of the unit called the Boundary Limestone. Later the platform was buried by a major influx of mud, which, together with a rise in sea level, put an end to carbonate production. Subsequent influxes of mud largely bypassed the platform and were deposited in the basin. It was during this stage that the Burgess Shale biota was buried.

The Cathedral Escarpment can be traced from the Walcott Quarry on Fossil Ridge to its outcrop on the front of Mount Field high over the Kicking Horse River, and from there across the Valley onto Mount Stephen. It extends for about 20 kilometers southeast through Yoho National Park. At a number of the places where it outcrops, fossils have been found preserved in a manner similar to those in the Walcott Quarry. The best-preserved fossils are confined to the shales close to the escarpment. Farther away the exceptional preservation is lost and a closely spaced cleavage penetrates the shales, preventing them from splitting parallel to the bedding. This cleavage does not develop where the shales are protected from tectonic deformation by the adjacent Cathedral Formation dolomites.

Because the Cathedral Escarpment appears to have played a

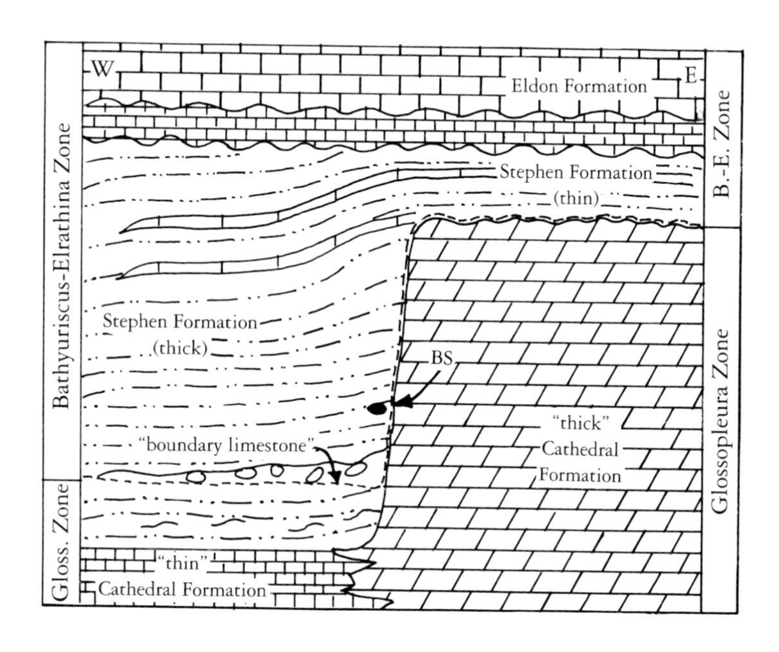

FIGURE 2.4. Diagrammatic cross section of the stratigraphy in the area of the Walcott Quarry showing the position of the boundary between the two trilobite zones, *Glossopleura* and *Bathyuriscus-Elrathina,* in relation to the Cathedral Escarpment. [Adapted from Figure 1 of Fritz (1990).]

critical role in the preservation of the Burgess Shale fossils, it has attracted considerable attention. Obviously the scale of the feature on the side of Fossil Ridge today does not provide a direct indication of the height of the escarpment when fossils were deposited. One way of estimating the height of the escarpment when the Burgess Shale animals were buried is to identify evolutionary changes in the trilobites in the basin and correlate them with similar changes on the top of the reef, making some allowance for subsequent dewatering and compaction of the shales. A change that can be used in this way occurs in the Boundary Limestone, well down in the Stephen Formation. Here trilobites characteristic of the *Glossopleura* Zone occur at the base of the limestone, and those of the *Bathyuriscus-Elrathina* Zone at the top (Figure 2.4). The same change occurs at the top of the escarpment, where the dolomites of the Cathedral Formation give way again to shales, suggesting that the height of the cliff was about 160 meters when the Burgess Shale animals were buried.

To define the height of the escarpment, it is essential that the change in trilobite faunas should have occurred simultaneously in

FIGURE 2.5. The back wall of the Walcott Quarry showing the near-horizontal continuous layers of the Phyllopod Bed. The coarser lower part of each event horizon weathers to a light color; the finer top is dark gray.

the shales in the basin and on the carbonate platform, representing, for example, the extinction of some trilobites and the appearance of others. If, on the other hand, the trilobites changed in response to some environmental fluctuation, this is less likely to have happened at the same time in the basin and on the platform, and it might give an exaggerated indication of the relief on the scarp. Because of these difficulties, we cannot be certain of the exact height of the cliff. Indeed, trilobite expert Rolf Ludvigsen has even offered a radical alternative to the escarpment model—that the Burgess Shale animals might have been deposited on the deeper part of a gently sloping ramp—but his idea is not consistent with the sedimentological evidence. The high scarp towering over the Burgess Shale localities would have provided sheltered areas on the seafloor, low in oxygen, where rapid deposition of sediment might take place.

Transport and Burial

When you stand in the Walcott Quarry on Fossil Ridge and look at the layers of shale exposed and weathered in the back wall, two observations immediately strike you. The first is that the beds are laterally continuous across the quarry (Figure 2.5). They are not obviously disrupted by burrowing and mixing of the sediment, and it is easy to pick out individual layers and follow them along. Clearly these sediments were deposited in bottom waters that were hostile to invertebrates living on or in the sediment. The second striking feature is the clear distinction between the layers. Here is a catalog of sedimentation events, each dumping slightly coarser material at the base, now orange-colored resulting from a higher concentration of calcium and iron. The sediment becomes increasingly finer upward to the top, where the color is dark gray. The thickness of these units varies, but each represents an influx of suspended sediment transported by a current.

The sediment layers were, of course, much thicker when originally deposited and have since undergone dewatering and compaction. The turbulent flow is evidenced by the disposition of the fossils in the rock. The animals were dumped at a variety of angles to the bedding. Certain more hydrodynamically stable attitudes predominate, but rare specimens—of the arthropod *Sidneyia,* for example—ended up enclosed in the mud standing on their heads and are compacted head to tail. *Sidneyia* (Illustrations 149–151) is one of the larger arthropods, up to 15 centimeters in length, and this gives an idea of the thickness of sediment originally laid down. The evidence for turbulent transport, and the absence of signs of animal activity in the layers that produced the best soft-bodied fossils, Walcott's Phyllopod Bed, clearly indicate that the organisms did not live where they are preserved. We have to imagine them living in a "pre-slide" environment (of which we have little direct evidence) before they were picked up and transported in a cloud of sediment (Figure 2.6). They were then buried in the "post-slide" environment, which is where the fossils are found today. The animals were probably killed during transport and burial, through a sudden change in temperature or suffocation in the sediment.

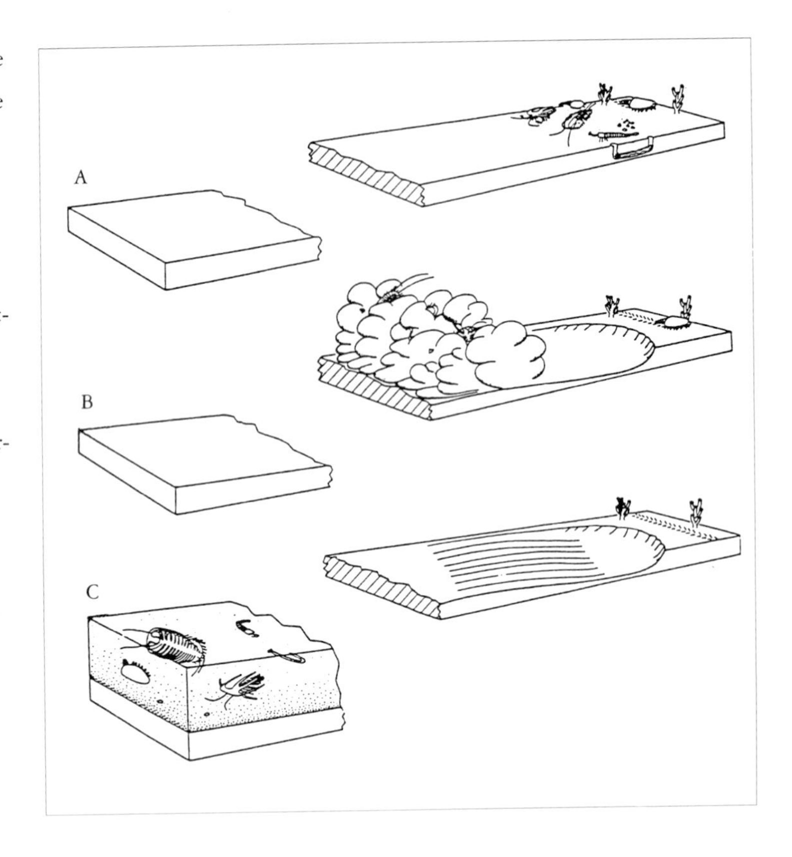

FIGURE 2.6. A sequence of diagrams illustrating the contrast between the pre-slide environment (on the right) and the post-slide environment (on the left). The animals were transported from their original habitat in well-lit muddy bottom waters (A) by a turbulent cloud of sediment (B) to the area now represented by the Walcott Quarry and similar localities (C). [From Figure 3.8 of Whittington (1985b), which was adapted, in turn, from Whittington (1980b).]

What do we know of the pre-slide environment, the living habitat of the Burgess Shale community? The likely living strategies of the various animals, some of which were soft-sediment burrowers, others feeding on organic material in the mud, indicate that they inhabited a muddy bottom site. Most of the Burgess Shale animals lived on the sea bottom, and they include forms that were anchored or sessile, or burrowed in the substrate, as well as those that moved about. The flow that transported them may have been triggered by storms or earth movements, or simply by instability of the sediment pile. It is unlikely that burrowing animals were eroded out of the mud in which they lived and transported away; they are presumably buried in the sediment that they occupied in life. A small proportion of the Burgess Shale animals appears to have swum within the water column (nekton). These are rarely preserved, however, compared with most of the bottom dwellers. They were less likely to be caught up and transported in turbulent clouds of sediment and may even have managed to swim upward and escape to safety.

If we imagine the looming submarine cliff of the Cathedral Escarpment in Cambrian times, we might expect fragments and larger blocks of limestone to break off and tumble into the basin alongside. But as Douglas Stewart has pointed out, after carbonate sedimentation ceased and the platform was buried by an influx of mud, there was no longer a source of carbonate input. Thus, sediment and animals may have been deposited by currents that traveled off the top of the escarpment or parallel to the front. The condition of most of the animals, which show little or no evidence of any damage during transport and burial, might be mistaken as evidence that the biota was not transported far. But experiments on freshly killed worms and shrimps tumbled in a barrel show that they can survive transport over the equivalent of several kilometers without any visible deterioration.

The Burgess Shale community includes a variety of algae that must have lived in the photic zone, to enable photosynthesis to take place. The greatest depth to which light penetrates is some 90 meters. Hence, if the fossils were deposited at a depth of 160 meters at the base of a vertical cliff, the minimum transport distance was 70 meters. However, given that the biota may have been transported some distance on the platform or along the front of the submarine reef, the distance traveled was probably much greater.

Preservation of the Fossils

Soft tissues (i.e., those that are not mineralized in life) are usually preserved in the fossil record in one of two ways. Labile tissues like muscle, which are easily metabolized (i.e., broken down) by microorganisms, decay very rapidly and morphological detail is lost unless the tissue is replicated by a mineral. This type of process is exemplified by the Cretaceous Santana Formation of Brazil, where details such as muscle fibrils and banding, and even cell nuclei, are preserved in calcium phosphate in shrimps, fish, and pterosaurs. At the other end of the spectrum are more decay-resistant tissues like cuticles, which become altered to complex, essentially inert, organic macromolecules. The earliest communities of terrestrial plants and arthropods, which can be extracted from fine-grained nonmarine sediments of Silurian and Devonian age, are preserved in this way.

One of the striking features of well-preserved Burgess Shale fossils is their high reflectivity under incident light. Analysis of the surface of preserved soft tissues reveals a composition similar to mica (a calcium aluminosilicate). However, using delicate extraction techniques involving hydrofluoric acid, Nick Butterfield, then a graduate student at Harvard, demonstrated that at least the more decay-resistant tissues of the Burgess Shale fossils are preserved as a residue of altered original organic carbon. Nor is this preservation confined to just a few tissues. Butterfield isolated sclerites of *Wiwaxia,* setae and body-wall cuticle of the polychaete *Canadia,* cuticle of the priapulid worm *Ottoia,* fragments of the arthropod *Marrella,* and other unidentified scraps of organic material. It appears that these organic residues are covered by a film of aluminosilicates that represent the original clay minerals that were in contact with the carcass. Even delicate tissues that are easily broken down are preserved—many specimens show traces of gut tissues and muscles. In this respect the preservation of the Burgess Shale fossils is anomalous. Under normal circumstances, all but the most resistant tissues decay rapidly even in the absence of oxygen. The morphology is lost unless it is replicated by early diagenetic minerals, and there is no evidence that this has occurred in the Burgess Shale fossils.

There is clear evidence that the Burgess Shale animals have decayed to some degree, although this varies considerably from specimen to specimen. Some, like the arthropod *Marrella,* may show a dark stain around the rear of the body that represents seepage of fluids (Illustration 97). The priapulid worm *Ottoia* displays a range of decay stages, from the detachment of the body wall from the outer cuticle (Illustration 72) to the loss of much of the internal anatomy. The chordate *Pikaia* usually shows shrinkage of the body muscles (Illustration 162). If this decay had taken place before transport, the carcasses would have been broken up by the turbulent currents; it must have occurred after they were buried. In spite of this kind of evidence for decay, however, evidence of labile tissues frequently survives. Something must have acted to inhibit microbial activity.

Butterfield suggested that the mud in which the Burgess Shale fossils are buried may have acted as an agent to prevent decay. Its role, however, must have gone beyond simply smothering the fauna and eliminating scavengers and oxygen. Anaerobic microbes are the primary agent of decay in marine sediments. Butterfield noted that clay minerals prevent enzymatic reactions and stabilize structural polymers. The turbulent transport and deposition of the Burgess Shale animals ensured that mud came into contact with all the spaces in a carcass; indeed, in at least some cases, it even penetrated the body cavity, presumably through rupturing of the wall tissues. More research needs to be done on this aspect of the preservation of the Burgess Shale fossils. Although it is likely that clay minerals played a role in preventing decay, it is probable that only the more robust tissues survived as an organic film. More labile structures like muscle would probably not yield an organic residue even with the most careful acid preparation. However, even in that case, clay minerals probably became aligned on the surface of the tissue before it decayed completely, thus preserving the outline of the morphology.

Evidence for the early processes involved in the preservation of the Burgess Shale fossils is all but obliterated by later diagenetic changes. Other minerals, such as barium sulphate and cerium phosphate, may occur in association with the aluminosilicate film that covers the carbon residue forming the fossils. The remains of hard parts may also be altered. The inarticulate brachiopods retain their original phosphatic composition, and some of the sponges remain siliceous, but analyses of the trilobite *Olenoides* have shown that the calcite exoskeleton is replaced by illite and chlorite. This alteration presumably occurred relatively late in the diagenetic history of the fossils. The trilobites and brachiopods are commonly cracked and fractured as a result of overburden pressure. This suggests that the shells remained brittle and did not dissolve away at an early stage (as a result of a decay-induced increase in acidity, for example). Shells may also be partly replaced by pyrite, which occurs in many Burgess Shale specimens, but rarely in association with the soft parts. The pyrite takes the form of framboids, and although its formation tends to be the result of anaerobic processes, it is likely to have formed at too late a stage to reflect conditions at the time of burial.

The Burgess Shale Community

Modern marine communities are dominated by animals that lack biomineralized skeletons, which may make up as much as 60% of the species and individuals present and have a very low potential for fossilization. The importance of the Burgess Shale and similar Cambrian biotas lies therefore in the complete preservation, which provides critical evidence of the soft-bodied organisms that evolved during the Cambrian radiation. Indeed, in the Burgess Shale community as many as 86% of genera were without a biomineralized skeleton and are therefore not represented at other Cambrian localities, where the soft-bodied component has been lost through decay (Figure 2.7). These percentages emphasize the significance of the Burgess Shale fossils. It is important to realize, however, that the shelly component of the fauna, the trilobites, brachiopods, and hyoliths, is typical of more usual Cambrian assemblages. Clearly, only the preservation of the Burgess Shale fauna is unusual; the soft-bodied animals were widely distributed but are not usually represented in the fossil record.

Because the Burgess Shale preserves soft-bodied organisms as well as those with biomineralized tissues, the collections made by Walcott, Raymond, and the Geological Survey of Canada provide a unique basis for exploring the ecology of a Cambrian community. This aspect of the fauna was studied by Simon Conway Morris, who worked systematically through all the available Burgess Shale material, examining more than 65,000 specimens on over 30,000 slabs of rock! In doing so, he carried out as complete a census of a diverse Paleozoic community as is ever likely to be

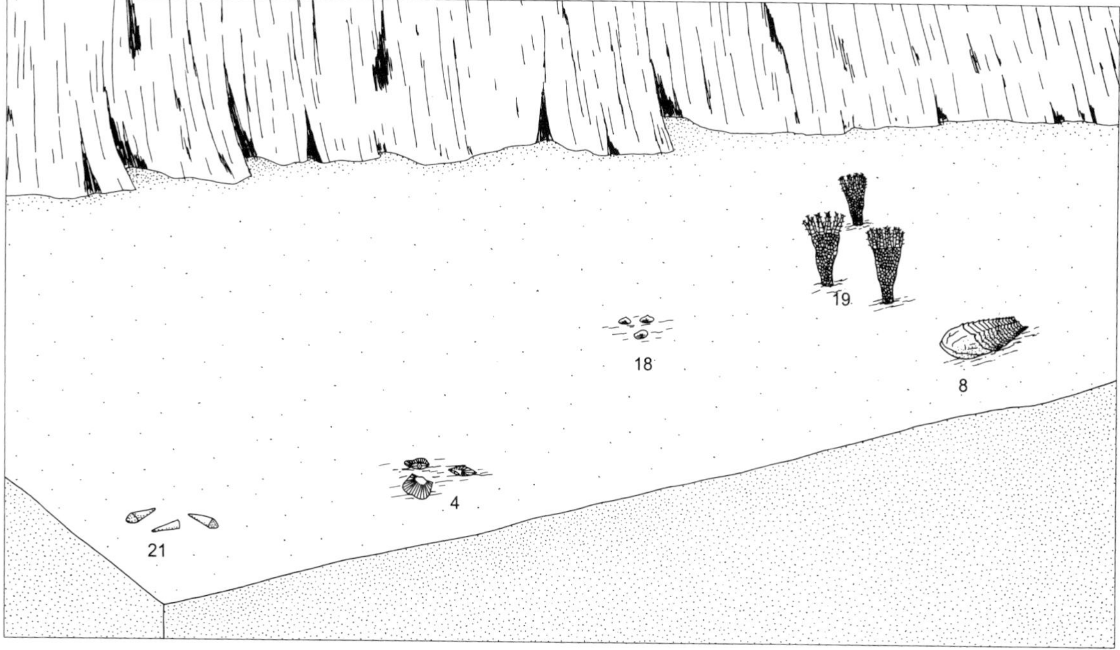

FIGURE 2.7. The top diagram shows a restoration of representative animals from the Burgess Shale community. As many as 86% of the genera present lacked a biomineralized skeleton. The bottom diagram shows the equivalent assemblage preserved at a more usual Cambrian locality where normal decay processes have operated. Sponges: 1, *Vauxia;* 2, *Choia;* 3, *Pirania.* Brachiopod: 4, *Nisusia.* Polychaete: 5, *Burgessochaeta.* Priapulids: 6, *Ottoia;* 7, *Louisella.* Trilobite: 8, *Olenoides.* Other arthropods: 9, *Sidneyia;* 10, *Leanchoilia;* 11, *Marrella;* 12, *Canadaspis;* 13, *Molaria;* 14, *Burgessia;* 15, *Yohoia;* 16, *Waptia;* 17, *Aysheaia.* Mollusc: 18, *Scenella.* Echinoderm: 19, *Echmatocrinus.* Chordate: 20, *Pikaia.* Others: 21, *Haplophrentis;* 22, *Opabinia;* 23, *Dinomischus;* 24, *Wiwaxia;* 25, *Anomalocaris.* [From Figure 3 of Briggs (1991), which was adapted, in turn, from Conway Morris and Whittington (1985).]

achieved. The specimens, however, include not only live animals that were carried in the turbulent, sediment-laden currents, but also shells and discarded molts that had accumulated in the mud before the flows were initiated. To understand the ecology of the living community, it is important to distinguish between these two categories.

Conway Morris estimated that just over 60% of individual Burgess Shale specimens represented organisms that were transported alive. We can deduce their life habits on the basis of morphology, as well as on comparisons with similar living forms. The rudderlike tail of *Odaraia* (Illustrations 103, 105) indicates that it was a swimmer; the sponges, like their modern relatives, presumably fed by filtering particles out of the water. In this way the animals can be subdivided into those that lived in or on the muddy substrate (i.e., were infaunal or epifaunal forms) and those that occupied the waters above. Equally, the bottom dwellers can be further subdivided into those, like the arthropods, that actively moved about (vagrant), in contrast to sponges, for example, that remained attached to the substrate (sessile). Most of the Burgess Shale animals lived on the surface of the sediment. Of those that lived within it, the priapulids, particularly *Ottoia* (Illustrations 71, 72), were the dominant vagrant form. The most important sessile form was an animal similar to modern acorn worms (which has not yet been reinvestigated) that presumably lived in a permanent burrow. Significant among animals living in the water column was *Eldonia* (Illustrations 158–160), a pelagic (floating) sea cucumber (holothuroidean).

The large spinose grasping limbs of *Anomalocaris* (Illustration 164), with its circular jaw and batteries of teeth (Illustration 166), show that it was a predator. The feeding strategies of many of the animals, however, are more difficult to determine. In this muddy bottom setting, most individuals (over 60%) were deposit feeders, consuming organic matter in the sediment itself (this category is dominated by arthropods). Just over 30% were filter feeders, capturing suspended particles in the water. Most of them, like the sponges, fed at a level more than 10 millimeters above the level of the sediment, presumably to avoid clogging up the filtering apparatus with mud. Less than 10% were predators and scavengers.

The impact made by different organisms on the ecosystem may not be accurately represented simply by percentages of individuals. Although the predator *Anomalocaris,* for example, was relatively rare in the Burgess Shale, some individuals reached a length of half a meter, compared with the thousands of specimens of *Marrella* (Illustrations 96, 97) that are less than 2 centimeters long. More realistic assessments of their ecological importance, therefore, may be obtained by taking the relative sizes of the different animals into account. Where the proportions of feeding categories are expressed as biovolumes (using length as a measure), the three categories (deposit feeders, filterers, predators and scavengers) are more nearly equal, reflecting the much larger size of the predatory animals. Modern soft-bottom environments are likewise dominated by deposit feeders, but different animals are important—polychaetes and infaunal bivalves.

Other Burgess Shale–type Faunas

Walcott's Burgess Shale is not unique. Burgess Shale animals are present at over 30 other localities ranging through Lower and Middle Cambrian in age, and not only in North America, but in Greenland, China, Australia, Siberia, Spain, and Poland (Figure 2.8). This observation is important in revealing a pattern of evolution during the Cambrian. It shows that the Burgess Shale–type faunas were widespread, particularly in deeper waters, and that a number of the animals had a long history. It also has significant implications for our understanding of the preservation of these assemblages.

The preservation of soft-bodied animals is not evenly distributed through the fossil record. When the numbers of exceptionally preserved faunas are related to the area of outcrop (which is clearly the most important bias affecting their occurrence) for each period of geological time, it is clear that there are significantly higher numbers in the Cambrian and the Jurassic. The high number of

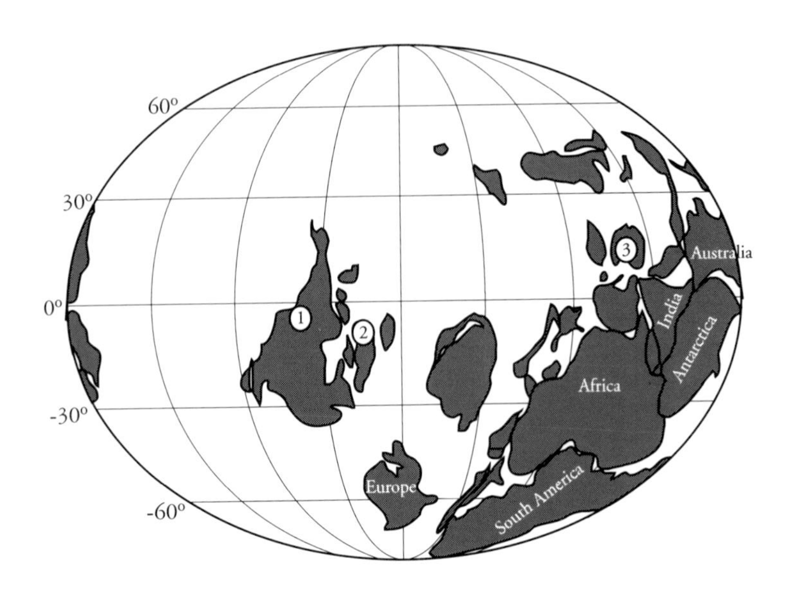

FIGURE 2.8. Paleogeographic reconstruction of Early Cambrian continental positions. The localities of the Burgess Shale (1), Sirius Passet (2), and Chengjiang (3) soft-bodied faunas are marked.

Jurassic biotas (e.g., Holzmaden and Solnhofen in Germany) can be explained by a concentration of restricted marine basins at that time. A more fundamental evolutionary control, however, may have operated in the Cambrian. A critical factor in the preservation of soft-bodied fossils is protection of the carcasses from destruction by scavengers. The thickness of sediment required to eliminate scavengers depends on how deep they can burrow. Thus, if there were fewer deep burrowers in Cambrian times than in later periods, the chances of soft-tissue preservation would be increased. There is some evidence that deep burrowers radiated from nearshore shallow-water environments to offshore deeper-water settings after the Cambrian and, furthermore, that depth of burrowing increased through the late Proterozoic and early Paleozoic. Thus the anomalously high number of exceptionally preserved faunas in the Cambrian may reflect a low diversity of burrowers, particularly in deeper water. Not all the Burgess Shale–type faunas, however, occur in offshore settings; the Chengjiang Fauna of China may be from shallower water. Furthermore, preliminary observations show that some of the Burgess Shale–type faunas are preserved in a manner different from that of the fossils in Walcott's

Phyllopod Bed, including, for example, mineralized muscle tissues. New discoveries of soft-bodied Cambrian faunas are providing more information on the Cambrian radiation. We also need to investigate more fully the preservation of these fossils so that we can understand not only the specimens but also the biases that determine what survives to enter the fossil record.

Further Reading

The preservation of the Burgess Shale fossils is treated by Whittington (1971a, 1980b, 1985b) and Conway Morris (1986, 1990b). Fritz (1971) established the detailed biostratigraphy of the Stephen Formation that supports the escarpment model (see Ludvigsen [1989, 1990]; Aitken and McIlreath [1990]; Fritz [1990] for discussion of an alternative model). Stewart (1991) and Stewart et al. (1993) discussed the truncation model for the Cathedral Escarpment. The discovery of other localities along the Cathedral Escarpment was reported by Collins et al. (1983). Butterfield (1990a) isolated organic remains of the Burgess Shale animals. Briggs and Williams (1981) considered the effects of flattening on the outline of the fossils. Conway Morris (1986) presented a detailed analysis of the structure of the Burgess Shale community, and Briggs and Whittington (1985a) considered the feeding strategies in the arthropods. The distribution of Burgess Shale–type faunas in the Cambrian has been discussed by Conway Morris (1985b, 1989b) and Allison and Briggs (1993a).

The Cambrian Radiation

And so, if you wish to ask the question of the ages — why do humans exist? — a major part of the answer, touching those aspects of the issue that science can treat at all, must be: because Pikaia *survived the Burgess decimation.*

— GOULD, 1989, *WONDERFUL LIFE*, P. 323

When Charles Darwin wrote *The Origin of Species* in 1859, the sudden appearance of animal fossils at the beginning of the Cambrian was of particular concern to him. It was at odds with his view that the diversification of life on earth through natural selection had required a long period of time. Darwin's theory predicted that the major groups of animals should gradually diverge during evolution. He knew that the sudden appearance of fossils would be used by his opponents as a powerful argument against his theories of descent with modification and natural selection. Consequently, he argued that a long period of time, unrepresented in the fossil record, must have preceded the Cambrian to allow the various major groups of animals to diverge. At that time the strata that we now regard as Cambrian were still subsumed within the concept of the Silurian, so Darwin wrote,

> I cannot doubt that all the Silurian trilobites have descended from some one crustacean, which must have lived long before the Silurian age. . . . Consequently, if my theory be true, it is indisputable that before the lowest Silurian strata was deposited, long periods elapsed, as long as, or probably far longer than, the whole interval from the Silurian to the present day. . . . The case must at present remain inexplicable; and may be truely urged as a valid argument against the views here entertained (*The Origin of Species,* 1859, pp. 313–314).

One solution to Darwin's dilemma was to postulate a major hiatus in the sedimentary rock record at the base of the Cambrian and to explain the sudden appearance of fossils as an artifact of preservation. This was the view promoted by Walcott, who argued that the ancestry of the Cambrian fauna was concealed in sediments that were laid down during what he termed the Lipalian Period and are now buried beneath the oceans.

> The apparently abrupt appearance of the Lower Cambrian fauna is therefore to be explained by the absence on our present land areas of the sediments, and hence the faunas of the Lipalian period (Walcott 1910, p. 15).

The nature of the Cambrian radiation has remained controversial since Darwin's day, but has received particular attention in the last 20 years as part of renewed interest in the initial radiation of animal life. We now know that no lengthy interval of nondeposition is represented below the base of the Cambrian. Equally, research has revealed that the rocks of the Precambrian are not as barren of fossils as Walcott supposed. There is evidence for a long period of Precambrian evolution, but the appearance of diverse shelly fossils near the base of the Cambrian remains abrupt and not simply an artifact of inadequate preservation.

The rate at which the first metazoans evolved and radiated remains a controversial issue. Virtually all of the phyla and classes of animals that have biomineralized skeletons, and are therefore readily preserved, first appeared during a geologically short interval of about 20 million years from the latest Proterozoic (the Vendian) to the earliest Cambrian (Figures 3.1, 3.2). (Systematists have grouped organisms into a heirarchy based on evolutionary relationships, beginning with kingdom as the most inclusive unit and ranging down through the progressively more restricted levels of phylum, class, order, and family to the genus and species.) But the Cambrian radiation involved far more than just the development of hard skeletons. Groups lacking a biomineralized skeleton, including many of those represented in the Burgess Shale, also di-

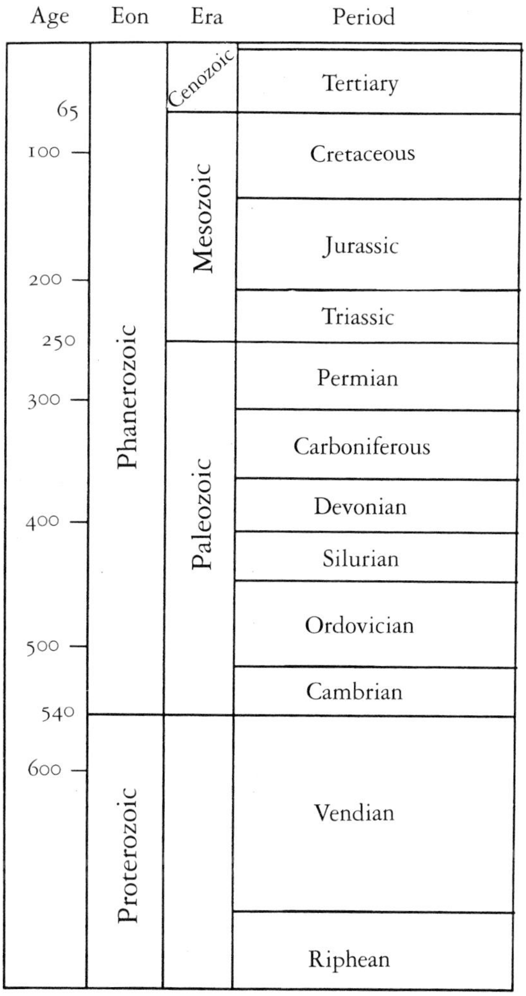

Age: 65, 100, 200, 250, 300, 400, 500, 540, 600

Eon	Era	Period
Phanerozoic	Cenozoic	Tertiary
	Mesozoic	Cretaceous
		Jurassic
		Triassic
	Paleozoic	Permian
		Carboniferous
		Devonian
		Silurian
		Ordovician
		Cambrian
Proterozoic		Vendian
		Riphean

FIGURE 3.1. Geologic time scale.

versified, as did a variety of single-celled organisms. This rapid burst of evolutionary innovation established all the major body plans that are present in the modern fauna, but the relationships of some of the other groups that appeared in the Cambrian remain unclear. Paleontologists continue to debate how rapidly the metazoan radiation occurred, what biological or physical events triggered it, and what lessons this event holds for our understanding of evolutionary processes and the history of life.

Many Cambrian animals lacked a mineralized skeleton and are therefore only preserved under the unusual conditions that pre-

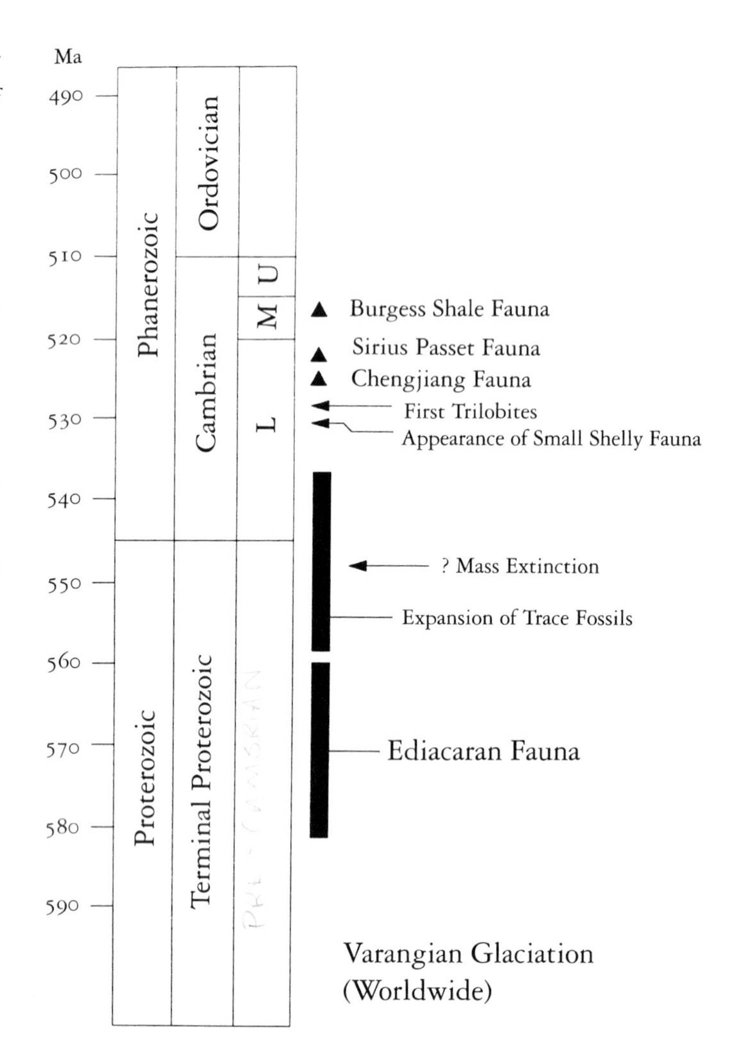

FIGURE 3.2. Major physical and biological events of the Neoproterozoic (latest Precambrian) and Cambrian. The time scale is based on Bowring et al. (1993). Note that selection of rocks in Newfoundland as the definitive section for the Neoproterozoic/Cambrian boundary places the boundary much earlier than the first appearance of trilobites or the first diverse small shelly fossils.

vailed in the Burgess Shale and similar deposits. The bizarre *Opabinia* (Illustrations 173–175), with its five pedunculate eyes and long flexible "proboscis" ending in grasping spines, and *Anomalocaris* (Illustrations 164–166), perhaps the most fearsome predator of Cambrian seas, provide us with a glimpse of what might have been had these animals persisted into the modern oceans. The Burgess Shale remains the most significant fossil discovery to our understanding of the metazoan radiation, but it has confronted paleontologists with as many questions as it resolves.

The End of the Proterozoic

Our story begins about 2 billion years ago, some 1,500 million years before the animals of the Burgess Shale were entombed. The fossils of the Proterozoic, as the last interval of Precambrian time is known, are not readily preserved. Occurrences are limited to relatively rare assemblages of single and aggregated cells enclosed in chert (and protected by the durability of the silica of which it is composed), occasional discoveries of larger cysts, and some trace fossils. Thick organic-walled cysts, known as acritarchs, are thought to have been produced by marine algae. Because prokaryotes do not produce such cysts, these acritarchs represent the earliest record of eukaryotes—and some of them occur in rocks as old as 2.1 billion years. The appearance of eukaryotes is an event of major evolutionary significance because, in contrast to the simpler prokaryotes, they have a discrete nucleus separating the DNA from the rest of the cell, as well as organelles such as chloroplasts and mitochondria. Although the reasons remain unclear, the rate of morphologic diversification is much higher in advanced eukaryotes (which include organisms from amoebas and simple algae to humans) than among any other group. Molecular and some paleontologic evidence suggests that a major radiation of eukaryotes into a variety of more complex forms took place about 1 billion years ago, giving rise to the lineages that eventually led to fungi, plants, and animals.

There are no fossil animals in rocks as old as a billion years. Reliable trace fossils, such as trails and burrows, are known from rocks about 650–700 million years old; more doubtful examples have been reported ranging from 700 to 1,000 million years in age. The first well-documented animal fossils are the impressions known as Ediacaran biotas, named after the locality in Australia where they were first discovered.

The Ediacaran Biota

In 1946 R. C. Sprigg, an Australian geologist, discovered abundant impressions of unusual "jellyfish" in the Ediacara Hills of South Australia. He recognized that these animals were soft-bodied and represented some of the oldest animal fossils yet found.

Extensive fieldwork by Sprigg, and later by Martin Glaessner and other geologists from the South Australian Museum and the University of Adelaide, revealed an assemblage of these soft-bodied impressions and associated trace fossils that became known as the Ediacaran Fauna. Ediacaran fossils have subsequently been found in Vendian rocks on every continent except Antarctica. These Proterozoic fossils fall into four major types. Most abundant are circular impressions reminiscent of jellyfish and other medusoid animals. The second most common type is trace fossils, a range of horizontal tracks and burrows formed by wormlike animals. Third, there are a number of benthic forms whose affinities with Cambrian and later animals remain unclear. Finally, many attached, frondlike organisms have also been discovered.

The higher taxonomic affinities of the Ediacaran Fauna remain controversial. Some animals, particularly the medusoids, display a very simple grade of organization and probably had a body wall made up of only two layers of cells (i.e., they are diploblastic, with ectoderm and endoderm). They may be coelenterates, related to modern jellyfish and corals, although many of the fossils are so simple that paleontologists are uncertain whether the similarities indicate relationship or are just the result of convergent evolution. Other Ediacaran animals have a more complicated organization and were likely triploblastic, with an additional layer of cells (the mesoderm) with the potential to develop into organ systems. These forms may be related to echinoderms, annelid worms, and arthropods.

In 1983 the German paleobiologist Adolf Seilacher offered a challenging alternative to the more conventional interpretation of the Ediacaran animals. Seilacher suggested that most of the Ediacaran forms, apart from the trace fossils, represent an independent radiation of animal-like organisms. He recognized a commonality of design; the animals appear to be constructed like an air mattress, in a fashion quite different from any modern metazoans. This structure, which presumably evolved to maximize surface area for feeding and respiration, is exemplified by the large, flat *Dickinsonia,* which reached dimensions of up to 1 meter. Seilacher interpreted the Ediacaran organisms as members of a distinct lineage that he called vendobionts rather than metazoans. He regarded them as a failed evolutionary experiment that was terminated by the advent of predators on such large sessile organisms. Seilacher's novel hypothesis has yet to gain wide acceptance. However, although most of the Ediacaran fossils are still widely regarded as true metazoans, the systematic affinities of many of them with Cambrian and later groups are far from clear.

A prolonged Late Proterozoic glacial period preceded the main radiation of the Ediacaran Fauna. Evidence of the last part of this episode, named the Varangian glaciation (after the region of northern Norway where it was first recognized), has been found on most continents in rocks from 610 to 590 million years old. Sediment sequences in the Mackenzie Mountains of western Canada display evidence of several different glacial episodes that bracket the earliest occurrence of Ediacaran-like fossils in that region. The oldest Ediacaran assemblages, like that on Mistaken Point in the Avalon Peninsula of Newfoundland, are generally composed of less-complex animals than later examples, such as the original discovery in the Ediacara Hills. Thus, although these animals began to diversify during the glacial epoch, they did not reach maximum levels of diversity or complexity until the glaciers had receded. Whether or not the Varangian glaciation played a role in the onset of the metazoan radiation is a subject of debate among paleontologists.

Most of the Ediacaran organisms disappear from the fossil record well before the beginning of the Cambrian. Some paleontologists argue that this loss represents the first mass extinction in the history of animals. It is not clear, however, to what extent the absence of Ediacaran forms in later sedimentary rocks simply reflects the loss of the conditions that favored their preservation. The increase in the diversity of tracks, trails, and burrows that occurs toward the end of the Proterozoic may herald an increase in scavengers and bioturbators. Indeed, the Proterozoic-Cambrian boundary itself is now recognized by the first occurrence of a distinctive horizontal burrow known as *Phycodes paedum.* Burrowing and scavenging would have promoted the degradation of carcasses and greatly reduced the chances of preservation. We cannot tell how abruptly the Ediacaran Faunas became extinct, but only a very small number are represented by possible survivors in the Burgess Shale (e.g., *Thaumaptilon* [Illustrations 40, 41]).

The Cambrian Explosion

Although the increase in metazoans is the most striking feature of the Cambrian radiation, it is also marked by a rapid diversification of algae and protists. Darwin and his contemporaries were quite familiar with the profusion of trilobites that marked the base of the Cambrian, but subsequent work has revealed that many other groups either appear in the fossil record at that time or diversify significantly. These taxa include a variety of acritarchs, radiolarians, foraminiferans, and calcareous algae and a range of metazoans, with and without biomineralized shells. The diversity and abundance of trace fossils also increased markedly during that interval. Early Cambrian body fossils show that most of the metazoan groups had reached an advanced stage of construction; they are eucoelomates, like the annelids, molluscs, and echinoderms, with a body cavity lined by mesodermal tissue. The analysis of differences in the genetic material (ribosomal RNA) of living animals suggests that the different eucoelomate groups diverged rapidly early in their history, evidently near the base of the Cambrian.

The main ingredients for the Cambrian radiation were assembled in the Vendian: Ediacaran metazoans, simple behavior patterns as revealed by trace fossils, and the first small shells. The Cambrian, however, witnessed a pronounced diversification. More varied trace fossils start to appear first. They include branching and spiraling burrows, U-shaped and more complex laminations known as spreite that record migration through the sediment, and trails and resting traces. These testify to the evolution of more-advanced behavior patterns. The first diverse shelly organisms come on the scene later. They are known collectively as small shelly fossils and include a variety of tiny cones, tubes, spines, and plates. Many are composed of calcium phosphate and can be collected in the residue when limestones are dissolved in acid. Some, which look like the shells of tiny snails, correspond to a single organism. Others, called sclerites, unite to form a skeleton of different elements (the scleritome) that protected the exposed parts of an animal with a kind of armor. Of course, once the animal died and began to decay the scleritome disarticulated. Only exceptionally preserved specimens allow paleontologists to reconstruct these primitive creatures. *Wiwaxia* from the Burgess Shale (Illustrations 178–180), one of the late examples of this kind of skeleton, provides evidence of the complete scleritome, although the sclerites were not biomineralized. Although small shelly fossils persist through the Cambrian, the number of species begins to decline during the middle of the Lower Cambrian, and by the Middle Cambrian they are fairly insignificant.

As the small shelly fossils begin to disappear, the first trilobites are found, along with a number of other arthropod groups, inarticulate brachiopods, various echinoderms, and an aberrant group of sponges with a conical calcareous skeleton, known as archaeocyathids. This marks the development of typical Cambrian assemblages. Archaeocyathids and trilobites are the most abundant Lower Cambrian fossils; other groups are a less significant part of the marine fauna until the Middle Cambrian.

The diversification of so many different lineages during the late Proterozoic and earliest Cambrian has prompted a range of hypotheses to explain this sudden burst of evolutionary innovation. The search for a cause has naturally focused on changes in the physical environment as a way of accounting for simultaneous change across the spectrum of different groups of organisms and ecosystems. For a time the debate concentrated on the appearance of mineralized skeletons, which provide the most dramatic evidence of the Cambrian radiation in the rock record. Skeletons might have evolved in response to the attainment of a critical threshold in levels of atmospheric oxygen or in the chemistry of the oceans. Skeletons, however, are only one manifestation of the Cambrian radiation; any hypothesis also has to account for a diversification of soft-bodied organisms and for the increase in behavioral complexity evident in the trace fossils. Oxygen levels could have had an impact beyond the evolution of skeletons; a certain concentration would have been necessary to permit larger, more complex animals to evolve. But changes in continental configurations, in ocean currents, and in climate (in response, for example, to glaciation) are also candidates for triggering the radiation.

Another suite of explanations involves factors intrinsic to life itself, rather than responses to environmental perturbations. The evolution of larger size may have initiated other evolutionary changes, such as an increase in complexity or the appearance of skeletons. The development of particular life strategies may have accelerated diversification—predation, for example, may have prompted the acquisition of skeletons for protection. Genetic mechanisms may even have differed in the early Cambrian from those that prevail today; more genetic flexibility could have promoted variation and accelerated diversification. In spite of the variety of hypotheses that have been offered to explain the Cambrian radiation, however, no clear explanation has yet emerged. The emergence of metazoans remains the major unresolved enigma in the history of life.

The Significance of the Burgess Shale Fauna

What role does the Burgess Shale fauna play in understanding the Cambrian radiation? Most obviously it gives us an unrivaled insight into the large number of Cambrian organisms lacking a mineralized skeleton that we would otherwise have missed. Over 80% of Burgess Shale genera are soft-bodied and therefore absent from contemporaneous shelly assemblages. Thus the Burgess Shale affords much more complete data than any other locality on the range of Cambrian organisms. For this reason it provides critical evidence of the results of early metazoan evolution.

Although Charles Walcott was impressed with the unusual morphologies of many of the Burgess Shale fossils, he tended to assign them to existing families and orders, taxa that frequently also included living species. The investigations of the Cambridge group revealed unusual morphologies and showed that placement of a number of these animals in accepted taxa was far from straightforward. Emphasis on some of the more bizarre attributes of the Burgess Shale fossils, at least by comparison with living animals, led to claims for a number of additional phyla (perhaps as many as 20). It follows that during the early Cambrian levels of diversification (at least by this measure) far exceeded anything since. Briggs and colleagues have focused on morphologic similarities, rather than differences, between Cambrian and later animals. Their reexamination of relationships, using cladistics (a technique now widely applied by taxonomists), shows that the Burgess Shale arthropods, at least, may be interpreted as early offshoots of the major modern groups. In addition, quantitative comparisons of form suggest that the range of morphology evident among Cambrian animals may be little greater than that among modern groups. Indeed, the limits of morphological evolution appear to have been established during the Cambrian and persisted to the present day.

The Burgess Shale fauna has dramatically expanded our knowledge of the Cambrian radiation. Only in the past 25 years, however, have paleontologists begun to explore fully the significance of Walcott's discovery to our understanding of the Cambrian radiation or, more generally, of the history of life. The research is still far from complete. There is considerable debate over many of the issues raised by new analyses of the Burgess Shale animals. Was the level of morphologic innovation higher during the Cambrian than subsequently, or is this impression simply an artifact of the way we classify animals? What triggered the metazoan radiation? Why did it begin when it did rather than earlier or later? Was it triggered by climatic change associated with the Varangian glaciation or by some other environmental shift? Alternatively, did the explosion of metazoan diversity simply reflect an exponential phase in their evolution, requiring nothing more than the existence of animals themselves? Scientists are actively debating all of these questions and have yet to reach a consensus on any of them. The broad spectrum of possibilities raised by recent studies of the Burgess Shale, however, demonstrates how single discoveries, like the one made by Walcott in 1909, can dramatically change our view of the history of life on earth.

Further Reading

The Ediacaran Fauna is discussed by Glaessner (1984); other pertinent references to the Ediacaran include Knoll (1992) and Schopf and Klein (1992). Recent references to the Cambrian radiation include Conway Morris (1992, 1993), Lipps and Signor (1992), Whittington (1980b), Valentine and Erwin (1987), and Valentine et al. (1991). The debate about morphological disparity in the Cambrian is addressed in Gould (1991a) and in the papers by Briggs et al. (1992a,b, 1993).

The Fossils of the Burgess Shale

This section includes illustrations, reconstructions, and discussions of all of the major types of fossils from the Burgess Shale. There are representatives of 85 of the 125 recognized genera. This selection is by far the most comprehensive set of photographs of the Burgess Shale organisms published outside the technical literature. It provides an unrivaled suite of images of Cambrian life. The text accompanying the illustrations aims to provide, with a minimum of technical detail, an outline of the morphology, mode of life, and affinities of the organism. The taxa are arranged in systematic (evolutionary) order, beginning with the Cyanobacteria. Within each higher taxonomic group, the taxa are arranged alphabetically. A complete list of all currently accepted species described from the Burgess Shale follows the illustrations.

We have also included, for the specialist in search of further data, the following information: the identity of the species, the author and date of the original description, the museum number of the specimen, the size of the organism, the artist who drew or redrew the reconstruction, the proportion of the Burgess Shale assemblage that it represents, where it occurs, where it is described, and additional relevant literature.

The proportions of the algae are not given. Conway Morris (1986) estimated that specimens of algae account for some 11.3% of all Burgess Shale fossils, but this is based on counting each slab, even with multiple algal pieces, as a single specimen. Estimates for the proportions of different animal taxa are more accurate. They are based on Conway Morris's (1986) estimate that 40,368 individual animals were alive at the time of burial. Thus the percentages give an indication of the numerical importance of different taxa in the original faunal community. Animals with no preserved soft parts do not contribute to the analysis; it is assumed that none was buried alive. The figures quoted are based on Conway Morris et al. (1982) and Conway Morris (1986).

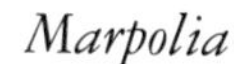

2

Marpolia

Marpolia appears to be very similar to a modern cladophoran alga, with a dense, twisted mass of filaments. The form of individual specimens varies considerably, apparently depending on their attitude to the bedding when the cloud of sediment carrying them settled to the seafloor. The lack of an attachment structure for *Marpolia* suggests that it may have been a floating mass or, if the structure simply was not preserved, it may have grown attached to various objects as do many modern cladophoran algae. *Marpolia* is very common on some bedding planes, where it almost completely covers the surface of the slab, as in Illustration 1. Elsewhere only a few stray filaments are found. In his original description of *Marpolia,* Walcott suggested that this form was a blue-green alga, but noted that it might also represent a member of the Chlorophycea (green algae).

Marpolia spissa Walcott, 1919. USNM 194191. Size: individual tufts average 3–6 cm. Isham reconstruction. Occurrence: Middle Cambrian Stephen Formation Burgess Shale, *Ogygopsis* Shale, and adjacent localities (Collins et al. 1983). Description: Walcott (1919). Other important references: Walton (1923), Whittington (1985b), Conway Morris and Robison (1988). Note: the Burgess Shale algae were redescribed in a thesis by Satterthwait (1976).

1 (×2)

3 (×2.5)

Algae

CHLOROPHYTA (Green Algae)

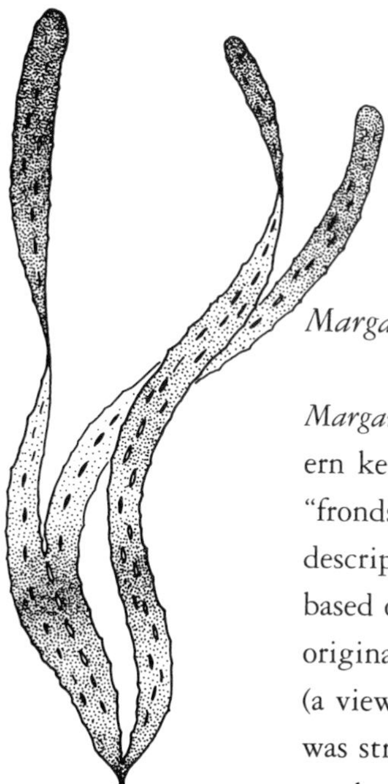

Margaretia

Margaretia appears to be a thin, frondlike alga, perhaps like modern kelp, with multiple strands attached to a narrow base. The "fronds" were perforated by a network of small oval holes. The description of this genus was published after Walcott's death, based on his notes that were assembled by Charles Resser. In the original notes Walcott believed the fossils to represent an alga (a view that is generally accepted), but later notes show that he was struck by the similarity between *Margaretia* and alcyonarian corals. Further discussion of the affinities of this genus awaits restudy of the specimens.

4

Margaretia dorus Walcott, 1931. USNM 83922. Size: 12.1 cm. Isham reconstruction. Occurrence: Middle Cambrian Stephen Formation Burgess Shale and adjacent localities (Collins et al. 1983). Description: Walcott (1931). Other important reference: Conway Morris and Robison (1988).

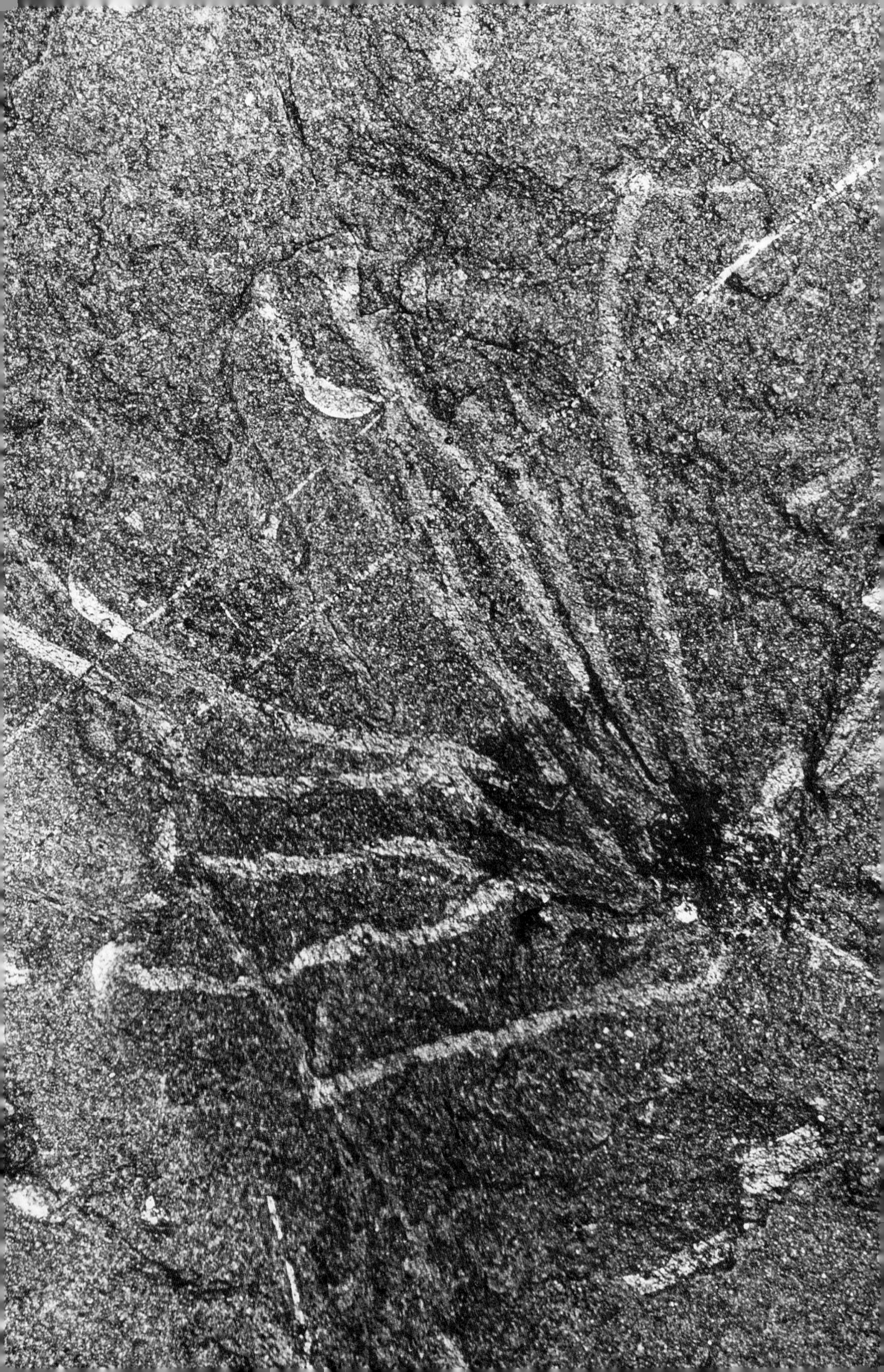

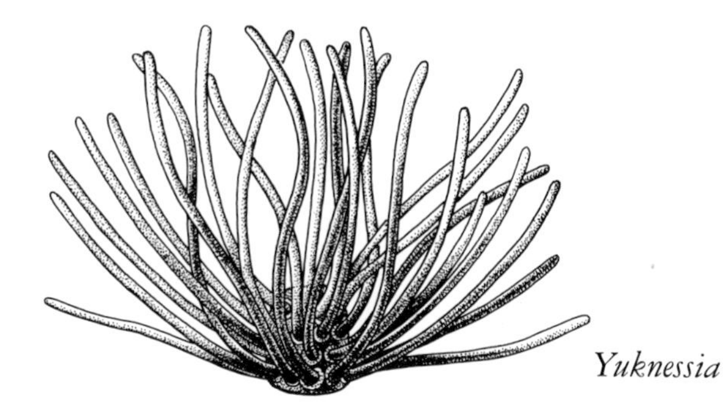

Yuknessia

6

Only three good specimens are known of this unusual alga, which consisted of a hollow, central body covered with small, closely arranged conical plates. The plates formed the attachments for long, flexible, and unbranched stipes that radiated from the body. *Yuknessia* was probably attached to the bottom. Like most of the algae from the Burgess Shale, this form is not well studied. Walcott suggested that *Yuknessia* was a green alga, but with considerable doubt, noting that it lacked any of the structures usually found in members of that group.

Yuknessia simplex Walcott, 1919. USNM 35408. Size: 21 mm. Isham reconstruction. Occurrence: Middle Cambrian Stephen Formation Burgess Shale, *Ogygopsis* Shale, and adjacent localities. Description: Walcott (1919). Other important reference: Conway Morris and Robison (1988).

5 (×7)

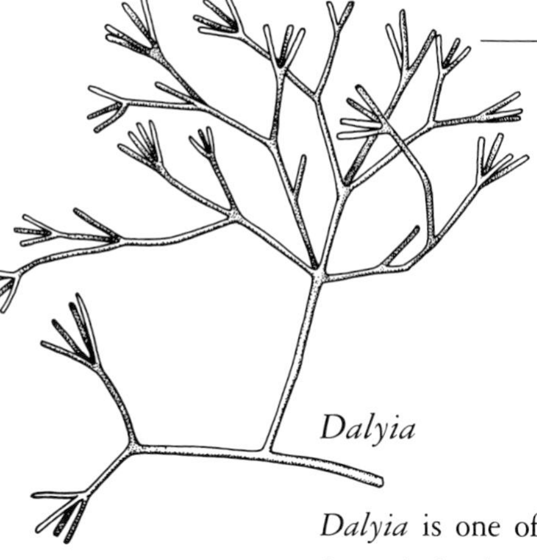

Dalyia

8

Dalyia is one of the more beautiful algae of the Burgess Shale. Several slender stems branched from the central stem and ended in a whorl of short, thin branchlets. The stems are generally smooth, but some specimens show a faint trace of transverse lines. Little else is known of this genus.

Dalyia racemata Walcott, 1919. USNM 35419. Size: 48 mm. Isham reconstruction. Occurrence: Middle Cambrian Stephen Formation Burgess Shale, *Ogygopsis* Shale, and adjacent localities. Description: Walcott (1919).

7 (×5)

Waputikia

Waputikia differs markedly from the other algae of the Burgess Shale with its large central stem interrupted by large branches, which in turn have a profusion of smaller branches and filaments. This is one of the most highly branched species within the collection. The surface of the fossils is smooth and almost shiny, without a hint of internal structure. All of the specimens known are fragmentary, the largest reaching a length of about 6 cm. The whole organism would have been much larger, but the actual size is difficult to determine. *Waputikia* commonly occurs with *Morania,* a form that Walcott assigned to the blue-green algae, but *Waputikia* is believed to belong to the Rhodophyta (red algae).

Waputikia ramosa Walcott, 1919. USNM 277815. Size: 19 mm. Isham reconstruction. Occurrence: Middle Cambrian Stephen Formation Burgess Shale. Description: Walcott (1919).

9 (×5)

11 (×6.5)

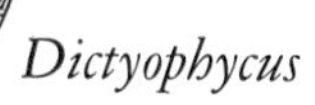

Dictyophycus

12

The fossil specimens of *Dictyophycus* consist of a mesh of very delicate fibers, with occasional circular pores. The living alga probably looked much like the reconstruction shown here (Illustration 12), a soft, frondlike alga. However, as with many of the other algae, much of the sheet decayed, leaving behind only the delicate fibers that supported it. Many of the fibers were broken during transport, and their base or point of attachment is missing. *Dictyophycus* has not been formally redescribed and hence its affinities are not well understood.

Dictyophycus gracilis Ruedemann, 1931. USNM 83483b. Size: 25 mm. Isham reconstruction. Occurrence: Middle Cambrian Stephen Formation Burgess Shale. Description: Ruedemann (1931).

Phylum Porifera

CLASS DEMOSPONGIA (Demosponges)

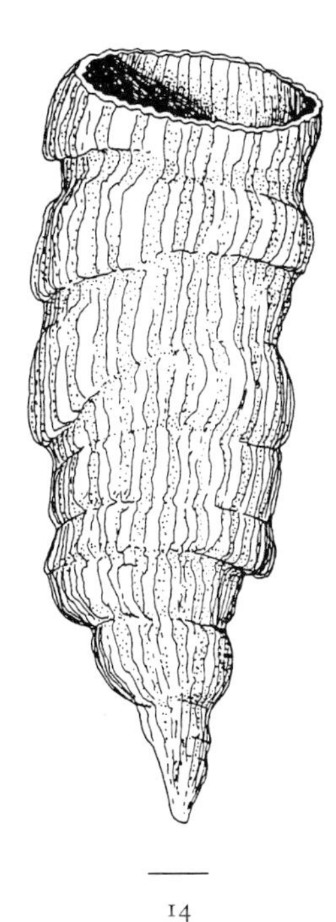

14

Capsospongia

This is a rare sponge; only two specimens are known. *Capsospongia* was conical, with a narrow base and undulating sides. The simple linear spicules that composed the skeleton were arranged into closely packed vertical columns connected by short horizontal spicules. Water currents presumably entered the sponge through the undulating wall and exited at the open end of the cone.

This demosponge belongs to one of the major families of the early Paleozoic, the Anthaspidellidae. Walcott originally named the genus *Corralia* but that name had already been used for a spiderlike arachnid, so a new genus, *Capsospongia,* had to be erected to accommodate the specimens.

Capsospongia undulata (Walcott, 1920). USNM 66479. Size: length 60 mm. Reconstruction from Rigby (1986). Proportion of total Burgess Shale assemblage in terms of numbers of individuals: <0.01%. Occurrence: Middle Cambrian Stephen Formation Burgess Shale. Description: Rigby (1986).

13 (×4)

15 (×6)

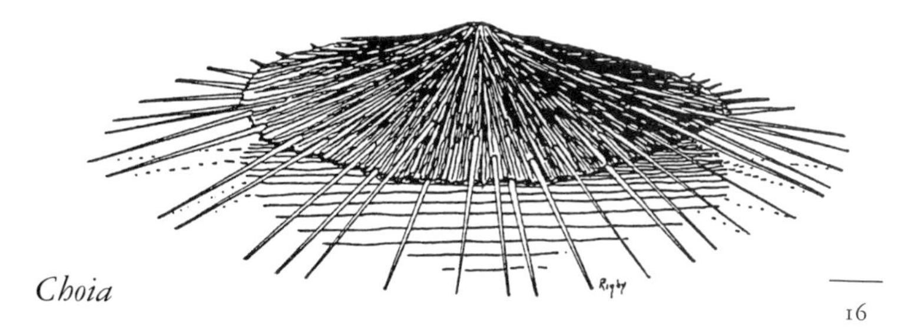

Choia

16

Choia is an unusual sponge, consisting of a small, thin disk with radiating spines, some of which extended far beyond the margin, giving the impression of a small, thatched hat. The nearly flat convex surface, from which the spines radiated, appears to be the upper surface, and the concave surface lay on the seafloor. This orientation of *Choia,* the opposite of that suggested by Walcott, would have been more stable in a current, making the sponge less likely to be overturned by wave action. Water currents appear to have entered the sponge parallel to the long spines, passed through, and exited near the center. *Choia* was an unattached sponge that simply lay on the substrate and filtered food particles out of the water. Several different species of *Choia* have been described from the Middle Cambrian, but only two are known from the Burgess Shale. This demosponge is placed in its own family, the Choiidae, within the Monaxonida.

Choia carteri Walcott, 1920. USNM 66482. Size: 28 mm, including spines. Reconstruction from Rigby (1986). Proportion of total Burgess Shale assemblage in terms of numbers of individuals: <0.1%. Occurrence: Middle Cambrian Stephen Formation Burgess Shale, *Ogygopsis* Shale, and adjacent localities (Collins et al. 1983), as well as several localities in the Middle Cambrian of Utah. Description: Walcott (1920), Rigby (1986).

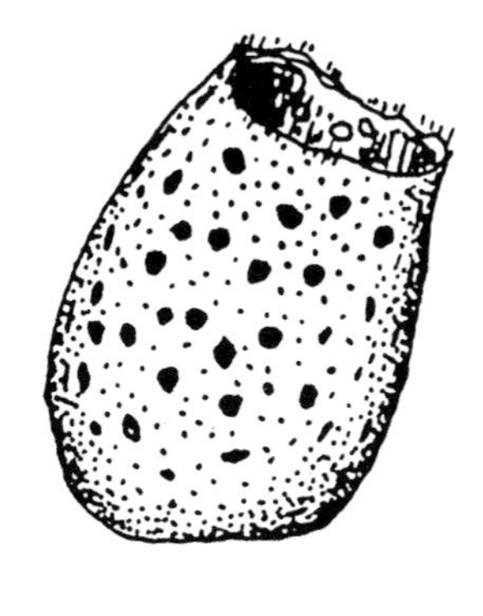

18

Crumillospongia

Crumilla is Latin for a small leather money purse, which describes the shape of this sponge quite well. It was saclike or globular with a thin wall pierced by small, circular holes of two different sizes. These holes were the openings for canals through the interior of the sponge. The canal system in the interior of *Crumillospongia* was far better developed than that in most Cambrian sponges. The spicules were long and straight (monaxial) and arranged in parallel vertical columns. The outer surface of the sponge was a regular thatch of spicules. Water currents entered through the openings in the wall, passed through the sponge, where food particles were removed, and then exited through the exhalent opening at the top. No evidence of an attachment structure has been found, so it is unclear whether or not this sponge lived anchored to the substrate.

The demosponge *Crumillospongia* appears to be related to the large genus *Hazelia* and to *Falospongia,* which also occur in the Burgess Shale, and all three genera are grouped into the Family Hazeliidae. The saclike shape of *Crumillospongia* easily differentiates it from the broad, open cones of *Hazelia* (Illustrations 21–24).

Crumillospongia biporosa Rigby, 1986. USNM 66778. Size: 21 mm. Reconstruction from Rigby (1986). Proportion of total Burgess Shale assemblage in terms of numbers of individuals: <0.01%. Occurrence: Middle Cambrian Stephen Formation Burgess Shale. Description: Rigby (1986).

17 (×7)

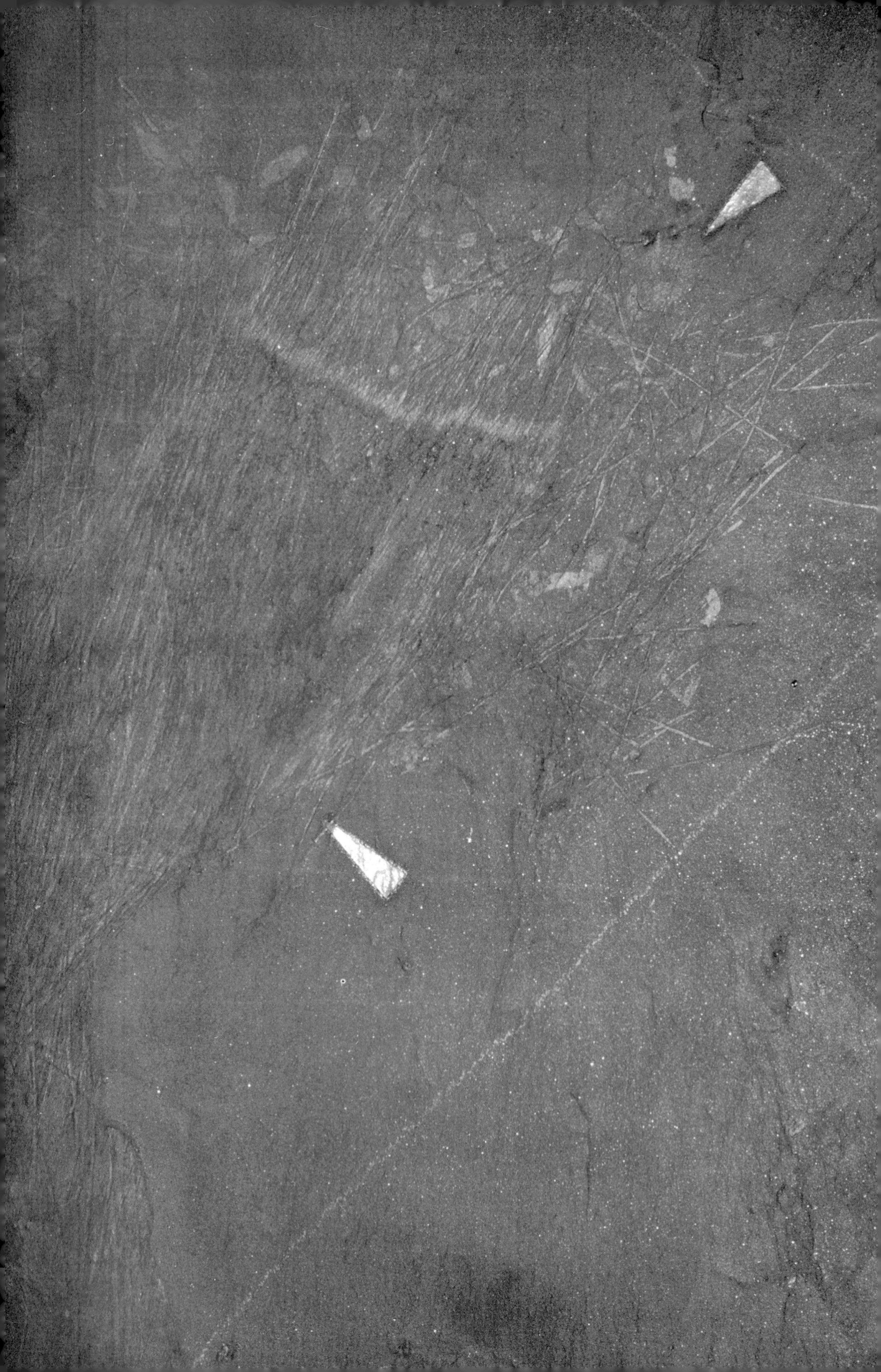

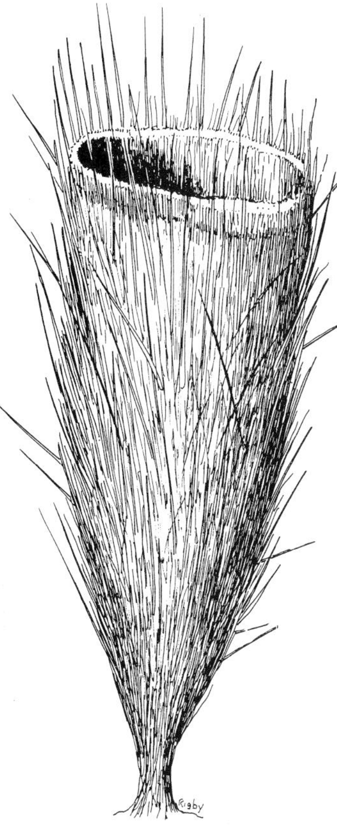

20

19 (×1)

Halichondrites

Halichondrites was a thin-walled sponge that began as a cone and developed into a long tube. A variety of different-sized spicules were present, but the major part of the skeleton consisted of simple vertically arranged spicules that formed a sort of hairy thatch. In fact, this sponge can best be described as hirsute. *Halichondrites* is the largest sponge in the Burgess Shale, and one of the largest known from the Middle Cambrian. No canals are obvious on the surface of the sponge, so water must have entered through small pores between the thatch before exiting through the top of the cone. The illustrated specimen, the only moderately complete example ever recovered, was folded over onto itself during burial. Because the base of the specimen is missing, the means of attachment to the seafloor is unknown. Other fragments of *Halichondrites* have been recovered from the Burgess Shale, indicating that the sponge broke apart during transport.

The demosponge *Halichondrites* may have evolved from an early species of *Leptomitus* (Illustrations 25, 26) by an increase in the size of both the individual spicules and the sponge as a whole. The affinities of *Halichondrites* have been the subject of some debate. Walcott considered the sponge to be so unlike other Cambrian sponges that he established a new suborder for this genus alone. Later, *Halichondrites* was grouped with *Leptomitus,* but more recently it has been placed in a separate family, the Halichondritidae.

Halichondrites elissa Walcott, 1920. USNM 66447. Size: 21.5 cm. Reconstruction from Rigby (1986). Proportion of total Burgess Shale assemblage in terms of numbers of individuals: <0.01%. Occurrence: Middle Cambrian Stephen Formation Burgess Shale. Description: Rigby (1986).

Hazelia

Species of *Hazelia* ranged in morphology from broad, cup-shaped forms; to long cones; to branching, club-shaped forms. All shared a moderately thin wall consisting of small, closely spaced spicules that diverged toward the wall, producing a plumose pattern. Small canals pierced the wall, allowing water to enter the sponge. Two species are illustrated. The specimen of *H. delicatula* shows three conical-cylindrical branches (Illustration 24). Although *H. delicatula* is similar in form to *Vauxia* (Illustrations 31, 32), the skeleton of delicate tufts of spicules is distinctly different from the double wall of fibers in that sponge. The specimen of *H. conferta* is a single conical specimen (Illustration 22); neither the top nor the base is complete. The skeleton is made up of two layers, one of vertically elongate spicules and one of radiating tufts. The former is more obvious in this specimen.

Nine species of *Hazelia* have been described from the Burgess Shale. This demosponge genus displays the most diverse morphology of any of the Burgess Shale sponges. It is closely related to *Falospongia* and *Crumillospongia,* and the three genera are placed together in the Family Hazeliidae.

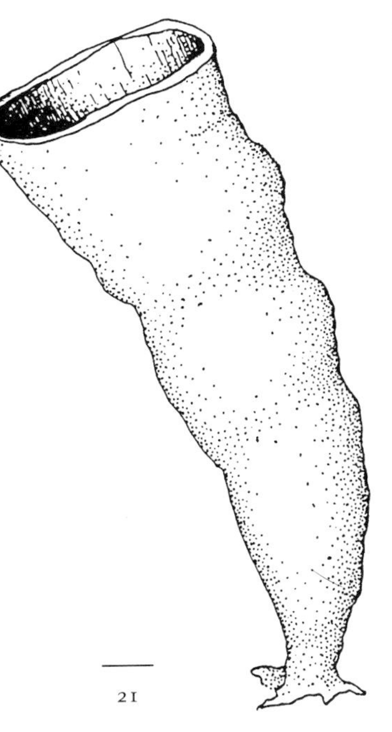

21

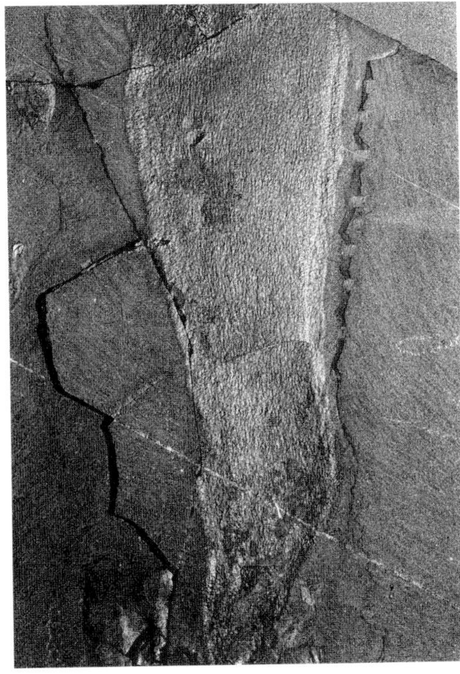

22 (×1)

Hazelia conferta Walcott, 1920. USNM 66469. Size: main branch 10 cm long. Reconstruction from Rigby (1986). Proportion of total Burgess Shale assemblage in terms of numbers of individuals: <0.1%. Occurrence: Middle Cambrian Stephen Formation Burgess Shale. Description: Rigby (1986).

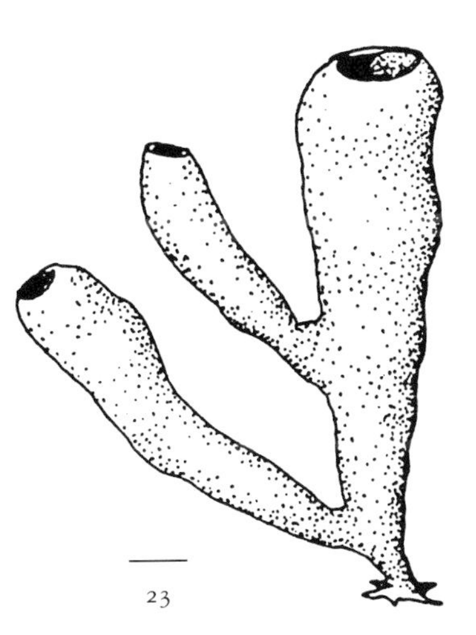

23

24 (×1)

Hazelia delicatula Walcott, 1920. USNM 66465. Size: main branch 66 mm long. Reconstruction from Rigby (1986). Proportion of total Burgess Shale assemblage in terms of numbers of individuals: <0.1%. Occurrence: Middle Cambrian Stephen Formation Burgess Shale. Other species of *Hazelia* have been recorded from the *Ogygopsis* Shale and adjacent localities (Collins et al. 1983). Description: Rigby (1986).

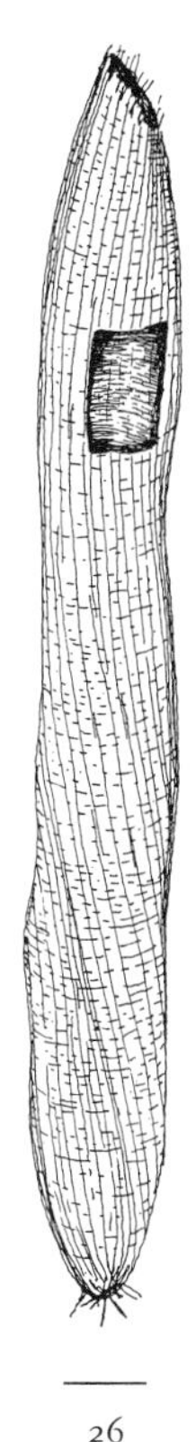

26

Leptomitus

Leptomitus was a very elongate, double-walled tubular sponge with a skeleton characterized by simple monaxial spicules arranged vertically, as shown in the illustration. The species of *Leptomitus* in the Burgess Shale have better-developed skeletons than those in earlier species. The skeleton was double-layered. The outer layer consisted of long, vertical spicules interspersed with densely packed short secondary vertical spicules. The inner layer was composed of a thatch of tiny horizontally arranged spicules. Wrinkling of the outer surface is apparent in many specimens and seems to result from uneven distribution of the primary vertical spicules. *Leptomitus* lived attached to the substrate and filtered water through the wall. The photograph shows only a portion of the entire specimen, which is 36 centimeters long.

Leptomitus is the earliest known demosponge and appears to be the root for the subsequent diversification of a variety of Middle Cambrian sponges. New types of sponges evolved from *Leptomitus* by elaboration and specialization of the skeleton. Genera derived from *Leptomitus* in this way include *Choia, Halichondrites, Hazelia, Pirania,* and *Wapkia. Leptomitus* is placed in the Family Leptomitidae with a few other genera of early sponges.

Leptomitus lineatus (Walcott, 1920). USNM 66448. Size: 36 cm. Reconstruction from Rigby (1986). Proportion of total Burgess Shale assemblage in terms of numbers of individuals: <0.1%. Occurrence: Middle Cambrian Stephen Formation Burgess Shale and adjacent localities (Collins et al. 1983). Description: Rigby (1986).

25 (×10)

27 (×4)

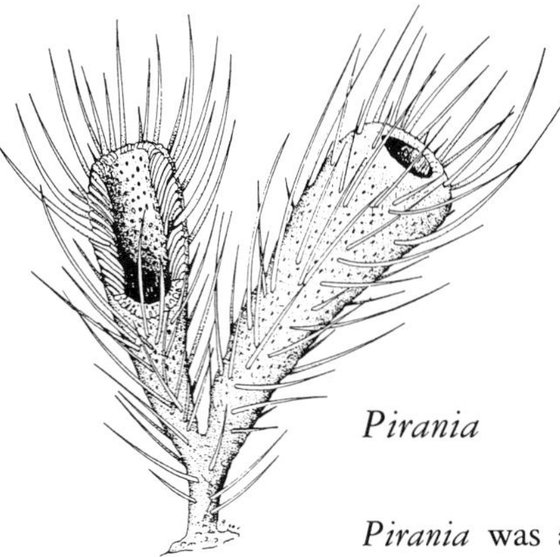

28

Pirania

Pirania was a branching, thick-walled cylindrical sponge with large marginal spicules coming off the external wall. Small canals pierced the thick walls parallel to the marginal spines, allowing water to flow into the relatively spacious interior of the sponge. The sponge had up to four branches.

Specimens of *Pirania* are often found with specimens of the articulate brachiopod *Nisusia* attached by their pedicle. Unlike most associations of fossils in the Burgess Shale, which are simply chance results of transport and deposition, these appear to be faithful records of the association of the sponge and these brachiopods during life. The sponge would have provided an attachment site for the brachiopods above the seafloor. The brachiopods may even have benefited, during feeding, from the currents generated by the sponge. *Pirania* may be related to *Hazelia* and the other sponges of the Family Hazeliidae, but is placed in its own family, the Piraniidae.

Pirania muricata Walcott, 1920. USNM 66495. Size: 32 mm. Reconstruction from Rigby (1986). Proportion of total Burgess Shale assemblage in terms of numbers of individuals: 0.32%. Occurrence: Middle Cambrian Stephen Formation Burgess Shale, *Ogygopsis* Shale, and adjacent localities (Collins et al. 1983). Description: Rigby (1986). Note: Whittington (1985b) illustrated brachiopods attached to *Pirania.*

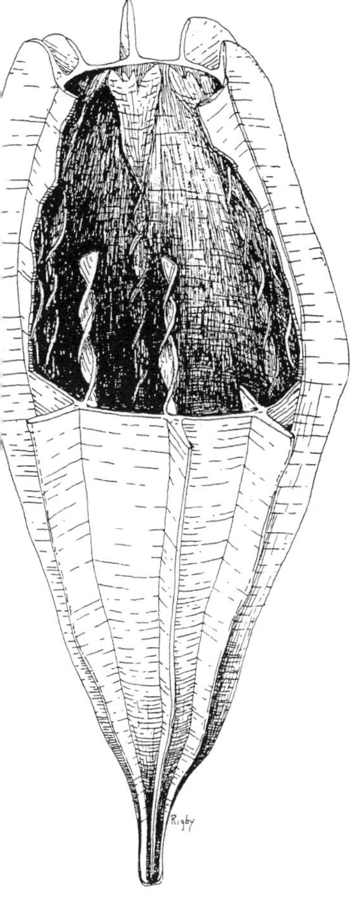

30

29 (×5)

Takakkawia

Takakkawia was a conical sponge with eight stiff, bladelike fins projecting radially from the outer surface that were connected on the interior to long, twisted, vertical ribbons of spicules. These spicules were elongate monaxial forms. The general shape of *Takakkawia* is similar to that of *Leptomitus* (Illustrations 25, 26), from which *Takakkawia* probably evolved, but *Leptomitus* lacks the fins and spiraling ribbons. The base of *Takakkawia* was very narrow, as shown in the illustration. These sponges appear to have lived on the seafloor. No pores or openings are evident in the walls of *Takakkawia,* so water must have seeped in between the spicules before exiting through the relatively large upper opening.

Takakkawia is such an unusual sponge that it is placed in a separate family, the Takakkawidae.

Takakkawia lineata Walcott, 1920. USNM 66539. Size: 40 mm. Reconstruction from Rigby (1986). Proportion of total Burgess Shale assemblage in terms of numbers of individuals: <0.1%. Occurrence: Middle Cambrian Stephen Formation Burgess Shale and south face of Mount Field. Description: Rigby (1986).

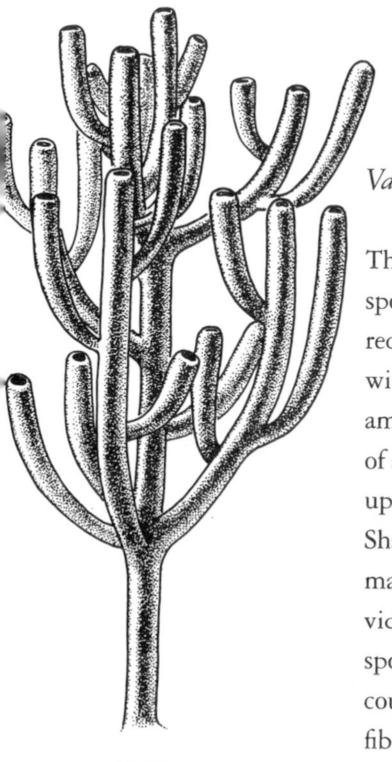

32

Vauxia

This beautiful, complexly branched sponge is the most common sponge in the Burgess Shale; several hundred specimens have been recovered. Specimens of *Vauxia* are conical to cylindrical, often with branches that produce a bushlike appearance, as in the example shown here. The skeleton of *Vauxia* was composed entirely of a tough organic substance like spongin, the material that makes up real bath sponges. Unlike all other sponges in the Burgess Shale, no discrete spicules are present. However, the fibers that made up the skeleton in *Vauxia* were fused into a net, which provided substantially more strength than in most of the other sponges found in the Burgess Shale. This tough framework accounts for the large number of complete specimens of *Vauxia.* The fibers in *Vauxia* have a central core that is highly unusual but is similar to that in the living sponge *Verongia.* In consequence, the several species of *Vauxia* are placed in the Family Vauxiidae within the demosponge Order Verongida.

Vauxia gracilenta Walcott, 1920. USNM 66511. Size: 31 mm. Isham reconstruction. Proportion of total Burgess Shale assemblage in terms of numbers of individuals: about 2% (all the sponges together represent 3.79%). Occurrence: Middle Cambrian Stephen Formation Burgess Shale. Description: Rigby (1986).

31 (×7)

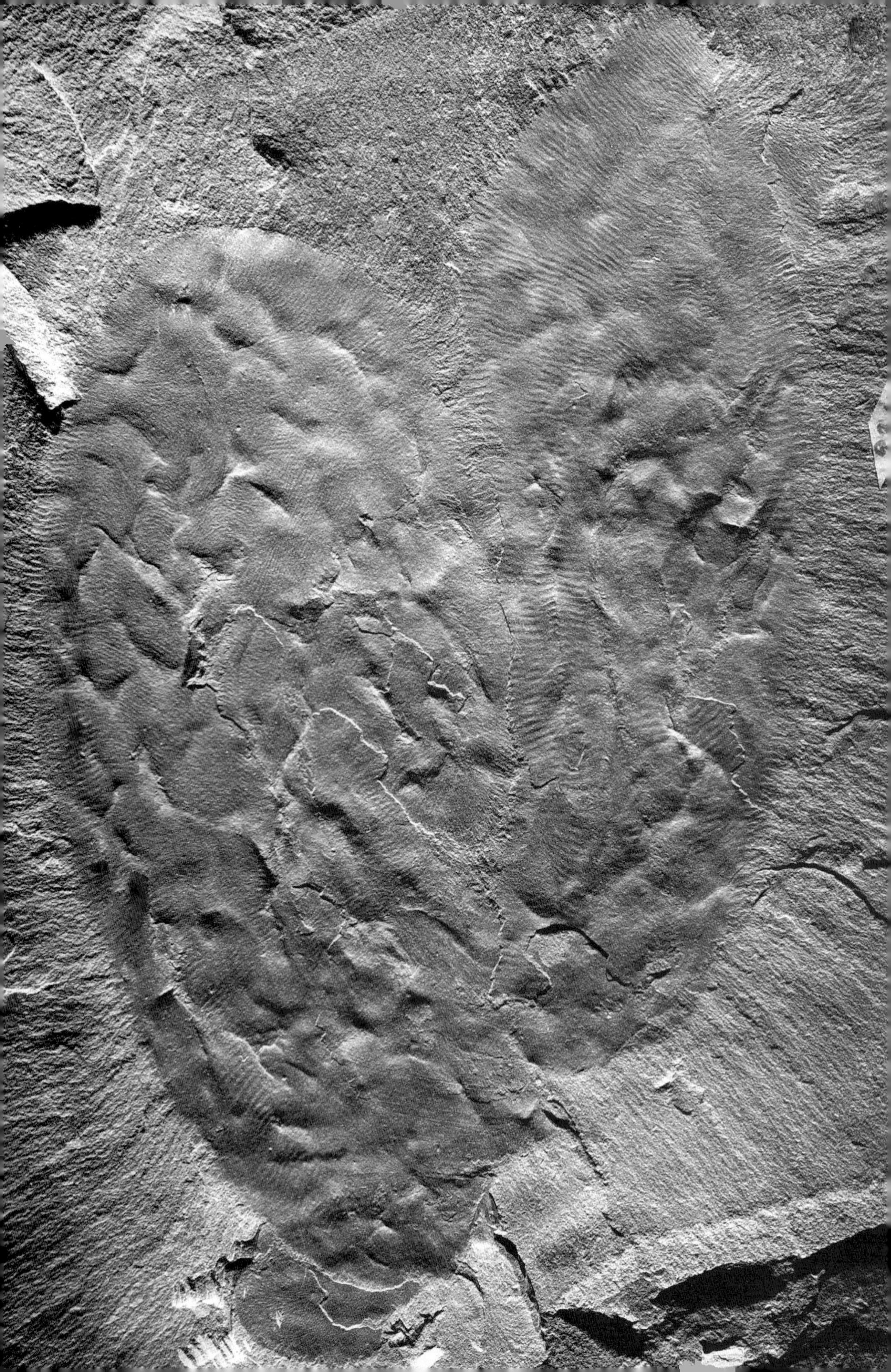

Wapkia

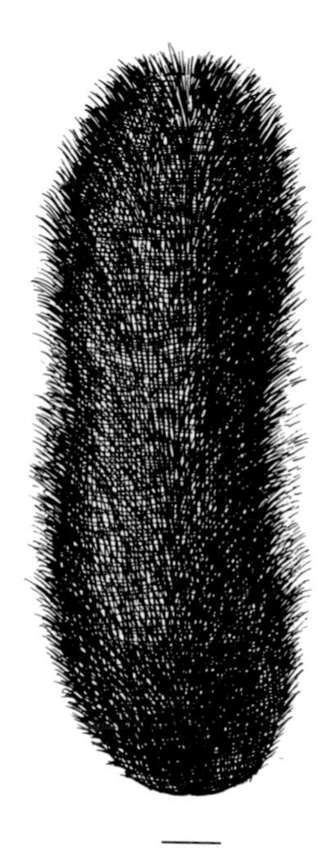

34

Wapkia is among the most complex of the Burgess Shale sponges (Rigby 1986). This large, oval form appears quite similar to *Leptomitus* (Illustrations 25, 26), as shown in the reconstruction. Many of the spicules were aligned in long vertical columns, as in *Leptomitus,* but the internal skeleton of *Wapkia* was far more complex. Rows of internal canals produced a wrinkled pattern on the outer surface of the sponge that is readily apparent in the illustration. The spicules of *Wapkia* were not fused into a network, which suggests that they were held in place by large amounts of a sponginlike material. *Wapkia* lived attached to the seafloor and fed by filtering water through its outer wall.

The affinities of *Wapkia* are unclear. It may have evolved, as did other Middle Cambrian sponges, by increasing the internal complexity of a *Leptomitus*-like form, or it may be derived from some other ancestor. *Wapkia* is such a distinctive demosponge that it is placed alone in the Family Wapkiidae.

Wapkia grandis Walcott, 1920. USNM 66461. Size: 21.3 cm. Isham reconstruction. Proportion of total Burgess Shale assemblage in terms of numbers of individuals: <0.1%. Occurrence: Middle Cambrian Stephen Formation Burgess Shale. Description: Rigby (1986). Other important reference: de Laubenfels (1955).

33 (×1)

Diagoniella

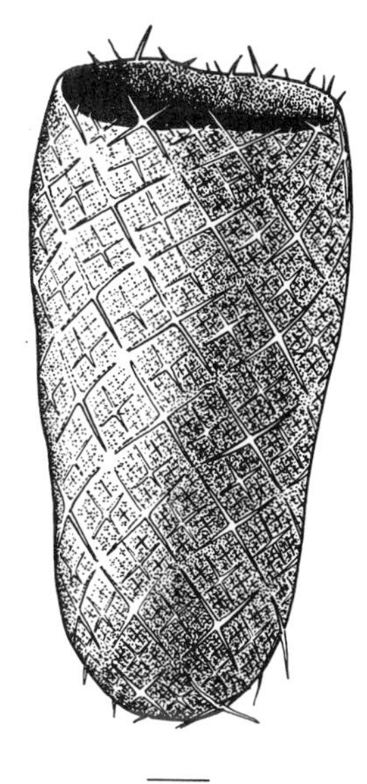

36

Diagoniella was a simple sac-shaped sponge in which the net of spicules was arrayed diagonally to the long axis. This sponge is known from only seven slabs of the Burgess Shale, and the spicules are covered by a dense film on all but a few specimens. The structure at the base of the specimens is not well preserved, but *Diagoniella* probably lived attached to the seafloor.

Diagoniella is one of two Burgess Shale sponges that belong to the Family Protospongiidae, a group of early and primitive members of the Class Hexactinellida. The hexactinellid sponges have six-rayed siliceous spicules. Unlike most later members of this class, the spicules of *Diagoniella* were not fused into a net, so this was a relatively fragile sponge.

Diagoniella hindei Walcott, 1920. USNM 66503. Size: 15 mm. Isham reconstruction. Proportion of total Burgess Shale assemblage in terms of numbers of individuals: <0.1%. Occurrence: Middle Cambrian Stephen Formation Burgess Shale. Description: Rigby (1986).

35 (×4)

37 (×2.5)

Protospongia

The Burgess Shale specimens of *Protospongia* are all fragments. Specimens from elsewhere, however, show that the shape of the sponge was globular to conical. The wall of *Protospongia* was thin and made up of a single layer of spicules called stauracts. These differ from the usual symmetrical six-rayed spicules of hexactinellid sponges: one of the pairs of opposing rays was reduced, giving the spicule the appearance of a simple cross. The spicules in *Protospongia* occurred in several ranks or orders of descending size, arranged in a rectangular pattern.

Protospongia is an early representative of the hexactinellid sponges. There is some scope for confusing it with the closely related Burgess Shale sponge *Diagoniella.* Both belong to the Family Protospongiidae.

Protospongia hicksi Hinde, 1887. USNM 66502. Size: the largest fragment from the Burgess Shale is about 5 by 5 cm. Proportion of total Burgess Shale assemblage in terms of numbers of individuals: $<0.1\%$. Occurrence: Middle Cambrian Stephen Formation Burgess Shale. Description: Rigby (1986).

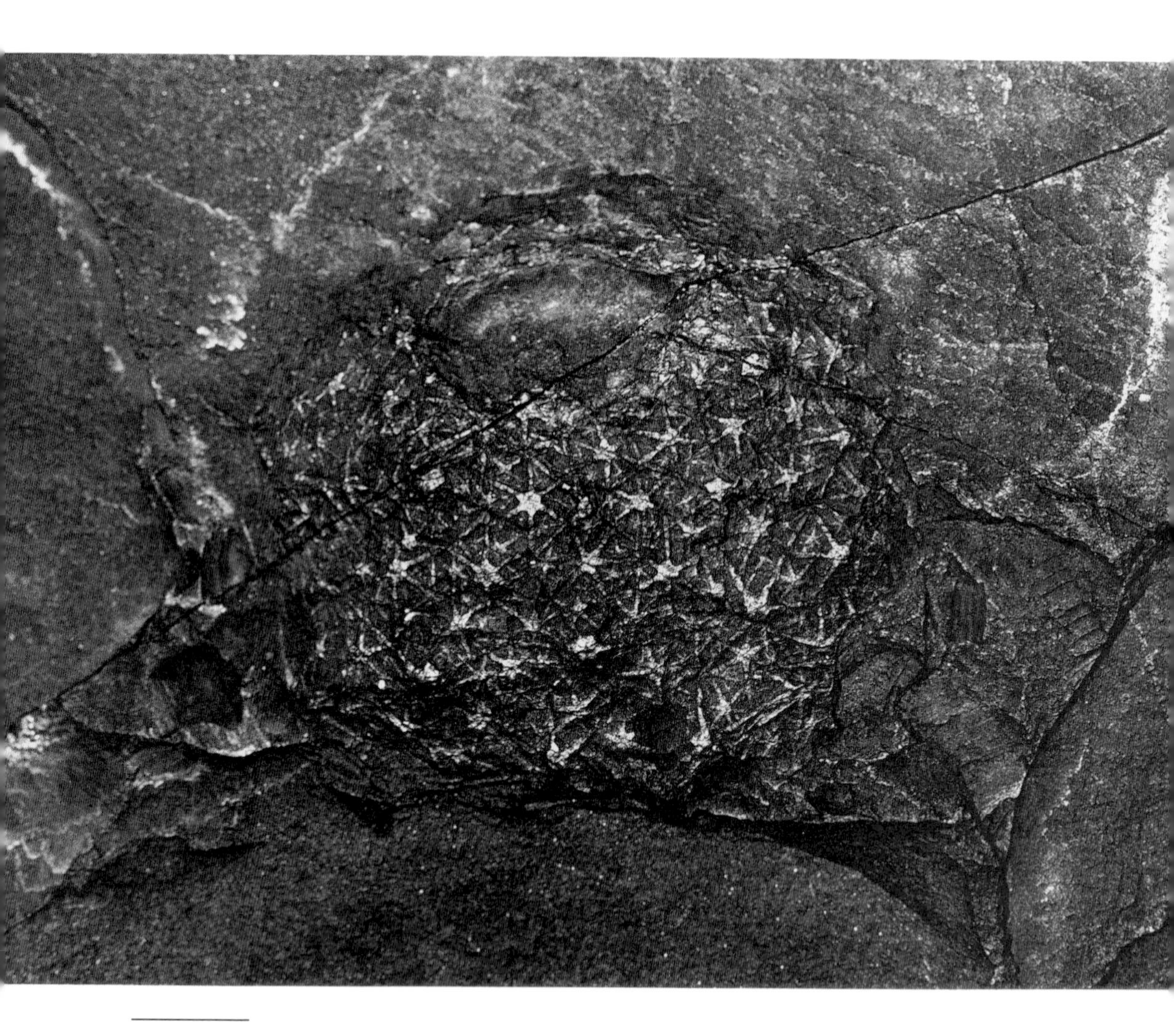

38 (×6)

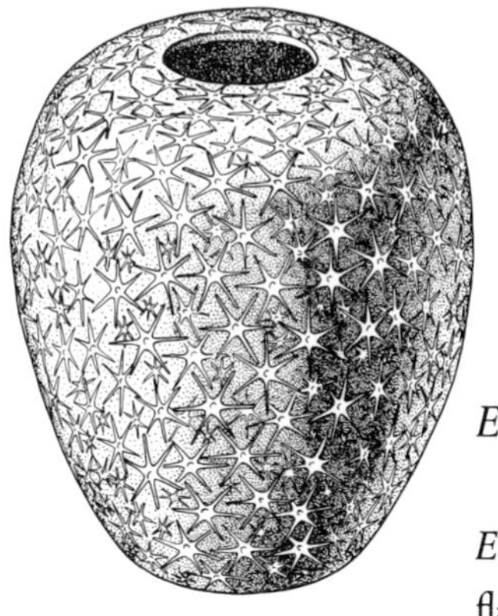

39

Eiffelia

Eiffelia was a complex, globular sponge. The top was somewhat flattened, with a wide central hole that served as the exit for water passing through the walls. The body of the sponge was supported by a mass of six-rayed spicules, the rays radiating in one plane from the central junction of the spicule. The spicules of *Eiffelia* were calcareous, unlike those of the other Burgess Shale sponges. Spongin was apparently lacking. These spicules, which occurred in at least four size categories, are clearly evident in the illustration. Like the other sponges of the Burgess Shale, *Eiffelia* was part of the sessile epifauna, living on the seafloor. Some specimens apparently lived directly on the seafloor, but at least one specimen has been found attached to an empty tube of the priapulid worm *Selkirkia.*

Eiffelia belongs to the calcareous sponges (Class Calcarea) and is placed in the Family Eiffeliidae along with a few sponges from younger rocks.

Eiffelia globosa Walcott, 1920. USNM 66522. Size: 16 mm. Isham reconstruction. Proportion of total Burgess Shale assemblage in terms of numbers of individuals: 0.04%. Occurrence: Middle Cambrian Stephen Formation Burgess Shale. Description: Rigby (1986). Note: *Eiffelia* attached to a *Selkirkia* tube is illustrated in Conway Morris et al. (1982).

Phylum Cnidaria

?CLASS ANTHOZOA

?Order Pennatulacea (Sea Pens and Sea Pansies)

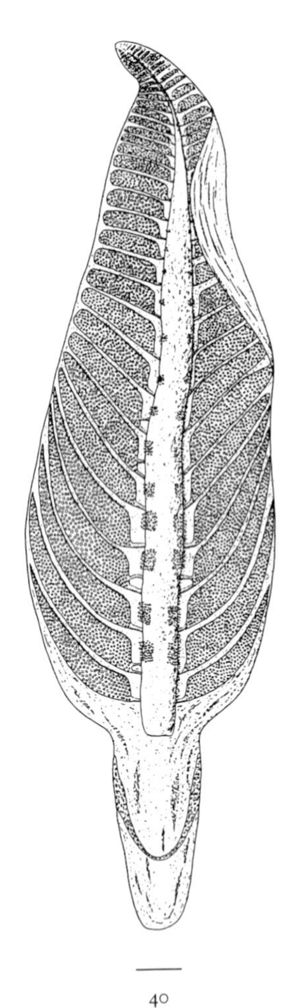

40

Thaumaptilon

This rare Burgess Shale animal is important as a possible link between the late Proterozoic Ediacaran animals and those of Cambrian and later times. *Thaumaptilon* was a leaflike animal with a broad central axis. Some 35 to 40 branches projected from each side of the axis, as far as the margin of the "leaf." There is some evidence that these branches were connected internally to the central axis by narrow canals. The branches appear to have formed cushionlike structures on the surface of the "leaf." They are covered by hundreds of tiny spots or blobs, which also occur in places flanking the central axis. The blobs may represent individual zooids, although they are too small to preserve evidence of tentacles. These zooids would have numbered in the thousands. The margin of the "leaf" is folded over in places, revealing the other side, which lacked structure and was simply covered by longitudinal ridges. *Thaumaptilon* terminated in a large, blunt holdfast. The form of *Thaumaptilon* indicates that it lived attached to the seabed with the holdfast buried in the sediment. The animal may have been able to adjust its position in the water by nuscular contractions of the central axis. If zooids were present, they presumably fed by capturing tiny suspended particles.

Frondlike Proterozoic animals from the Ediacaran Fauna have been interpreted either as the relatives of modern sea pens (pennatulaceans) or, in the revolutionary interpretation put forward by Seilacher, as representatives of a quite different type of organization, with a serial quilted structure. According to Seilacher's interpretation, these quilted forms, which he called the Vendobionta, disappeared before the end of the Proterozoic. A number of Ediacaran forms (*Charniodiscus, Vaizitsinia, Charnia*) are very similar to *Thaumaptilon* and may be related. *Thaumaptilon* is simi-

41 (×0.5)

lar to sea pens not only in its shape, but in the presence of zooids and a system of internal canals. Conway Morris, therefore, argued that an affinity with the cnidarians was likely for this animal. The remarkable preservation of the Burgess Shale fossils is not matched in the Ediacaran specimens, which are commonly found cast on the base of a layer of sandstone as an infilling of an impression left by the animal in the underlying mud. Thus, whether most of the Ediacaran organims became extinct, as argued by Seilacher, or survived to give rise to forms such as *Thaumaptilon* and modern sea pens, as advocated by Conway Morris, remains to be definitively resolved.

Thaumaptilon walcotti Conway Morris, 1993. USNM 468028. Size: 20 cm. Conway Morris reconstruction. Proportion of total Burgess Shale assemblage in terms of numbers of individuals: <0.01%. Occurrence: Middle Cambrian Stephen Formation Burgess Shale. Description: Conway Morris (1993). Other important references: Conway Morris (1989a), Seilacher (1992).

?Order Actiniaria (Sea Anemones)

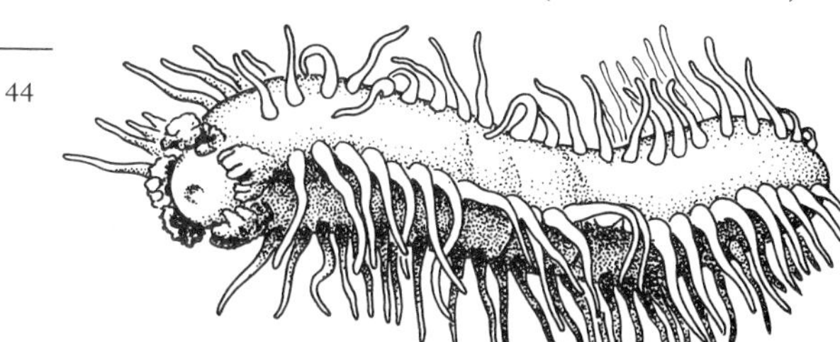

44

Mackenzia with *Portalia* (affinities unknown)

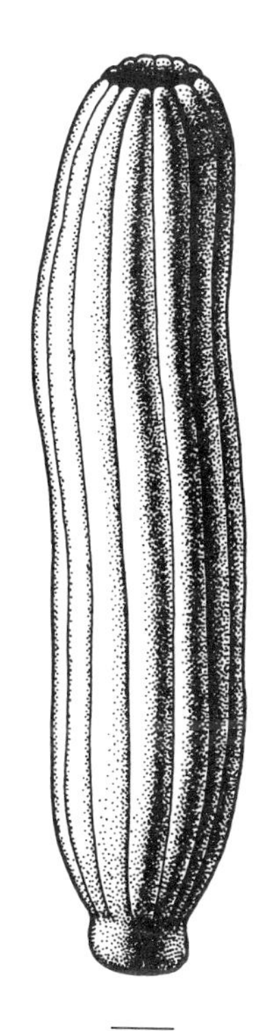

43

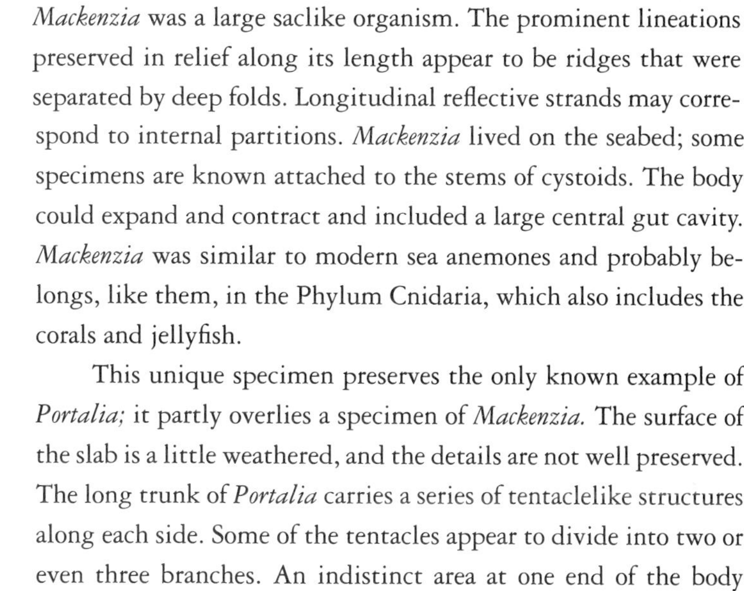

Mackenzia was a large saclike organism. The prominent lineations preserved in relief along its length appear to be ridges that were separated by deep folds. Longitudinal reflective strands may correspond to internal partitions. *Mackenzia* lived on the seabed; some specimens are known attached to the stems of cystoids. The body could expand and contract and included a large central gut cavity. *Mackenzia* was similar to modern sea anemones and probably belongs, like them, in the Phylum Cnidaria, which also includes the corals and jellyfish.

This unique specimen preserves the only known example of *Portalia;* it partly overlies a specimen of *Mackenzia.* The surface of the slab is a little weathered, and the details are not well preserved. The long trunk of *Portalia* carries a series of tentaclelike structures along each side. Some of the tentacles appear to divide into two or even three branches. An indistinct area at one end of the body may represent the head. The wide trace along the trunk axis is presumably the gut. There is little basis for speculation about the likely mode of life of *Portalia.* Walcott regarded it as an echinoderm (a holothurian, or sea cucumber), but this view was disputed by some later authors. Further consideration of the affinities of this strange animal await a redescription of the specimen.

Mackenzia costalis Walcott, 1911c; *Portalia mira* Walcott, 1918a. USNM 83927. Size: *Mackenzia,* 85 mm, up to 16 cm long; *Portalia,* 93 mm long. Isham reconstruction. Proportion of total Burgess Shale assemblage in terms of numbers of individuals: about 0.2% and <0.01%, respectively. Occurrence: Middle Cambrian Stephen Formation Burgess Shale. Description: for *Mackenzia,* see Briggs and Conway Morris (1986) and Conway Morris (1989a, 1993); *Portalia* has yet to be redescribed.

42 (×0.5)

45 (×2)

Phylum Ctenophora (Comb Jellies)

Fasciculus

Fasciculus was originally described on the basis of a single specimen and tentatively interpreted as a coelenterate (Simonetta and Delle Cave 1978a). A number of additional specimens have come to light over the past decade in the Stephen Formation on Mount Stephen. These new specimens provide some new information about one of the most enigmatic fossils from the Burgess Shale. *Fasciculus* was bilaterally symmetrical and included a series of flexible elongate bands with many closely spaced transverse structures. These bands are very reminiscent of the comb rows of ctenophores or comb jellies, but far more bands are present in *Fasciculus* than the eight associated with modern examples of this group. Little is known of the internal anatomy of the animal, and hence the affinities of *Fasciculus* remain uncertain.

Fasciculus vesanus Simonetta and Delle Cave, 1978a. USNM 202151. Size: about 8 cm across. Proportion of total Burgess Shale assemblage in terms of numbers of individuals: <0.01%. Occurrence: Middle Cambrian Stephen Formation Burgess Shale and locality 9 of Collins et al. (1983). Description: Simonetta and Della Cave (1978a); awaiting redescription by Conway Morris and Collins. Other important reference: Briggs and Conway Morris (1986).

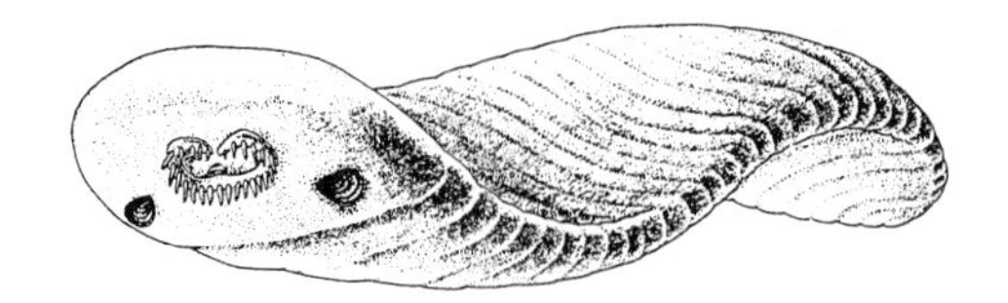

46

Odontogriphus

The aptly named *Odontogriphus* (literally "toothed riddle") is one of the rarest of the Burgess Shale animals. The only known specimen appears like a reflective film of tissue on the surface of the rock. The body was wide and flat, and the trunk annulated. Within the head region was a small structure shaped like a figure eight on its side, which carries traces of about 25 toothlike elements. Flanking this feeding apparatus was a pair of small bundles of lamellae, termed palps, that are difficult to pick out in the illustration. *Odontogriphus* is thought to have been a swimmer, using wavelike ripples of the body for propulsion. The toothlike structures arranged around the mouth may have supported tentacles for use in feeding. The palps may have been sensory. The toothlike structures in *Odontogriphus* have been compared with phosphatic microfossils known as conodont elements, which are common in Paleozoic sedimentary rocks. Indeed, it was even suggested that *Odontogriphus* might provide the long-sought evidence for the soft tissue morphology of the conodont animal. However, genuine conodont animals with preserved soft tissues have since been discovered in the Carboniferous of Scotland, which show that those formerly problematic fossils belong with the chordates.

The outline of the feeding apparatus in *Odontogriphus* is very similar to that in lophophorates (such as brachiopods, phoronid worms, and bryozoans). On this basis, *Odontogriphus* is assigned to the Superphylum Lophophorata.

47 (×2.5)

Odontogriphus omalus Conway Morris, 1976a. USNM 196169. Illustration size: about 6 cm long. Marianne Collins reconstruction. Proportion of total Burgess Shale assemblage in terms of numbers of individuals: <0.01%. Occurrence: Middle Cambrian Stephen Formation Burgess Shale. Description: Conway Morris (1976a). Note: Genuine conodont animals were described by Briggs et al. (1983) and Aldridge et al. (1986, 1993).

48 (×4)

Superphylum Lophophorata
Phylum Brachiopoda (Lamp Shells)
CLASS INARTICULATA (Inartiaculates)

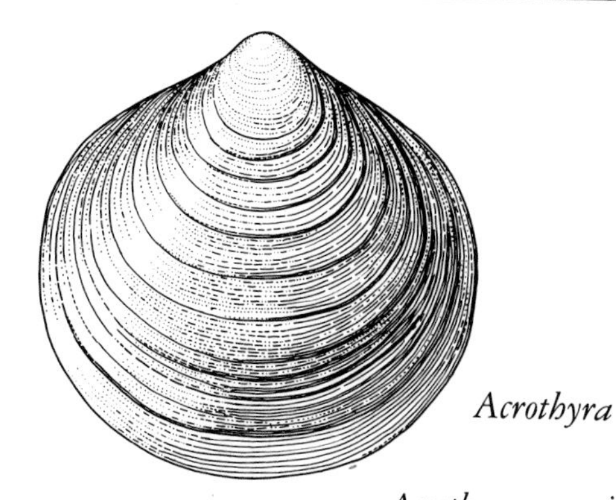

Acrothyra

49

Acrothyra gregaria is, as the species name implies, one of the more gregarious fossils found in the Burgess Shale fauna. As the illustration shows, slabs are often found that are covered with specimens of this brachiopod. The soft parts of *Acrothyra* are not preserved. *Acrothyra,* like all of the inarticulate brachiopods described here (other than *Micromitra*), apparently lived buried in the seafloor with only the upper part of the valves exposed. Water was pumped in through a gape in the valves, through the filaments of the lophophore where food particles were collected, and then out of the shell.

Acrothyra gregaria Walcott, 1924a. USNM 280969. Size: 2–9 mm. Isham reconstruction. Proportion of total Burgess Shale assemblage in terms of numbers of individuals: <1%. Occurrence: Middle Cambrian Stephen Formation Burgess Shale. Description: Walcott (1924a).

50 (×8)

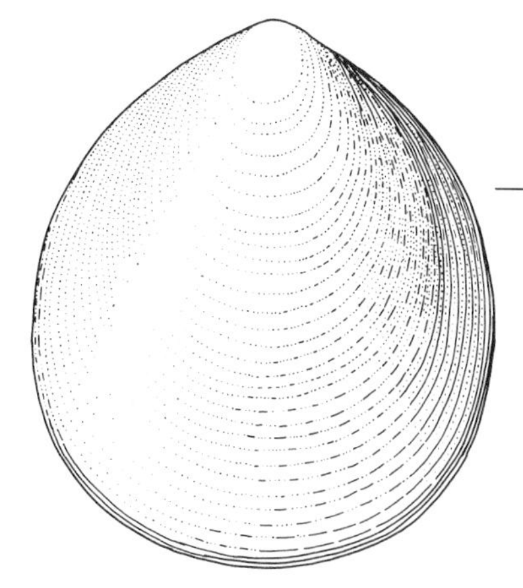

Lingulella

51

A small, fragile, inarticulate brachiopod, *Lingulella* had an elliptical to nearly circular shell. The only ornament on the shell was very fine growth lines. Although earlier workers believed that the hard shells had been dissolved away, recent work demonstrates that they retain their original calcium phosphate composition. No soft parts are preserved in most of these shelly fossils.

Lingulella waptaensis Walcott, 1924a. USNM 281746. Size: 4–6 mm. Isham reconstruction. Proportion of total Burgess Shale assemblage in terms of numbers of individuals: <1% (all the brachiopods together represent 0.56%). Occurrence: Middle Cambrian Stephen Formation Burgess Shale. Description: Walcott (1924a).

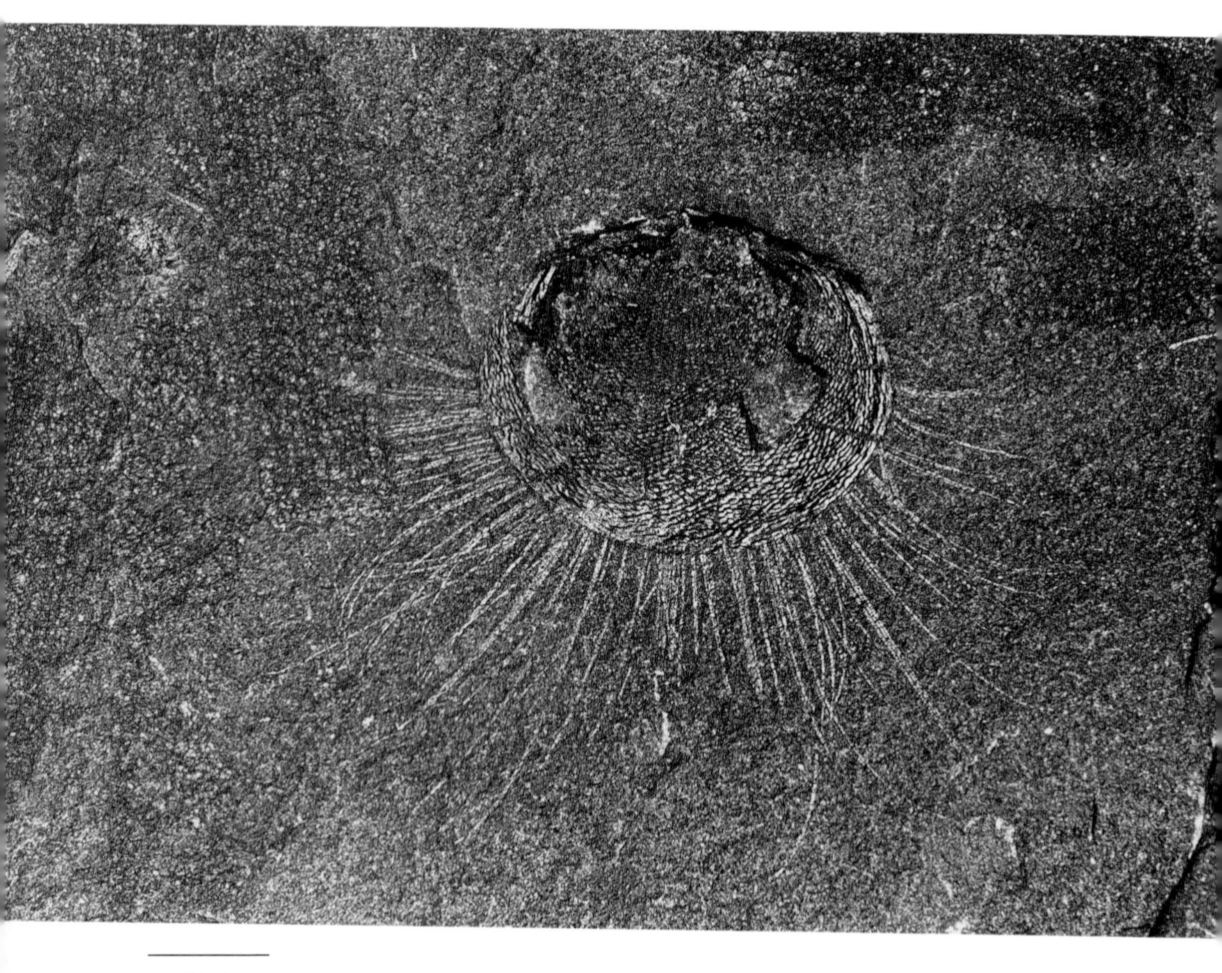

52 (×11)

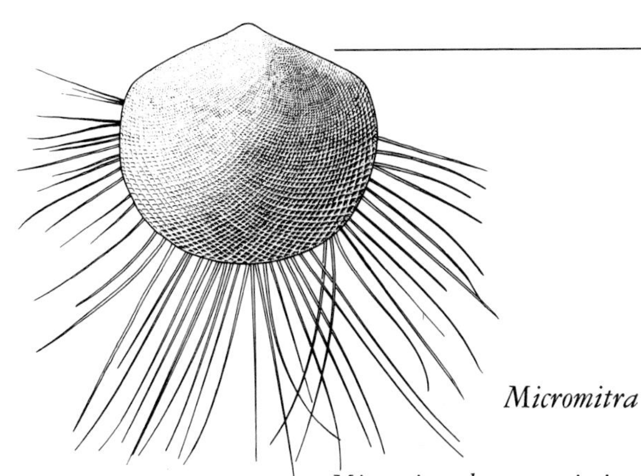

53

Micromitra

Micromitra burgessensis is the most ornate of the Burgess Shale brachiopods. This and other species of the genus are widespread throughout the Lower and Middle Cambrian of western North America, but few are as beautifully preserved as this specimen. The ornament is composed of fine raised lines that cut obliquely across the shell, dividing the surface into small diamonds. This distinctive sculpture allows the brachiopod to be identified readily even from fragmentary remains, and many hundreds of individuals occur in the Burgess Shale. This illustration shows the delicate setae that fringe the mantle, extending beyond the margin of the shell, as well as the exquisite ornament on the shell itself. The fine setae of *Micromitra* suggest that this species was an epifaunal suspension feeder and did not live buried in the sediment. Indeed, several specimens have been found attached to the sponge *Pirania* (Illustration 27). Living above the seafloor would have reduced the problem of mud clogging the filter-feeding apparatus.

Micromitra burgessensis Resser, 1938. USNM 59801. Size: 6 mm. Isham reconstruction. Proportion of total Burgess Shale assemblage in terms of numbers of individuals: <1%. Occurrence: Middle Cambrian Stephen Formation Burgess Shale. Description: Walcott (1912d, 1924a), Resser (1938). Note: Whittington (1985b) illustrated brachiopods attached to *Pirania.*

54 (×7)

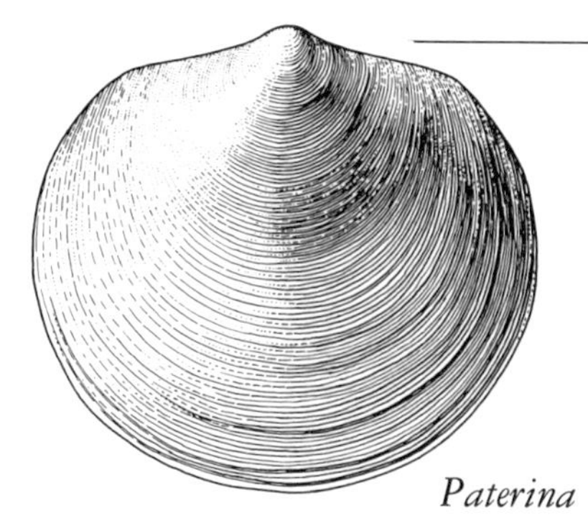

Paterina

55

These small, shiny black inarticulate brachiopod shells with prominent growth lines were originally assigned by Walcott to *Micromitra,* but the distinctive ornament led later paleontologists to recognize them as a different genus and species. The shell was composed of calcium phosphate; the soft tissues are unknown. Most of the specimens are flattened and distorted by the compression of the rock, but this particular specimen is relatively undistorted. *Paterina* was an infaunal suspension feeder living at the surface of the sediment.

Paterina zenobia (Walcott, 1924a). USNM 58311. Size: 11 mm. Isham reconstruction. Proportion of total Burgess Shale assemblage in terms of numbers of individuals: <1%. Occurrence: Middle Cambrian Stephen Formation Burgess Shale. Description: Walcott (1924a).

56 (×6)

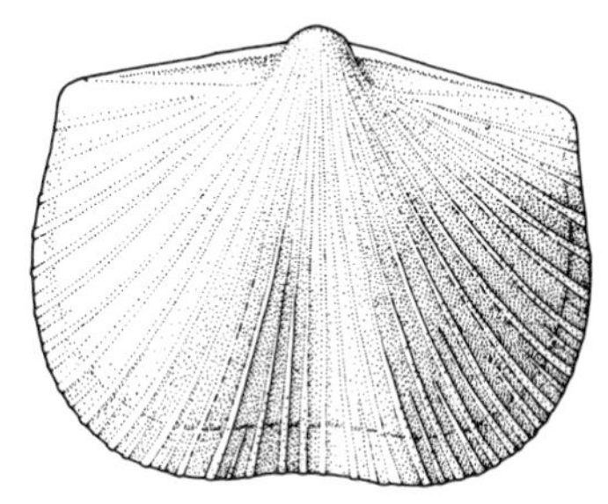

Diraphora

57

Articulate brachiopods were relatively minor players during the Cambrian, when they were overshadowed by their inarticulate cousins. *Diraphora* is one of two genera of articulate brachiopods found in the Burgess Shale (the other is *Nisusia*). *Diraphora* is another component of the calcified fauna of the Burgess Shale that is often overlooked because of the magnificent preservation of the soft-bodied animals. The shell of this articulate brachiopod has been replaced by clay minerals (some impressions of the internal structures have been found in other specimens). The fine lines, or costae, radiate from the hinge area of the brachiopod. *Diraphora* was an epifaunal suspension feeder, living attached to the substrate by a fleshy protruberance known as a pedicle and filtering food particles out of the water. There is some indication that *Diraphora* may have lived attached to sponges, as did *Micromitra* and *Nisusia*, but the evidence is not as strong as in the other two cases (Illustrations 27, 28). The articulate brachiopods of the Burgess Shale have not been restudied since Walcott's original descriptions.

Diraphora bellicostata (Walcott, 1924a). USNM 280949. Size: width 9 mm. Isham reconstruction. Proportion of total Burgess Shale assemblage in terms of numbers of individuals: <1%. Occurrence: Middle Cambrian Stephen Formation Burgess Shale. Description: Walcott (1924a).

58 (×4)

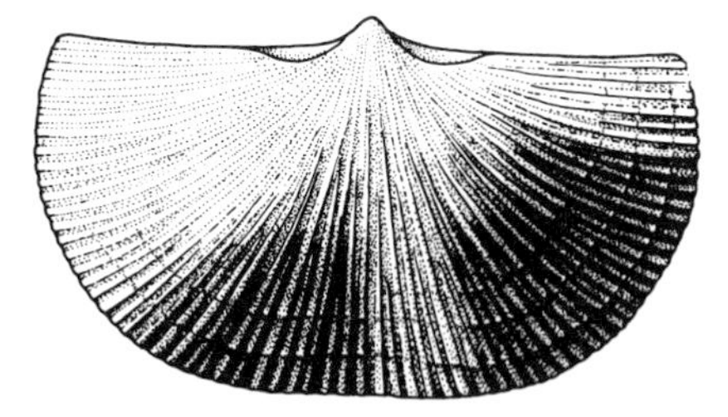

Nisusia

59

The hard shell of *Nisusia* has been replaced by clay minerals; none of the soft parts is preserved. The fine radiating ribs of *Nisusia* are clearly evident in this specimen. Like *Diraphora, Nisusia* was an epifaunal suspension feeder that pumped water through the mantle cavity enclosed by the two shells, removing organic matter with the filaments of its lophophore. A small specimen of *Nisusia* shows several long, slender, curved spines projecting from the outer margin of the shell. Larger specimens have small bumps in the same position, apparently remnants of spines in the adult forms. Some specimens of *Nisusia* have been found associated with the sponge *Pirania* (Illustration 27), indicating that the brachiopod may have supported itself on the sponge spicules with its spines.

Nisusia burgessensis Walcott, 1924a. USNM 69696. Size: width 22 mm. Isham reconstruction. Proportion of total Burgess Shale assemblage in terms of numbers of individuals: <1%. Occurrence: Middle Cambrian Stephen Formation Burgess Shale. Description: Walcott (1924a).

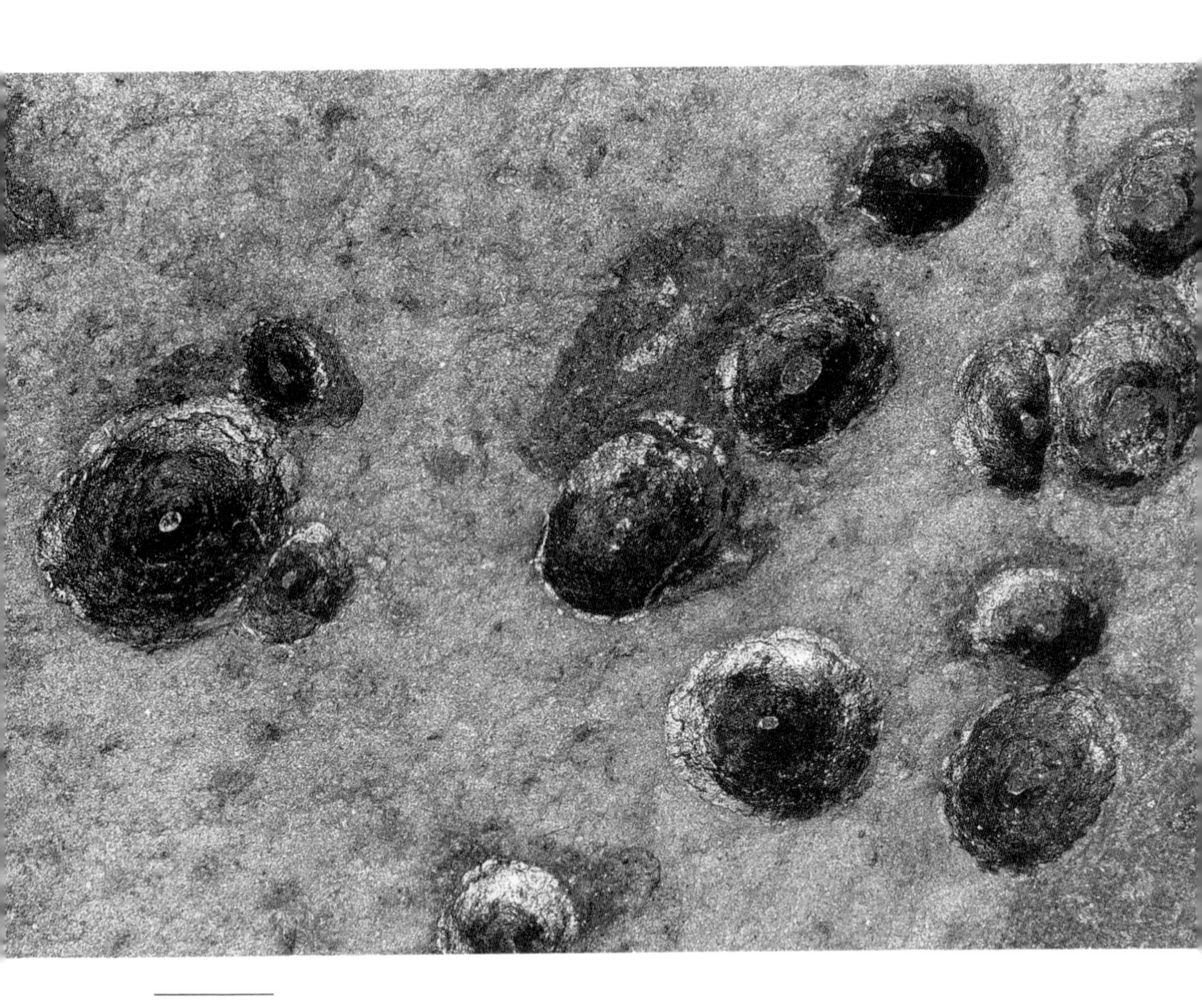

60 (×2)

?Phylum Mollusca (Molluscs)

CLASS HELCIONELLOIDA (Monoplacophora)

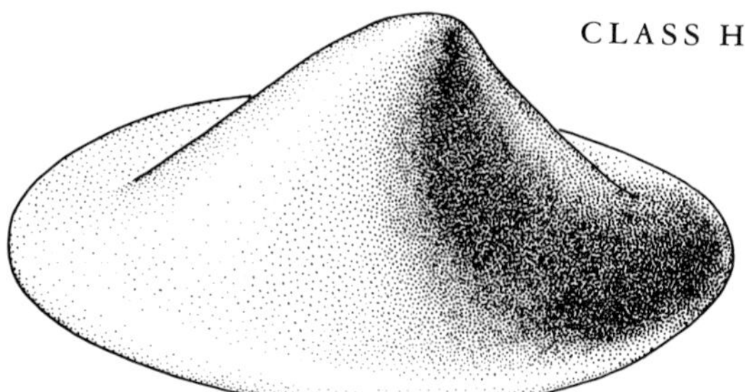

Scenella

61

Scenella is one of the most common fossils in the Burgess Shale. Walcott collected many slabs, each with 10 to 100 or more of these small cap-shaped fossils on the surface. He assigned these specimens to the monoplacophoran genus *Scenella,* but never described them. No soft parts are preserved. Monoplacophorans are molluscs, related to the gastropods, with a single shell covering a series of paired organs (gills, muscles) and a muscular foot. The affinities of the Burgess Shale form, however, are unclear. The shell lacks many of the features of true *Scenella,* including multiple paired muscle scars on the inner surface. More recently, some *Scenella* have been reinterpreted as a chondrophorine, a by-the-wind sailor or floating coelenterate.

Scenella was formerly assigned to the limpet-shaped tryblidid Monoplacophora. The Class Monoplacophora has recently been replaced by two classes, the Tergomya and Helcionelloida; *Scenella* is assigned to its own family, the Scenellidae, within the Class Helcionelloida.

Scenella amii (Matthew, 1902). USNM 277100. Size: 8 mm. Isham reconstruction. Proportion of total Burgess Shale assemblage in terms of numbers of individuals: <1%. Occurrence: Middle Cambrian Stephen Formation Burgess Shale. Description: Babcock and Robison (1988). Other important references: Knight (1941), Rasetti (1954). Note: Yochelson and Gil Cid (1984) discussed the chondrophorine hypothesis, which is favored by Babcock and Robison (1988); Peel (1991) reviewed the monoplacophoran molluscs described as *Scenella.*

Phylum Hyolitha (Hyoliths)

Haplophrentis

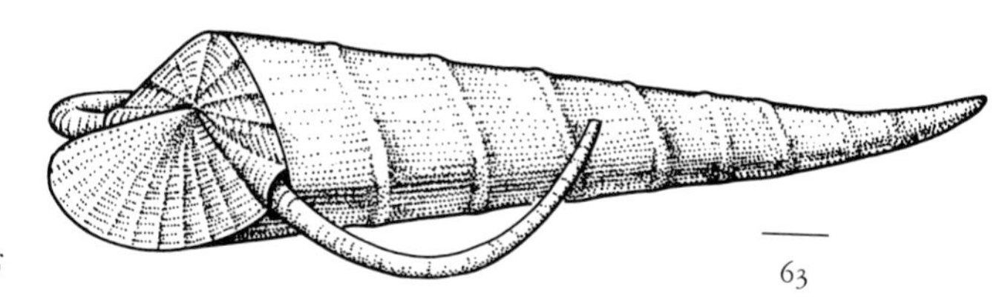

63

The mineralized skeleton of *Haplophrentis* consisted of three elements. The body was housed in a long pointed shell, conical in outline, but flat-bottomed. This conical shell was closed by a small lid or operculum. An unusual pair of curved appendages projected from the aperture. These appendages are known as "helens" (they were named by Charles Walcott for his daughter!). *Haplophrentis* lived an essentially sessile existence on the seafloor. The helens presumably stabilized the shell in the soft mud and may have worked rather inefficiently like oars to move the animal slowly along the surface. The specimen illustrated here is remarkable in that the various parts of the skeleton remain together; after the soft tissues decayed, the hard parts were readily scattered in the sediment. The soft parts of *Haplophrentis* are unknown, although traces of a sediment-filled gut have been found in related forms from other localities. The animal may have fed on organic material in the mud. It also provided food for other organisms. Specimens have been discovered lined up in the gut of the priapulid worm *Ottoia* (Illustration 73) and among other shell fragments in the gut of the arthropod *Sidneyia.*

The unusual morphology of hyolithids makes their affinities uncertain. Some authors regard them as molluscs, others as members of a separate phylum.

Haplophrentis carinatus (Matthew, 1899). USNM 57625. Size: 3–30 mm. Isham reconstruction. Proportion of total Burgess Shale assemblage in terms of numbers of individuals: 0.13%. Occurrence: Middle Cambrian Stephen Formation Burgess Shale and other localities. Description: Babcock and Robison (1988). Other important references: Yochelson (1961), Marek and Yochelson (1976), Runnegar (1980).

62 (×10)

64 (×2)

Phylum Priapulida (Priapulids)

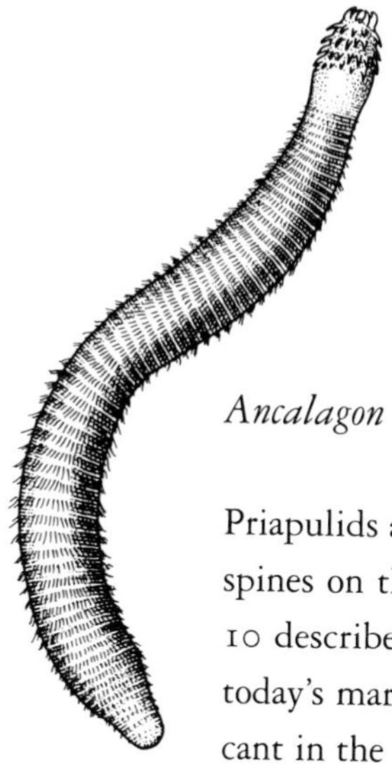

Ancalagon

65

Priapulids are short, fat, carnivorous worms that grasp prey using spines on the eversible proboscis and mouth. There are less than 10 described living species, so they are a very minor element of today's marine faunas. They are, however, relatively more significant in the Burgess Shale and other exceptionally preserved Cambrian biotas. Less than 20 specimens of *Ancalagon* are known, compared with over 50 times that number of the most abundant Burgess Shale priapulid, *Ottoia.* This well-preserved specimen shows the spines and hooks of the proboscis. A clear reflective trace of the wide gut runs the full length of the trunk. The cuticle of the trunk was annulated (although priapulids have no internal segmentation), but that is not clear on this specimen. Traces of tiny setae are evident, however, on the cuticle at the rear of the animal. *Ancalagon* was a burrowing predator. The evidence of the specimens indicates that the proboscis could not be everted to the same degree as that in other Burgess Shale priapulids.

Ancalagon differs from the other Burgess Shale priapulids and is not clearly related to any modern family. It is assigned to its own family, the Ancalagonidae.

Ancalagon minor (Walcott, 1911d). USNM 83939f. Size range: 3–11 cm. Isham reconstruction. Proportion of total Burgess Shale assemblage in terms of numbers of individuals: <0.1%. Occurrence: Middle Cambrian Stephen Formation Burgess Shale. Description: Conway Morris (1977d).

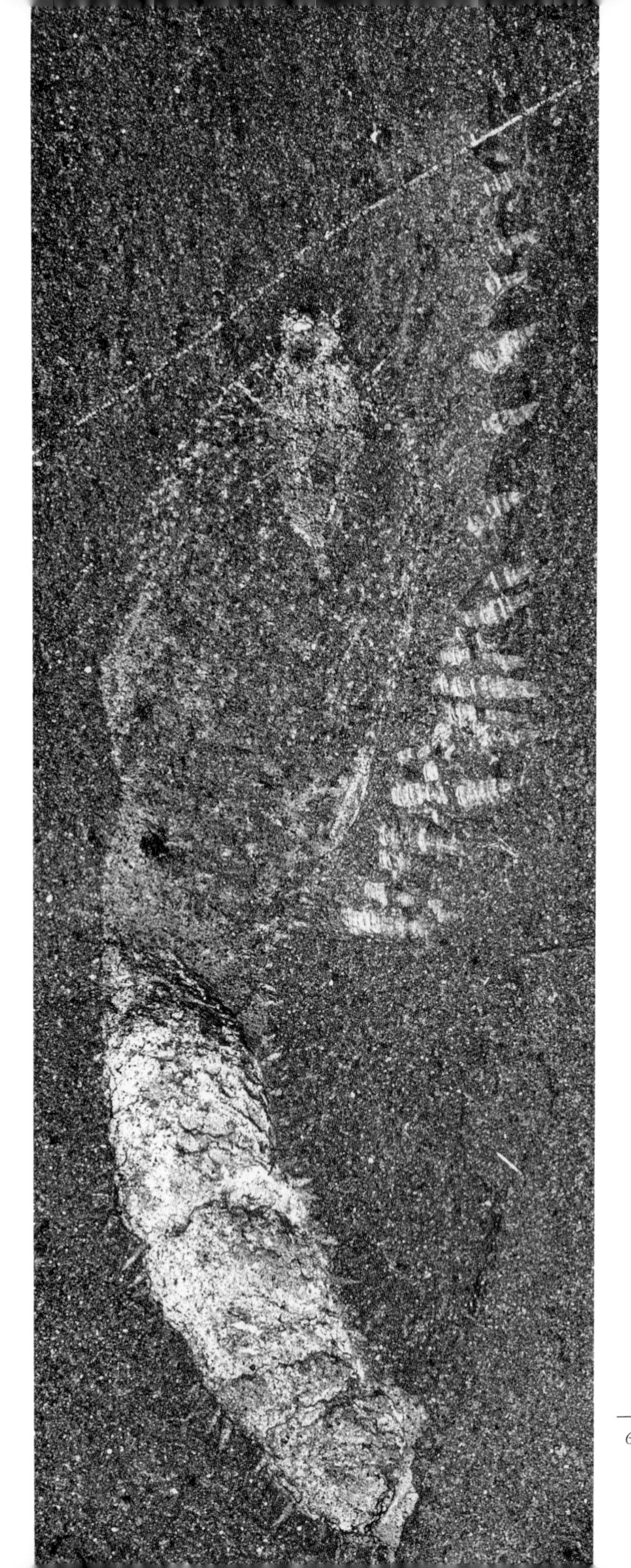

66 (×5)

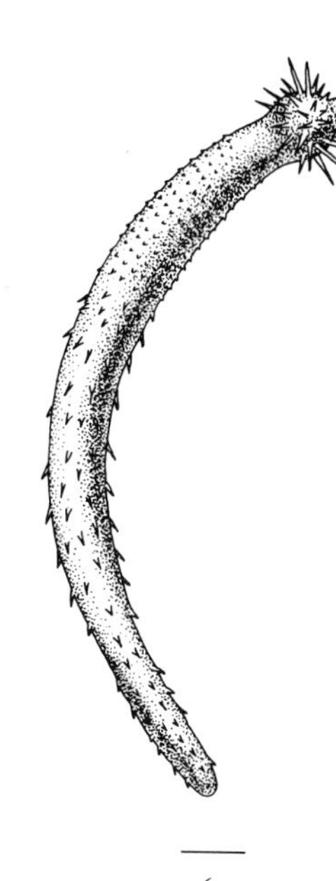

67

Fieldia

This is one of the rarer Burgess Shale priapulids. The trunk was subdivided into distinct anterior, central, and posterior parts. This specimen shows the proboscis, followed by a trace of the anterior part of the gut (perhaps the pharynx). The trunk was spinose. The swollen anterior section is not as strongly reflective as the narrow central part. The posterior part is broken off this slab. The central part of the trunk is usually filled with sediment, and its reflective preservation suggests that it was perhaps specialized in some way for digesting material from the mud. It was more resistant to decay than the rest of the animal. *Fieldia* was a burrower, but unlike the other Burgess Shale priapulids, it was probably a sediment feeder rather than a predator.

Fieldia differs from the other Burgess Shale priapulids and is not clearly related to any modern family. It is assigned to its own family, the Fieldiidae.

Fieldia lanceolata Walcott, 1912a. USNM 198605. Size range: 2.5–5 cm. Isham reconstruction. Proportion of total Burgess Shale assemblage in terms of numbers of individuals: <0.1%. Occurrence: Middle Cambrian Stephen Formation Burgess Shale. Description: Conway Morris (1977d).

68 (×0.5)

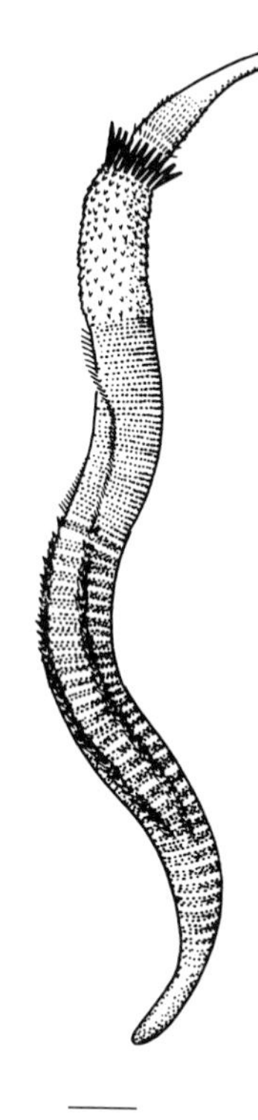

69

Louisella

This is the largest of the Burgess Shale priapulids. Adult specimens are between 15 and 26 cm long. This specimen shows the proboscis fully everted, with a reflective gut trace that extends the entire length of the body. The tip of the proboscis, which carries the mouth, is swollen and covered with fine spines. Behind this is a narrow, smooth length, but much larger spines are present farther back where the proboscis expands again. Beyond these long spines the cuticle is covered with conical papillae. Posterior of the proboscis the annulation of the trunk can be seen. The trunk of *Louisella* carried two longitudinal rows of papillae. *Louisella* was a burrower and, presumably, like modern priapulids, a predator. The rows of trunk papillae may have played a role in oxygen exchange. Such a specialized respiratory organ may have been necessary because of the large size of this priapulid.

Louisella differs from the other Burgess Shale priapulids and is not clearly related to any modern family. It is assigned to its own family, the Miskoiidae.

Louisella pedunculata Walcott, 1911d. USNM 57616. Size range: 15–26 cm, excluding proboscis. Isham reconstruction. Proportion of total Burgess Shale assemblage in terms of numbers of individuals: <0.5%. Occurrence: Middle Cambrian Stephen Formation Burgess Shale. Description: Conway Morris (1977d).

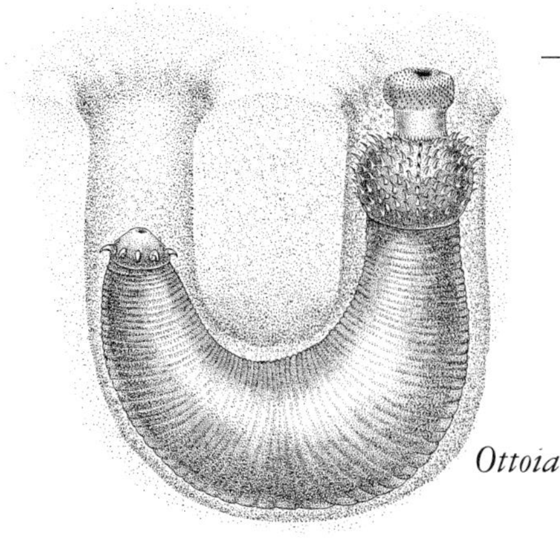

Ottoia

71

This is the most abundant of the Burgess Shale priapulids and is very common in the Raymond Quarry. Like modern priapulids, the body was divided into an anterior proboscis and posterior trunk. The proboscis is only partly everted in the specimen shown in Illustration 72. The tiny spines evident at the extremity are actually on the outside when the proboscis is fully extended. The much broader base of the proboscis was armed with an array of hooks. The remainder of the trunk was annulated, but this is only evident in the posterior part of this specimen. The internal organs are obscured by the reflectively preserved body wall. Along the margins it is clear that the body wall has pulled away from the overlying cuticle. *Ottoia* lived within the sediment, using the proboscis and the muscles of the body wall to burrow. It is usually curved, suggesting that it may have adopted a U shape in the mud.

72 (×1)

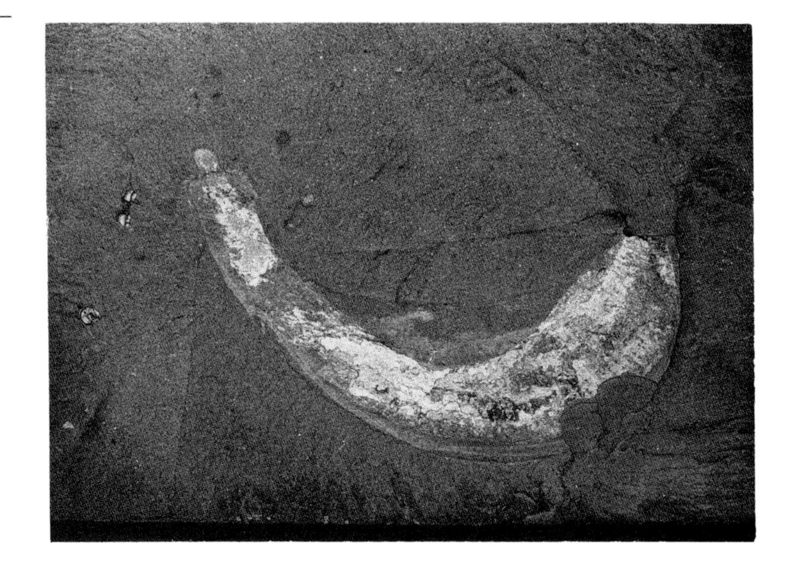

70 (×1)

The proboscis presumably projected out of the sediment for feeding, and an eversible tube at the posterior end may have carried the anus clear of the substrate.

Illustration 70 shows a slab preserving three specimens of *Ottoia,* which often occurs in such aggregations. In the individual on the right the proboscis is completely everted, showing the swollen extremity. The proboscis of the individual on the left, on the other hand, is completely withdrawn. The smallest specimen appears to show a small shell in the head region (but this may be a fortuitous superimposition).

Ottoia, like modern priapulids, was a carnivore. Over 30 specimens are known with *Haplophrentis* in the gut. The individual shown in Illustration 73 contains three shells, one of which is about to be expelled through the anus. Their consistent orientation indicates that they were actively hunted and usually swallowed apex last. As many as six have been recorded in a single specimen. One example of *Ottoia* is known with a trace of the proboscis of another individual in the gut. It appears that this Cambrian priapulid, like modern *Priapulus,* was a cannibal.

Ottoia differs from the other Burgess Shale priapulids and is not clearly related to any modern family. It is assigned to its own family, the Ottoiidae.

Ottoia prolifica (Walcott, 1911d). USNM 188609, 138288, 188604. Size: 2–16 cm. Marianne Collins reconstruction. Proportion of total Burgess Shale assemblage in terms of numbers of individuals: 3.7%. Occurrence: Middle Cambrian Stephen Formation Burgess Shale and other localities; Marjum Formation, Utah. A priapulid from the Lower Cambrian Chengjiang Fauna of China may be *Ottoia* (see Conway Morris [1989b]). Description: Conway Morris (1977d).

73 (×2.5)

Selkirkia

75

This priapulid is unusual among those of the Burgess Shale because it secreted an elongate outer rigid tube. The proboscis projected from the wider end of the tube, but it could be withdrawn completely into it. This specimen shows the proboscis partly everted. Like that of *Ottoia,* the proboscis of *Selkirkia* was covered by an array of spines. The tube conceals the trunk, but the reflective trace of the gut is evident through it. The narrow end of the tube was open. *Selkirkia* was a burrower, living in its tube (presumably oriented vertically) within the sediment. It was a carnivore, but, in contrast to *Ottoia,* recognizable prey has not been identified in the gut. About 80% of the specimens of *Selkirkia* consist only of the tube, which must have been composed of some toughened organic substance that was more resistant to decay than the rest of the tissues. Some of these empty tubes were used as attachment sites by other organisms, including brachiopods, sponges, and the crinoid *Echmatocrinus.*

Selkirkia differs from the other Burgess Shale priapulids and is not clearly related to any modern family. It is assigned to its own family, the Selkirkiidae.

Selkirkia columbia Conway Morris, 1977d. USNM 83941a. Size of tube: 3 mm–7.5 cm. Isham reconstruction. Proportion of total Burgess Shale assemblage in terms of numbers of individuals: 0.47%. Occurrence: Lower Cambrian; Middle Cambrian Stephen Formation Burgess Shale and other localities; Kinzers Formation, Pennsylvania (see Conway Morris [1989b]). Description: Conway Morris (1977d).

74 (×5.5)

Phylum Annelida

CLASS POLYCHAETA (Bristle Worms and their allies)

Burgessochaeta

This is the most abundant Burgess Shale polychaete. The head ended in a pair of long tentacles, which apparently could be extended and retracted. On this specimen they presumably project down into the sediment anteriorly or perhaps they are folded under the head. There were at least 24 trunk segments, each bearing a pair of appendages. The first pair consisted of a single branch, but the remainder were biramous. The two branches (neuropodium and notopodium) were identical, bearing 11 to 17 setae. This specimen shows highly reflective traces of the gut. Other specimens show that the gut could be everted anteriorly to form a proboscis. *Burgessochaeta* is thought to have used the setae to move through burrows within the sediment. The proboscis may have assisted in burrowing, and the tentacles in feeding. The lack of an obvious filling of sediment in the gut suggests that *Burgessochaeta* was not a deposit feeder. It may have removed food particles selectively from the sediment.

Burgessochaeta differs from the other Burgess Shale polychaetes and is not clearly related to any modern family. It is assigned to its own family, the Burgessochaetidae.

77

Burgessochaeta setigera (Walcott, 1911d). USNM 83930b. Size range: 2–5 cm. Isham reconstruction. Proportion of total Burgess Shale assemblage in terms of numbers of individuals: 0.94%. Occurrence: Middle Cambrian Stephen Formation Burgess Shale. Description: Conway Morris (1979a).

76 (×8)

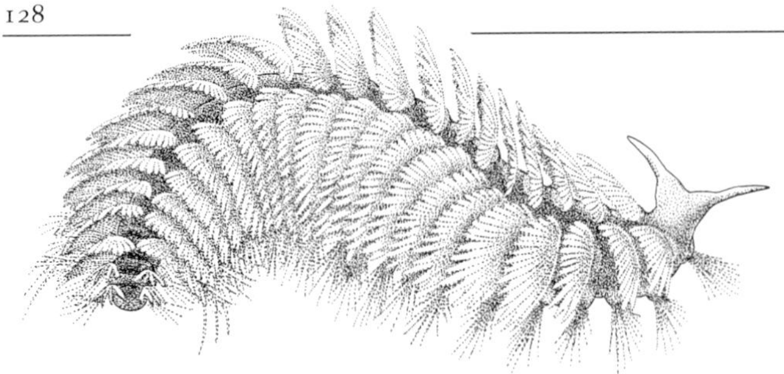

78

Canadia

The reflective preservation and clear outlines of the myriad of setae make specimens of *Canadia* some of the most spectacularly photogenic of Burgess Shale fossils. In one of the specimens shown here (Illustration 79), decay has loosened the setae and some have become detached and scattered around the carcass. The head (prostomium) bore a pair of long, slender, backward-curving tentacles. The gut could be everted anteriorly to form a proboscis. The trunk consisted of 20 to 22 segments, which became very small posteriorly. The first pair of limbs (parapodia) consisted of a single branch, but the remainder were biramous. The two branches were

79 (×2.5)

80 (×2)

very different. The notopodium typically carried 30 to 35 flattened setae that projected backward and covered the trunk. The neuropodium carried about 30 simple setae that projected laterally beyond the body outline. These overlapping bundles of laterally projecting setae are clearly seen in both the illustrated specimens. Some of those at the rear of the body are characteristically long. A small lobate structure (called a branchia) that projected at a level between the two branches of most parapodia was probably used for respiration. It is usually concealed by the setae, but where these have fallen away along the bottom of the partially decayed specimen, one or two branchiae are clearly evident (looking like tiny Christmas trees!). *Canadia* could use the limbs to walk on the substrate and to swim just above it. The tentacles may have been sensory. There is no filling of sediment in the gut, suggesting that this worm may have been a carnivore or scavenger. The proboscis may have been involved in food gathering.

Canadia differs from the other Burgess Shale polychaetes, but it shows some similarity to living palmyrid polychaetes. The differences are sufficient, however, to place it in a separate family, the Canadiidae, originally proposed by Walcott.

Canadia spinosa Walcott, 1911d. USNM 275517, USNM 83929c. Size range: 2–4.5 cm. Marianne Collins reconstruction. Proportion of total Burgess Shale assemblage in terms of numbers of individuals: 0.47%. Occurrence: Middle Cambrian Stephen Formation Burgess Shale. Description: Conway Morris (1979a).

81 (×5)

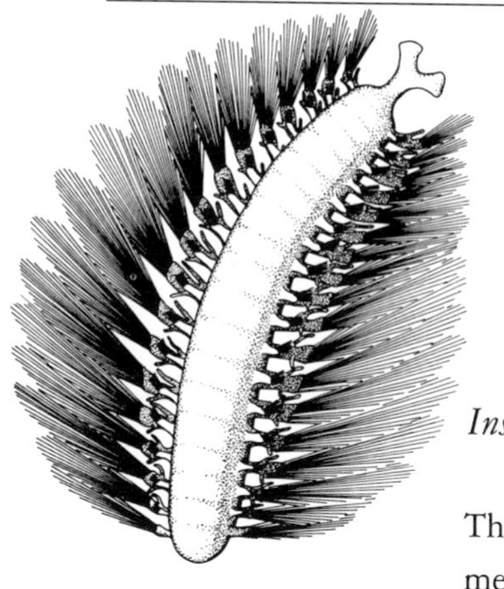

82

Insolicorypha

This is one of the rarest of Burgess Shale fossils: only a single specimen is known. Although it is tiny, the details are remarkably well preserved. The end interpreted as the head is unusual because it divides in two. Each of these projections is thought to have borne a sensory appendage. The trunk consisted of about 19 segments, but those at the posterior are not clear, because this part of the body has suffered some decay. The parapodia (apart from those of the first one or two segments) had two branches (i.e., they are biramous). The larger branch (the neuropodium) bore 30 to 40 simple setae extending out in a fan. Three tentaclelike cirri projected near the base. The much smaller second branch (the notopodium) is usually obscured, but one or two are evident, showing a bunch of about 10 setae. The large fan-shaped arrays of setae suggest that *Insolicorypha* may have been an active swimmer. This would explain its rarity. Pelagic animals, swimming in the water above the substrate, were less likely than bottom dwellers to be trapped by the rapidly moving clouds of sediment that buried the fauna.

Insolicorypha differs from the other Burgess Shale polychaetes and is not clearly related to any modern family. It is assigned to its own family, the Insolicoryphidae.

Insolicorypha psygma Conway Morris, 1979a. USNM 198712. Size: 9 mm. Isham reconstruction. Proportion of total Burgess Shale assemblage in terms of numbers of individuals: <0.01%. Occurrence: Middle Cambrian Stephen Formation Burgess Shale. Description: Conway Morris (1979a).

83 (×10)

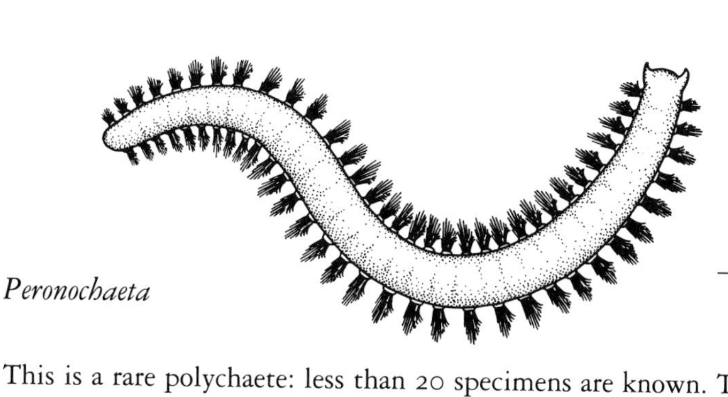

Peronochaeta

84

This is a rare polychaete: less than 20 specimens are known. The head (prostomium) bore a pair of small conical papillae at its anterior corners. The trunk consisted of up to 34 segments, all with similar one-branched (uniramous) parapodia. Each parapodium carried two types of setae, 15–20 long thin ones, and 2–4 flexed setae. *Peronochaeta* lacks a gut filling and may not have been a deposit feeder, living instead by scavenging. It used the long setae for locomotion either in or on the muddy substrate. The small flexed setae could have been used to grip the sediment during burrowing movement.

Peronochaeta cannot be accommodated in any family of polychaetes, fossil or recent. It is assigned to its own family, the Peronochaetidae.

Peronochaeta dubia (Walcott, 1911d). USNM 198718. Size range: 10–20 mm. Isham reconstruction. Proportion of total Burgess Shale assemblage in terms of numbers of individuals: <0.1%. Occurrence: Middle Cambrian Stephen Formation Burgess Shale. Description: Conway Morris (1979a).

85 (×6)

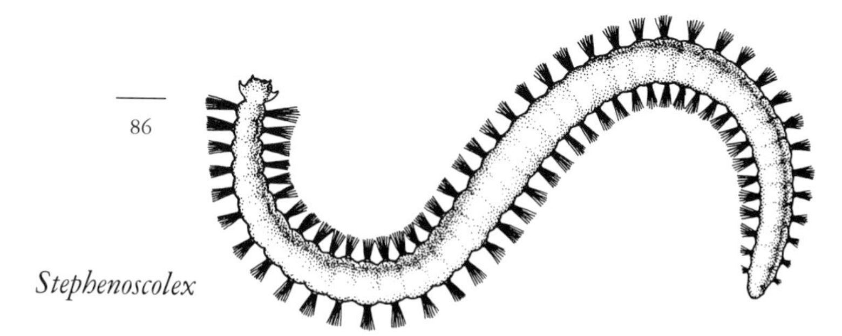

86

Stephenoscolex

This is one of the rarest of Burgess Shale fossils: only two specimens are known. Both are preserved in a highly reflective film (hence the species name *argutus,* which means "bright, shiny"). The head (prostomium) bore a number of small conical papillae. The limbs of the trunk (parapodia) consisted of just one branch that ended in a bunch of 10 to 15 straight setae. Twenty-one pairs of parapodia are evident, but additional pairs are obscured in the posterior part of the body. The trunk in that region appears to have been twisted and lies in a different orientation to the bedding; the parapodia may be compacted onto it and obscured by the reflective surface. There are few clues as to the mode of life of *Stephenoscolex,* but it probably moved about either in or on the surface of the muddy sediment.

Stephenoscolex differs from the other Burgess Shale polychaetes and is not clearly related to any modern family. It is assigned to its own family, the Stephenoscolecidae.

Stephenoscolex argutus Conway Morris, 1979a. USNM 83936b. Size: 32 mm. Isham reconstruction. Proportion of total Burgess Shale assemblage in terms of numbers of individuals: <0.01%. Occurrence: Middle Cambrian Stephen Formation Burgess Shale; equivocal record in the Spence Shale, Utah (see Conway Morris [1989b]). Description: Conway Morris (1979a).

Phylum Onychophora (Velvet Worms)

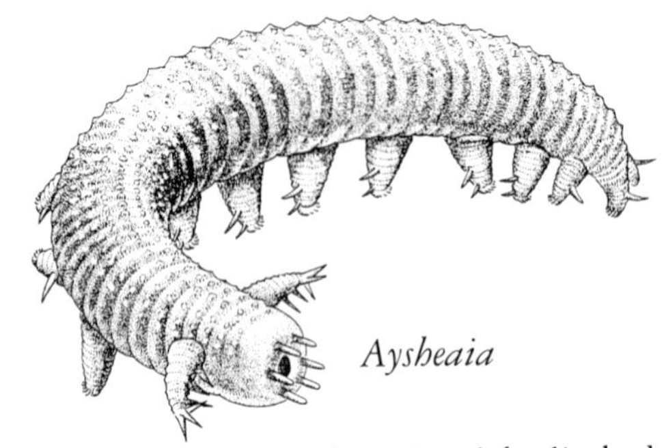

Aysheaia

87

Aysheaia is a lobe-limbed animal or lobopod. Both of the specimens in the photographs afford a view from the right side. The specimen shown in Illustration 88 appears to be walking, with the right limbs extending beyond the body. The trunk has been removed in two places to show how the left limbs are concealed beneath the body as a result of flattening of the specimen in an oblique orientation to bedding. The specimen in Illustration 89 is curved. The head shows three of the fingerlike projections (papillae) that surrounded the mouth. A pair of tapering limbs with long spines projects straight out from the side of the head; the left one is particularly well displayed on both these specimens. The trunk of *Aysheaia* was annulated, as were the 10 pairs of lobelike walking appendages. They end in little curved claws that tend to be highly reflective. Reflective traces of the gut can also be seen

88 (×2)

89 (×1.6)

on the curved specimen. The criss-cross pattern on the right side of part of the curved specimen (Illustration 89) is created by the spicules of a sponge that is compacted against it. This association of *Aysheaia* with sponge spicules is not uncommon and suggests that it may have fed on them. *Aysheaia* may have used the papillae around the mouth to penetrate the soft sponge tissue while holding on with the spiny head appendages and with the claws on the trunk limbs.

Aysheaia has been compared with the modern onychophorans, or "velvet worms," which live in forest litter in the Southern Hemisphere. A range of similar forms has now been described from the Lower Cambrian of China and elsewhere. They represent a primitive sister group of the arthropods.

Aysheaia pedunculata Walcott, 1911d. USNM 235880, 83942a. Size range: 1–6 cm. Marianne Collins reconstruction. Proportion of total Burgess Shale assemblage in terms of numbers of individuals: 0.05%. Occurrence: Middle Cambrian Stephen Formation Burgess Shale and locality 9 of Collins et al. (1983); Wheeler Formation (see Conway Morris [1989b]). Description: Whittington (1978). Other important reference: Robison (1985).

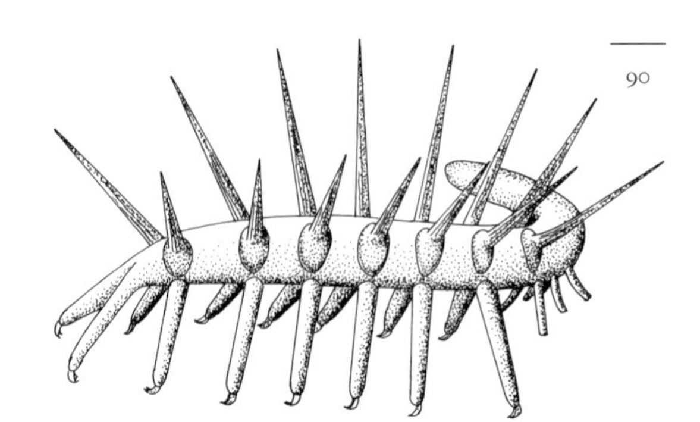

Hallucigenia

Hallucigenia has become one of the most notorious of the Burgess Shale animals. It was originally described by Walcott as a polychaete annelid. Conway Morris, however, observed that the specimens only show spines along one side of the trunk, unlike polychaetes, which have regularly spaced bundles of bristles on both sides. He named the animal *Hallucigenia* in recognition of its "bizarre and dream-like quality." His 1977 restoration depicted *Hallucigenia* walking on the spines, as if on stilts, with the seven dorsal tentacles waving in the water. The head was poorly defined, obscured by a dark stain. It seemed possible that each tentacle terminated in an individual mouth, connected by a narrow tube to the main gut, which ran the length of the trunk. Small wonder that *Hallucigenia* occupied center stage in the debate about how weird the Cambrian organisms are compared with those of today.

The discovery of a group of animals in the exceptionally preserved Lower Cambrian Chengjiang Fauna of China suggested a different interpretation of *Hallucigenia.* The Chengjiang Fauna includes a number of "armored lobopods," caterpillarlike animals with lobelike appendages and isolated plates on the dorsal surface, sometimes with spines. These lobopod animals suggested that the spines of *Hallucigenia* were actually designed to protect the dorsal side of the animal, and the tentacles were long limbs with claws at the tip: the previous restorations showed the animal upside down! But although the specimens clearly show that the spines were paired, only one set of these tentaclelike limbs was evident; if they were limbs, they too should be paired. In 1992 Ramsköld reported that he had revealed traces of the second row of limbs by carrying out very delicate preparation on one of the best specimens

91 (×3)

92 (×3)

of *Hallucigenia.* His work confirmed that the image of *Hallucigenia* that became an icon for the weirdness of the Burgess Shale fauna was both upside down and back to front!

Hallucigenia and the other armored lobopods can be grouped together with *Aysheaia* (which has no armor plates) in the Phylum Onychophora, a group that is represented today by the velvet worms like *Peripatus,* which live on land. Relationships within this group of Cambrian lobopods, and between them and the modern onychophorans, have yet to be completely resolved.

Hallucigenia sparsa (Walcott, 1911d). USNM 83935, 198658. Size range: 0.5–3 cm long. Baldaro reconstruction. Proportion of total Burgess Shale assemblage in terms of numbers of individuals: 0.1%. Occurrence: Middle Cambrian Stephen Formation Burgess Shale. Description: Conway Morris (1977a). Other important references: Ramsköld and Hou (1991), Ramsköld (1992).

Phylum Arthropoda
Primitive

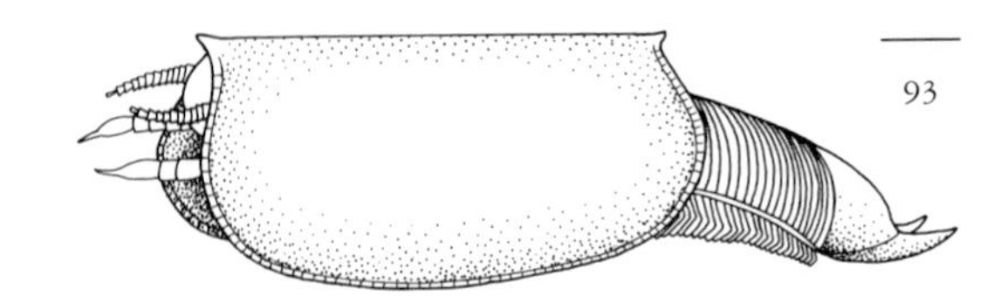
93

Branchiocaris

Branchiocaris is one of the rarest of the arthropods in the Walcott Quarry. Four specimens were collected by Walcott and an additional one by a Harvard expedition in 1930. The counterpart of this last specimen was found in the scree below the quarry by a Royal Ontario Museum party in 1975, 45 years later! *Branchiocaris* is now known from several other localities in British Columbia and elsewhere.

Branchiocaris had a large bivalved carapace, with a straight hinge line, which covered the anterior of the body. A narrow border followed the margins of the valves, with a series of small, irregularly spaced, elongate pits. In the specimen shown in Illustration 94, much of the carapace has been removed to reveal the trunk beneath, although the head remains largely obscured. The specimen is flattened in an oblique attitude. The outline of the left valve was complete before preparation; the right valve is folded beneath itself. The trunk was made up of over 40 divisions, separated by annulations. The appendages were large flaplike structures. There is some evidence that they were strengthened by a segmented ridge where they are attached to the trunk. There appear to be more limbs than there are divisions of the trunk. Thus these divisions may not have been true somites. The telson bore a pair of broad bladelike processes. The slightly darker band evident in the posterior part of the trunk of the specimen in Illustration 94 may represent the gut.

The specimen of *Branchiocaris* in Illustration 95 shows the head appendages. A pair of short, robust antennae curves forward; the left one is clearly evident. A pair of larger appendages flanks the antennae and terminates in what appears to be a claw. There is

94 (×1.5)

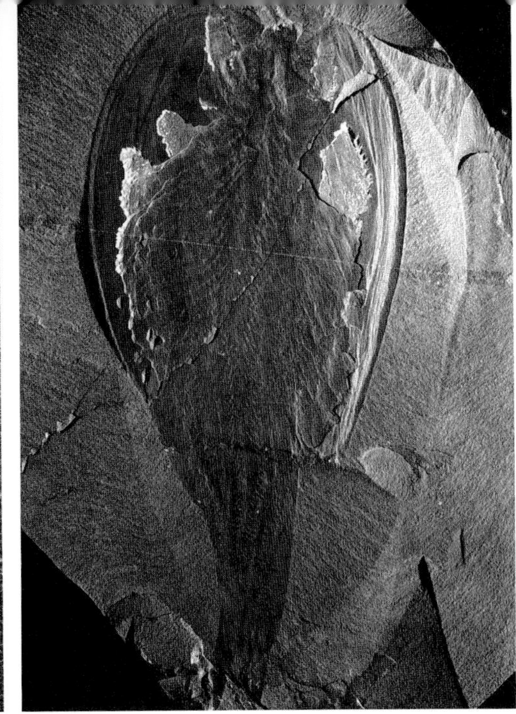

95 (×1.5)

no evidence of eyes. The long series of lamellate trunk appendages is evident, with traces of segmented structures near their attachment. The margins of two or three of the lamellae have been revealed by removing part of the overlying carapace. In contrast to the specimen in Illustration 94, this one is flattened dorsoventrally and is almost bilaterally symmetrical. The blades of the telson point directly posteriorly. *Branchiocaris* probably swam near the sea bottom, over the surface of the mud. Because it lacked eyes, it is unlikely to have been an active predator. It probably scavenged on carcasses or preyed on sessile animals, using the claws to transfer food directly to the mouth.

Branchiocaris is crustaceanlike, with its bivalved carapace and flaplike appendages, but much of its morphology is primitive, placing it near the origin of the Cambrian arthropods.

Branchiocaris pretiosa (Resser, 1929). USNM 80483, 189028a. Size range: about 7 to over 9 cm long. Baldaro reconstruction. Proportion of total Burgess Shale assemblage in terms of numbers of individuals: 0.01%. Occurrence: Lower Cambrian Chengjiang Fauna of China; Middle Cambrian Stephen Formation Burgess Shale and locality 9 of Collins et al. (1983); Marjum Formation, Utah; and possibly other localities (see Conway Morris [1989b]). Description: Briggs (1976). Other important references: Briggs and Robison (1984), Hou (1987).

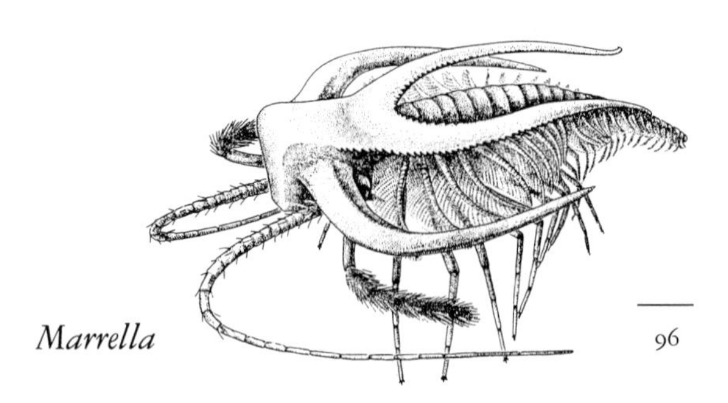

Marrella 96

Marrella, called the "lace crab" by Walcott, is the most abundant of all the Burgess Shale animals. A total of over 15,000 has been collected from the Walcott Quarry. *Marrella* was the first animal to be described by Harry Whittington during the restudy of the Burgess Shale, which started in the 1960s. He used it to demonstrate that the specimens had been transported in a turbulent cloud of sediment and buried at various angles in the mud. Combining the evidence from specimens preserved in different attitudes has allowed the Burgess Shale animals to be restored in three dimensions. The strange head shield of *Marrella* had two pairs of large curving spines, the rear pair extending back the full length of the body. There were two pairs of antennae, the first with a large number of uniform short segments, the second ending in a brushlike tip. The many trunk segments diminished in size toward the rear, each with a pair of biramous limbs. The dark stain that is seen surrounding the rear of many specimens is the result of fluids seeping from the body during early decay. *Marrella* presumably fed on small animals and organic particles as it moved over the surface of the sediment. The brushlike antennae may have been used to sweep particles toward the mouth. The feathery filaments on the outer branch of the limbs were used for respiration.

The morphology of *Marrella* is primitive, with a large number of body segments bearing identical limbs. It is the kind of arthropod that could have given rise to any of the three great aquatic arthropod groups—the crustaceans, chelicerates, or trilobites.

97 (×4.5)

Marrella splendens Walcott, 1912a. USNM 83486j. Size range: 2.5 to 19 mm. Marianne Collins reconstruction. Proportion of total Burgess Shale assemblage in terms of numbers of individuals: 37.4%. Occurrence: Middle Cambrian Stephen Formation Burgess Shale and *Ogygopsis* Shale (see Conway Morris [1989b]). Description: Whittington (1971b). Other important reference: Briggs and Whittington (1985a).

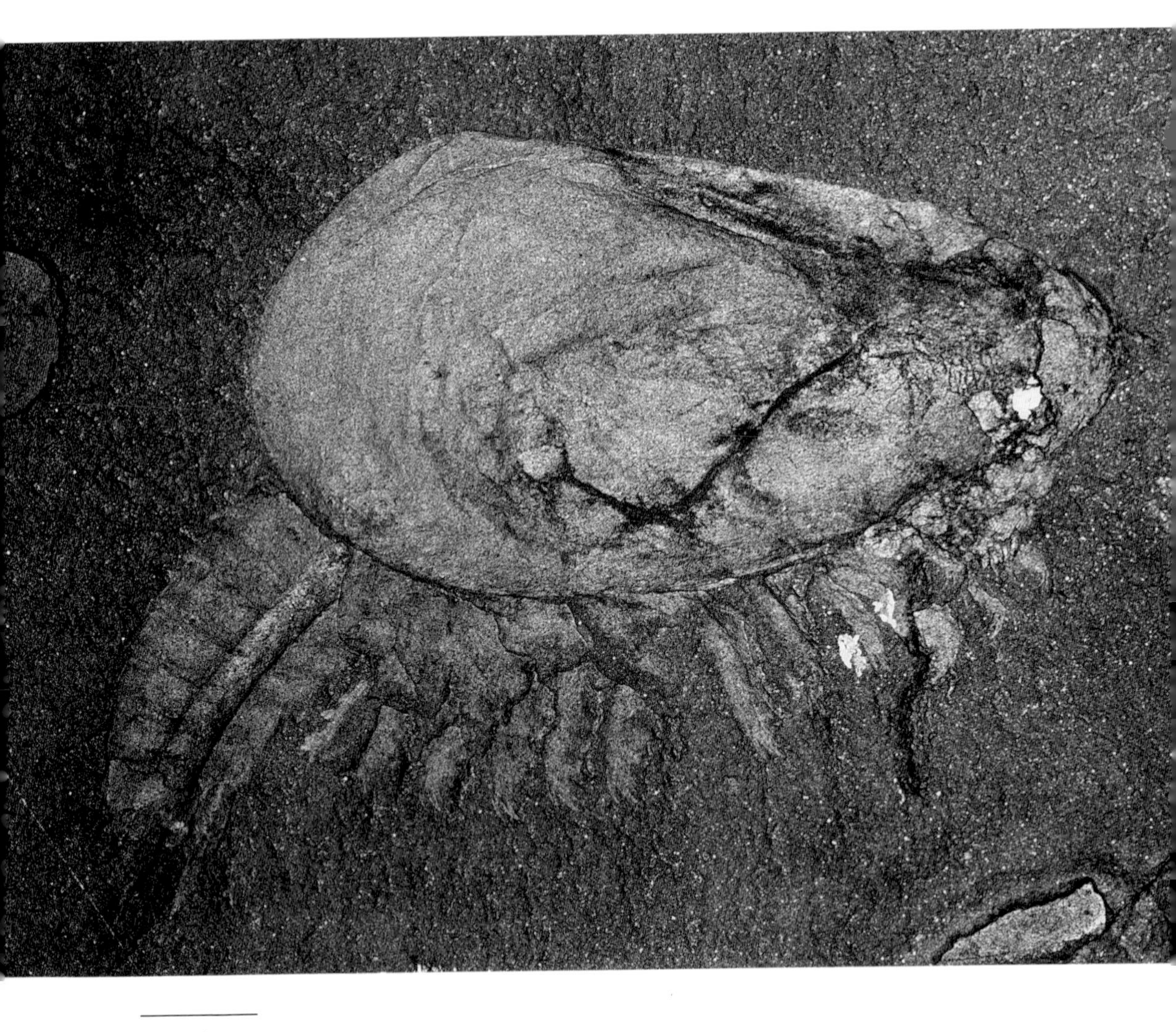

98 (×4)

Subphylum Crustacea and Crustaceanomorphs
(Crabs and their allies)

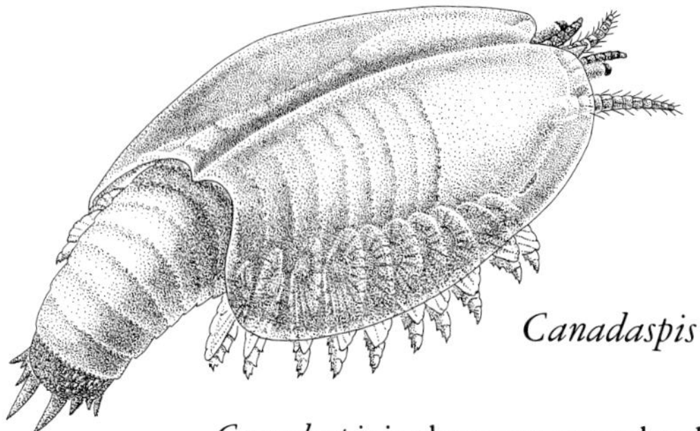

Canadaspis

99

Canadaspis is the most completely known of the crustaceans in the Burgess Shale. The carapace consisted of two valves connected by a straight hinge. The specimen in Illustration 98 shows the right valve, with the abdomen and the appendages of the thorax projecting beyond it. The gut trace is clearly picked out in relief. The limbs of *Canadaspis* were biramous. The inner branch, which was segmented and used for walking, is clearly displayed in this specimen, ending in small curved claws. Some of the outer flaplike gill branches are seen overlapping each other just forward of where the abdomen emerges from between the valves. The abdomen itself lacks limbs except for the spines of the telson, which can be seen projecting beyond the end of the gut trace, which marks the position of the anus. *Canadaspis* is thought to have used its limbs to churn up the sediment in search of the small animals and organic particles upon which it fed.

The specimen of *Canadaspis* shown in Illustrations 100 and 101 is compacted so that we are looking down on the right-hand side. The abdomen emerges from between the valves of the carapace. A number of the somites can be distinguished and, at the posterior end, the spines of the telson. Illustration 100 shows the specimen before preparation. Illustration 101 shows it after most of the right valve had been dissected away to reveal the flaplike gill branches of the limbs that lie beneath, overlapping in a series from front to back. *Canadaspis* undoubtedly used these flaps for swimming, as well as for oxygen exchange in respiration. This specimen preserves the limbs frozen in time, each successive flap a little farther along in the swimming stroke, which moved like a wave down the length of the thorax.

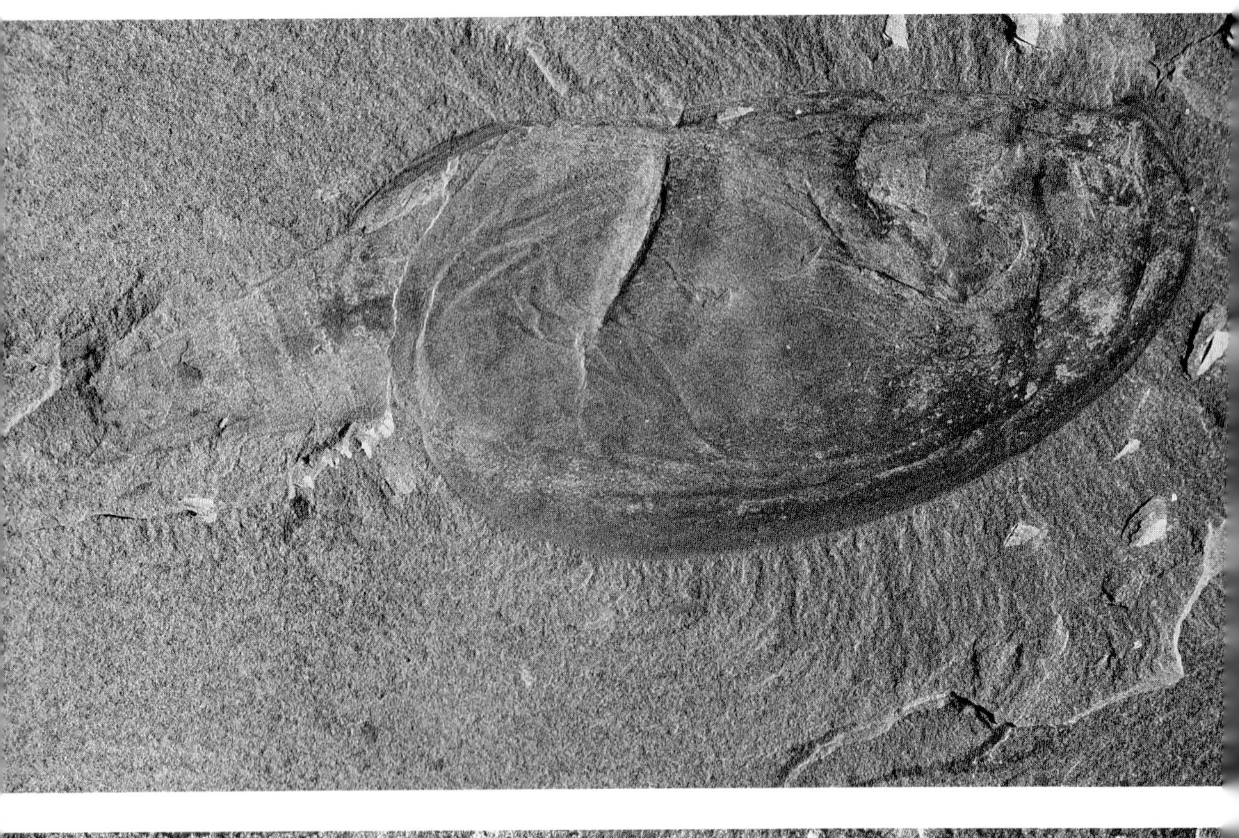

Canadaspis certainly looks like a crustacean—some living forms also have a bivalved carapace and a similar arrangement of appendages. The evidence that clinches its crustacean affinities, however, lies in the limbs of the head. Just a handful of the 4,000+ specimens show the two pairs of antennae, the mandibles, and the maxillae characteristic of crustaceans. Usually the smaller limbs are concealed under the carapace, where they are compacted into the outline of the head.

Canadaspis perfecta (Walcott, 1912a). USNM 57703, 213856. Size range: length of carapace from less than 10 to over 50 mm. Marianne Collins reconstruction. Proportion of total Burgess Shale assemblage in terms of numbers of individuals: 11.69%. Occurrence: Middle Cambrian, Spence Shale, Utah; Stephen Formation, *Ogygopsis* Shale, Burgess Shale (see Conway Morris [1989b]). Description: Briggs (1978a, 1992). Other important references: Dahl (1983, 1984).

100 (×4)

101 (×4)

102 (×4)

Isoxys

Isoxys, like *Tuzoia,* is known only from specimens of the valves. The specimen illustrated here shows the two valves attached along the straight hinge line. Note that even the slight variation in their orientation to bedding has resulted in a difference in outline. Reliable evidence of the soft parts of *Isoxys* has yet to be found. The Burgess Shale species, *I. acutangulus,* was described by Walcott in 1908 (before his great discovery) based on specimens from the *Ogygopsis* Shale on Mount Stephen. At that time Walcott tentatively referred *acutangulus* to *Anomalocaris,* reflecting his belief that what we now know to be the feeding appendage of *Anomalocaris* might be the body belonging to various carapaces, including *Isoxys.* In 1975 Simonetta and Delle Cave described a second species of *Isoxys* from the Burgess Shale, *I. longissimus,* which is characterized by extraordinarily long spines projecting from the anterior and posterior of the hinge line. Otherwise the Burgess Shale material of this genus has received little attention. *Isoxys* may have lived swimming in the water column, thus avoiding the clouds of sediment that trapped the fauna. In that case the specimens in the Burgess Shale are mainly valves of dead or molted individuals. *Isoxys* is one of the longer-ranging Burgess Shale taxa, occurring in at least 12 localities from the Lower Cambrian of China to the Middle Cambrian of Utah.

Isoxys acutangulus (Walcott, 1908a). USNM 189181. Size range: length of valves ranges from about 1 to over 3 cm. Proportion of total Burgess Shale assemblage in terms of numbers of individuals: none buried alive. Occurrence: Middle Cambrian Stephen Formation Burgess Shale and other localities (see Collins et al. [1983], Conway Morris [1989b]). Description: Walcott (1908a). Other important reference: Simonetta and Delle Cave (1975).

103

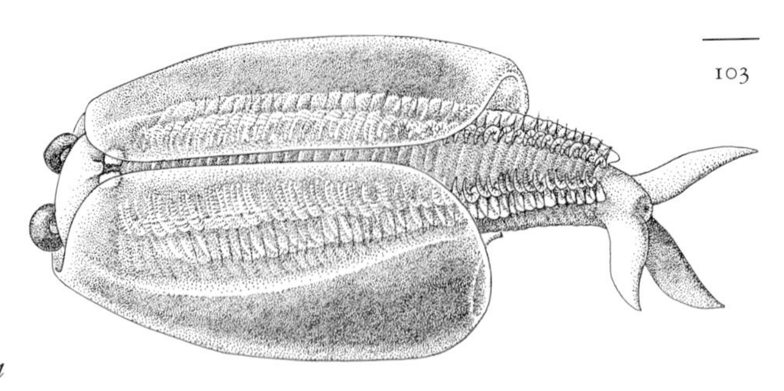

Odaraia

Odaraia is one of the most remarkable of the Burgess Shale arthropods in terms of its functional design. It had a pair of enormous eyes. The two valves met along the ventral margin so that the carapace formed a tube that opened at the front and rear. The telson had three blades or flukes, the lateral ones projecting horizontally, the median one vertically. The specimen in Illustration 105 is tilted down and forward so that the carapace extends beyond the eyes and the whole animal is foreshortened. The valves have broken away to reveal the eyes beneath. The carapace widens posteriorly and part of the trunk, and the telson, project beyond it. In the specimen in Illustration 104 the carapace has broken away to reveal the trunk beneath. The trunk bears a long series of similar biramous appendages. Most of the limbs of *Odaraia* were enclosed within the carapace and could not have come in contact with the sediment surface. The arthropod is interpreted as an active swimmer, using the large eyes to seek out shoals of small floating or swimming organisms. These were captured by the appendages, which sieved them out of a current of water passing through the tubelike carapace. The arthropod is most likely to have swum upside down, to minimize the uneven drag that would otherwise have occurred because of the slight gap at the junction between the valves. The telson was adapted to prevent rolling of the otherwise rather unstable animal in the water and to help in steering. The power for swimming was generated by the appendages. The limbs of the head in *Odaraia* are small and concealed by the carapace. There is some evidence, however, of small antennae and a strengthened mandible.

104 (×2)

Odaraia is related to the crustaceans.

105 (×2.5)

Odaraia alata Walcott, 1912a. USNM 213809, 189232. Size range: 6–15 cm. Marianne Collins reconstruction. Proportion of total Burgess Shale assemblage in terms of numbers of individuals: 0.06%. Occurrence: Middle Cambrian Stephen Formation Burgess Shale; a similar form was reported from the Lower Cambrian Chengjiang Fauna of China. Description: Briggs (1981a). Other important references: Briggs and Williams (1981), Hou and Sun (1988).

106 (×7)

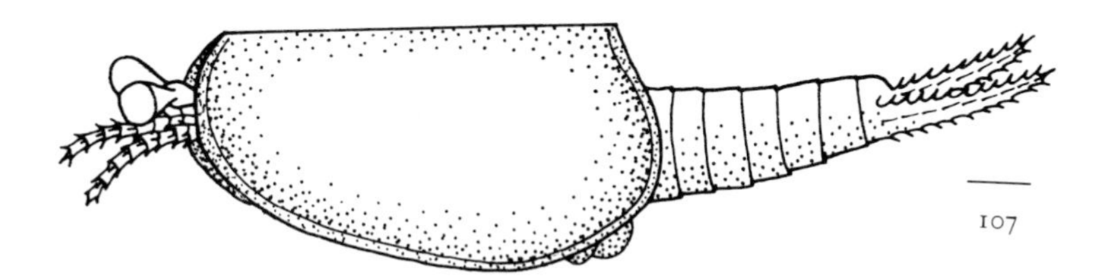

107

Perspicaris

Perspicaris was a bivalved arthropod. This specimen provides a slightly oblique view. The complete outline of the right valve can be seen, separated by the straight hinge line from the left valve, which is folded beneath itself. The head is obscured, but the eyes, which give *Perspicaris* its name (perspicax means "sharp sighted"), are clearly displayed. The abdomen extended beyond the carapace. It terminated in a telson that bore a pair of long bladelike appendages, fringed by tiny spines. The trunk limbs of *Perspicaris* are not exposed in this specimen, but another example shows them to have been large, flat lamellae. The rarity of this arthropod, together with its flaplike appendages and large eyes, suggests that it was a swimmer, living in the water column. Only occasional specimens were overwhelmed by the clouds of sediment that preserve the Burgess Shale fauna.

Perspicaris shows a number of similarities to *Canadaspis* and, like it, belongs to the Subphylum Crustacea.

Perspicaris dictynna (Simonetta and Delle Cave, 1975). USNM 189245. Size: average length 2.24 cm. Baldaro reconstruction. Proportion of total Burgess Shale assemblage in terms of numbers of individuals: <0.1%. Occurrence: Middle Cambrian Stephen Formation Burgess Shale and *Ogygopsis* Shale and a number of equivocal records including the Lower Cambrian Chengjiang Fauna (see Conway Morris [1989b]). Description: Briggs (1977).

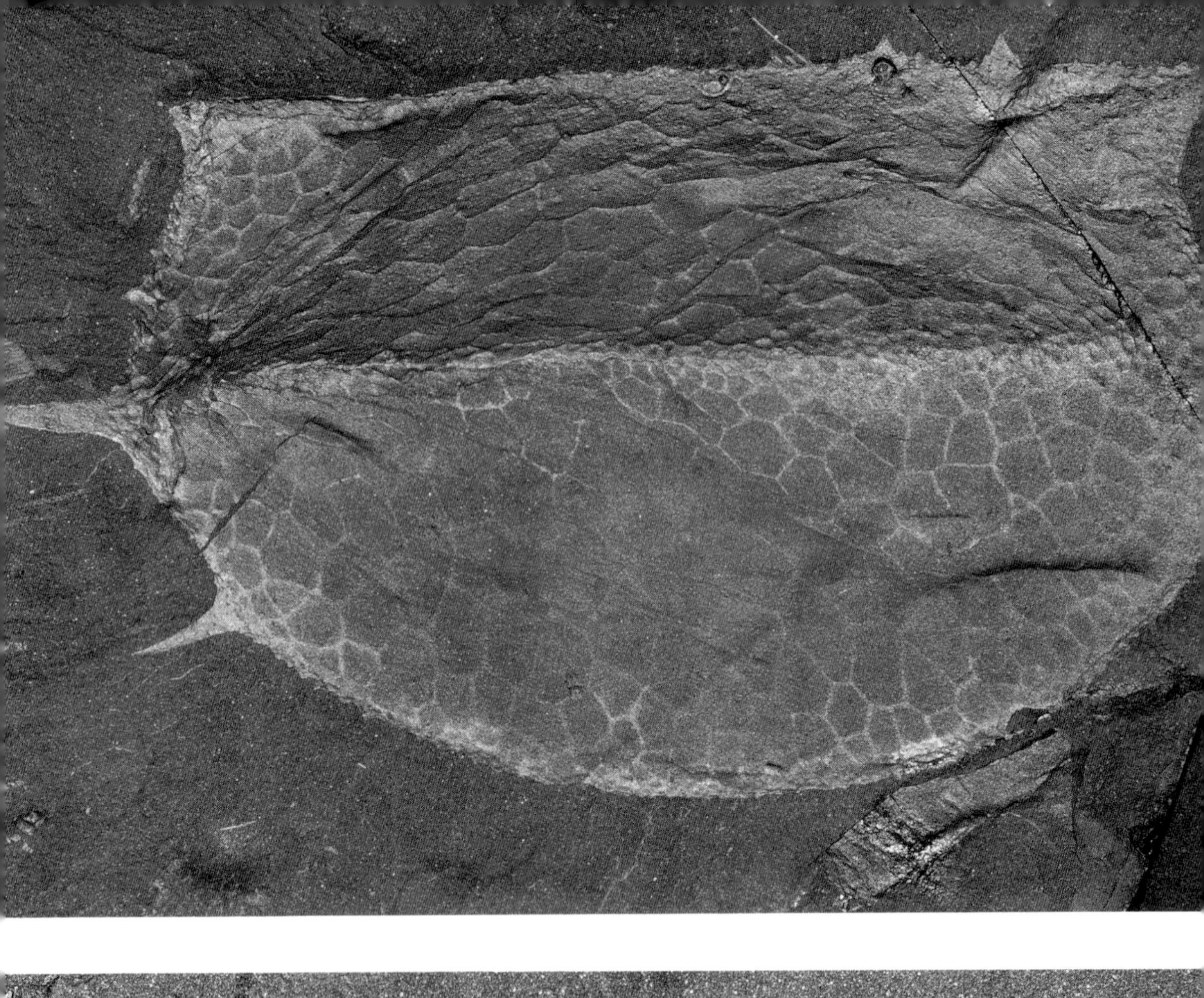

Tuzoia

The valves of *Tuzoia* remain one of the enigmas of the Burgess Shale. Although several tens of specimens are known, definitive evidence of the soft parts of this large arthropod has yet to be found. While the large feeding appendages of *Anomalocaris canadensis* were still mistakenly considered to represent the body of an arthropod, a number of authors suggested that *Tuzoia* might be the carapace of the same animal. Thus the restoration of the Burgess Shale fauna by the famous artist Charles R. Knight, published in *National Geographic Magazine* in 1942, shows *Tuzoia* swimming with an *Anomalocaris* appendage projecting from the valves in place of the trunk. The specimen of *Tuzoia* in Illustration 108 shows a single valve in lateral view; the specimen in Illustration 109 shows the two valves hinged together. The valves are characterized by a straight hinge line, a reticulate pattern on the surface that is variably developed, and spines around the margin. *Tuzoia* may have swum in the water column, and living individuals were rarely if ever trapped in the sediment flows that buried the Burgess Shale fauna. It is one of the longer-ranging Burgess Shale genera, occurring in at least 12 localities from the Lower Cambrian of China to the Middle Cambrian of Utah.

108 (×1.5)

Tuzoia awaits detailed systematic revision. Walcott described the genus based on just one species, *Tuzoia retifera,* in 1912. Resser, however, described three more species from the Burgess Shale in 1929, *T. burgessensis, T. canadensis,* and *T. praemorsa,* as well as a number of forms from other localities. The outline of the valves, the distribution of ridges, and the scale of reticulation on various parts of the valves vary depending on how the specimen is compacted. In 1975 Simonetta and Delle Cave suggested that *T.*

109 (×2)

burgessensis and *T. canadensis* are synonymous with Walcott's *T. retifera.* All the available Burgess Shale material of *Tuzoia* needs to be studied to determine how many species are present.

In the absence of evidence of the soft parts, the affinities of *Tuzoia* are uncertain. It may be related to the crustaceans.

Tuzoia burgessensis Resser, 1929. USNM 80477. *Tuzoia praemorsa* Resser, 1929. USNM 80488b. Size range: length of valves ranges from about 5 to about 16 cm. Proportion of total Burgess Shale assemblage in terms of numbers of individuals: none buried alive. Occurrence: Middle Cambrian Stephen Formation Burgess Shale and other localities (see Collins et al. [1983], Conway Morris [1989b]). Description: Walcott (1912a), Resser (1929). Other important reference: Simonetta and Delle Cave (1975).

110

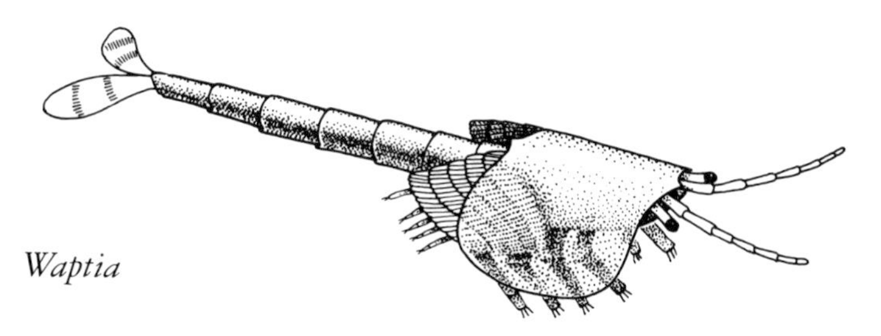

Waptia

One of the illustrated specimens shows the arthropod *Waptia* in dorsal view (Illustration 112), the other in lateral view (Illustration 111). A pair of antennae and eyes project in front of the carapace. Other small appendages were present in the head region, but they are usually concealed by compaction against the head or carapace. The valves of the carapace did not separate easily but folded along a median line that functioned as a hinge. The trunk appendages were attached to a series of short somites beneath the valves. The functions of walking and oxygen exchange were separated. The first four limbs consisted only of a walking limb, the following six of a gill branch with blade-shaped filaments. This difference is evident in the laterally flattened specimen. Some of the gill branches are also evident in the dorsal view, extending beyond the

111 (×1.5)

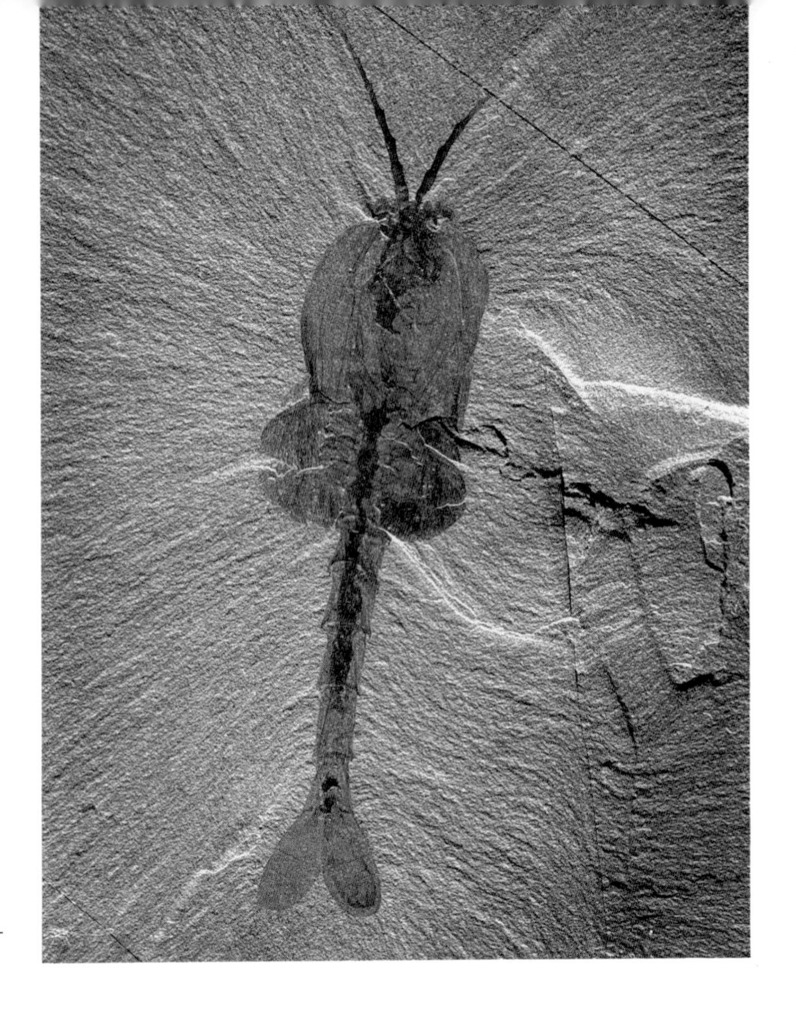

112 (×1.8)

carapace. The abdomen consisted of five somites and lacked limbs apart from two large segmented flaps at the extremity, which made up a caudal furca or tail fork attached to the long telson. Traces of the gut are evident in the dorsal view. *Waptia* lived on the sea bottom. It swam using the gill branches, stabilizing and steering itself with the telson flaps. It could balance on the substrate on the walking limbs. *Waptia* did not have strongly developed jaw appendages. It presumably fed on organic particles in the sediment.

Waptia has yet to be redescribed in detail. Preliminary studies suggest that it is a crustacean, but not one that fits readily into any of the modern crustacean groups.

Waptia fieldensis Walcott, 1912a. USNM 13823, 83948e. Size: usual length about 7.5 cm. Isham reconstruction. Proportion of total Burgess Shale assemblage in terms of numbers of individuals: 2.55%. Occurrence: Middle Cambrian Stephen Formation Burgess Shale. Description: Hughes in Conway Morris et al. (1982). Other important reference: Briggs (1983).

Subphylum Arachnomorpha
CLASS TRILOBITA (Trilobites)

The vast majority of trilobites in the fossil record are known only from the dorsal exoskeleton, because it alone was mineralized (in calcite) in life. It is not surprising, therefore, that some of the most celebrated Burgess Shale fossils are the trilobites that preserve other features—limbs and additional "soft" tissues. Most famous is *Olenoides,* perhaps the most completely known trilobite from anywhere. More unusual is *Naraoia,* a trilobite with an organically strengthened rather than a mineralized exoskeleton. Surprisingly, however, of the 13 Burgess Shale trilobite genera with calcified exoskeletons, only *Kootenia* and *Elrathina,* apart from *Olenoides,* preserve any evidence of soft parts. And although specimens of *Olenoides* with soft parts are relatively numerous, the limbs are very rarely preserved in the other two genera.

Why is soft-part preservation confined to so few of the Burgess Shale trilobites? In some cases the explanation may be simple: the trilobite was very rare. If others were represented only by fragments, we could explain them as the remains of molts or dead individuals that disarticulated before or during the sediment slides. But in most cases there is a significant proportion of complete exoskeletons. This suggests that some of the trilobites may have been buried alive and that the soft tissues decayed away in place. It is probably more than a coincidence that the trilobites with preserved appendages, *Olenoides* and *Naraoia,* are the largest and that their limbs are armed with spines. The limbs of these predators would have been thicker and more robust than those of the other trilobites and therefore more likely to be preserved. Such variation in preservation potential is evident even within *Olenoides,* where the thinner ventral cuticle of the body has largely disappeared even though the limbs survive.

The illustrations show examples of 11 of the 15 genera of

Burgess Shale trilobites. Omitted are the uncommon *Hanburia, Peronopsis, Spencella,* and *Tegopelte.* The mode of life of the Burgess Shale trilobites is very poorly known except for the completely preserved taxa *Olenoides* and *Naraoia,* which were predators. The limbs of *Kootenia* and *Elrathina* are too inadequately preserved to allow any meaningful deductions to be made. The agnostids *Ptychagnostus* and *Peronopsis* and the eodiscoid *Pagetia* are assumed to have been pelagic, floating or swimming in the water column. The remaining trilobites presumably lived on the seabed. The more abundant examples may have been deposit feeders on the muddy substrate, but even that is only speculation.

The major reference on the Burgess Shale trilobites is by Rasetti (1951). He (1963) assigned specimens to *Spencella* that he formerly (1951) tentatively identified as *Solenopleurella.* Whittington (1975b, 1980a) redescribed and interpreted *Olenoides.* Conway Morris (1986) considered the relative abundance of live and dead specimens. Whittington (1977, 1985a) described the soft-bodied trilobites *Naraoia* and *Tegopelte* and listed (1985b) the entire trilobite fauna.

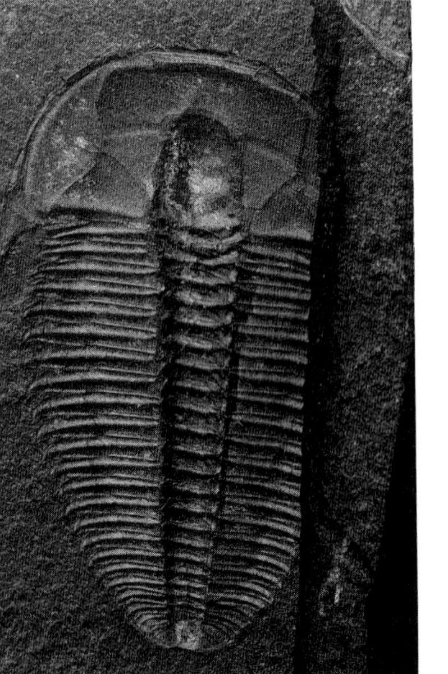

Chancia palliseri (Walcott, 1908b) (Ptychopariida). USNM 116236c. Size range: 30–36 mm. Occurrence: Middle Cambrian Stephen Formation Burgess Shale and *Ogygopsis* Shale. Description: Rasetti (1951).

---

113 (×2)

Ehmaniella burgessensis Rasetti, 1951 (Ptychopariida). USNM 116246a. Size range: up to 27.5 mm. Occurrence: Middle Cambrian Stephen Formation Burgess Shale and a large number of adjacent localities (see Rasetti [1951], Collins et al. [1983]). Description: Rasetti (1951).

114 (×3)

Ehmaniella waptaensis Rasetti, 1951 (Ptychopariida). USNM 116244b. Size range: up to 12 mm. Occurrence: Middle Cambrian Stephen Formation Burgess Shale. Description: Rasetti (1951).

115 (×8)

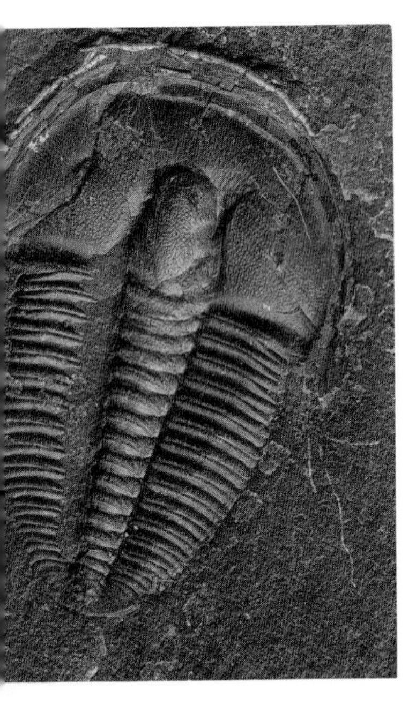

Elrathia permulta (Walcott, 1918b) (Ptychopariida). USNM 116240a. Very rare. Size range: up to at least 21 mm. Occurrence: Middle Cambrian Stephen Formation Burgess Shale. Description: Rasetti (1951).

116 (×3)

Elrathina cordillerae (Rominger, 1887) (Ptychopariida). USNM 116225. Size range: up to at least 20 mm. Occurrence: Middle Cambrian Stephen Formation Burgess Shale and *Ogygopsis* Shale. Description: Rasetti (1951).

117 (×4)

Kootenia burgessensis Resser, 1942 (Corynexochida). USNM 65511. Size range: up to at least 40 mm. Occurrence: Middle Cambrian Stephen Formation Burgess Shale and Mount Field. Description: Resser (1942).

118 (×1.5)

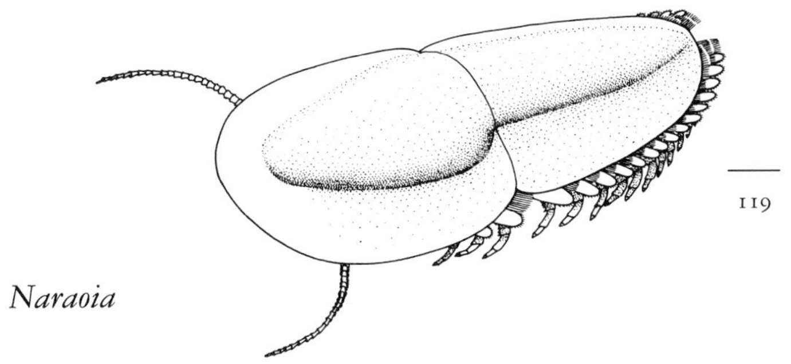

119

Naraoia

Naraoia is a remarkable trilobite in two main ways: unlike almost all other trilobites, the dorsal exoskeleton was not calcified, only organically strengthened; and the exoskeleton consisted of only two shields, rather than the cephalon, thorax, and pygidium in *Olenoides* and other trilobites.

The specimen of *Naraoia* in Illustration 120 is obliquely compacted so that the right side (particularly of the head shield) is distorted, whereas the limbs of the left side are all displayed. The limbs of the trilobite had two branches (i.e., they were biramous), one jointed and used mainly for walking, the other with a series of filaments for oxygen exchange. The gill branches consisted of rows of long filaments. Harry Whittington dissected away part of the head shield and gill filaments on this specimen to reveal some of the walking limbs beneath. This, and other specimens of *Naraoia,* reveal that these walking limbs carried a formidable array of spines. *Naraoia* appears to have been well equipped as a predator. It fed on worms and other soft-bodied creatures. Be-

120 (×2)

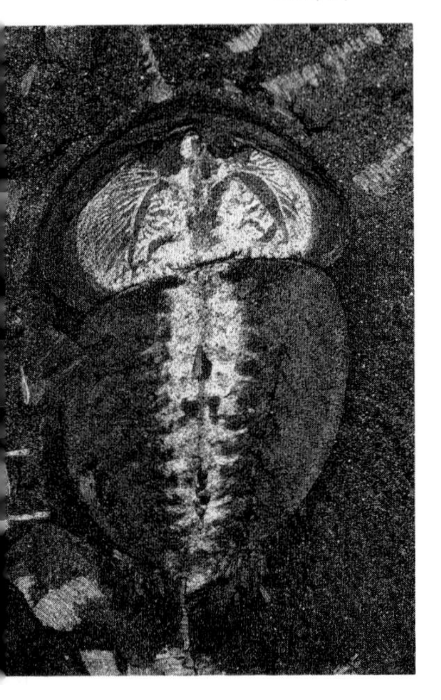

121 (×2.5)

cause the trilobites became extinct by the end of the Paleozoic, we rely on the evidence of remarkably preserved fossils, like those of the Burgess Shale, for glimpses of the soft-part morphology and mode of life of these arthropods.

But how do we know that *Naraoia* belongs with the trilobites? It does not look at all like *Olenoides.* The limbs of *Naraoia* were very like those of other trilobites, with two branches. Not only was each individual limb similar, but their arrangement was the same. Both *Naraoia* and *Olenoides* had a pair of antennae (the left one is evident in the specimen in Illustration 120) and three pairs of biramous limbs in the head, which were essentially the same as those in the trunk. The posterior shield of *Naraoia* is equivalent to both the thorax and pygidium in *Olenoides* and other trilobites. *Naraoia* evolved from the early trilobites at a stage before the exoskeleton became strengthened with calcium carbonate. The massive spiny limbs may have required the extra support of a fused thorax and pygidium for muscle attachment. In the specimen in Illustration 121, the gut is evident as a silver trace on the exoskeleton. In the head region two complex branching digestive glands, the gut diverticula, connect with what may be the stomach region. In the region of the posterior shield the reflective gut trace shows a series of lateral projections.

Naraoia compacta Walcott, 1912a (Nektaspida, Family Naraoiidae). USNM 83945b, 83945c. Size range: 9 to 40 mm. Isham reconstruction. Proportion of total Burgess Shale assemblage in terms of numbers of individuals: 0.32%. Occurrence: Lower Cambrian Chengjiang Fauna of China; Middle Cambrian Stephen Formation Burgess Shale and locality 9 of Collins et al. (1983); Marjum Formation, Utah; and other localities (see Conway Morris [1989b]). Description: Whittington (1977). Other important reference: Zhang and Hou (1985).

Olenoides

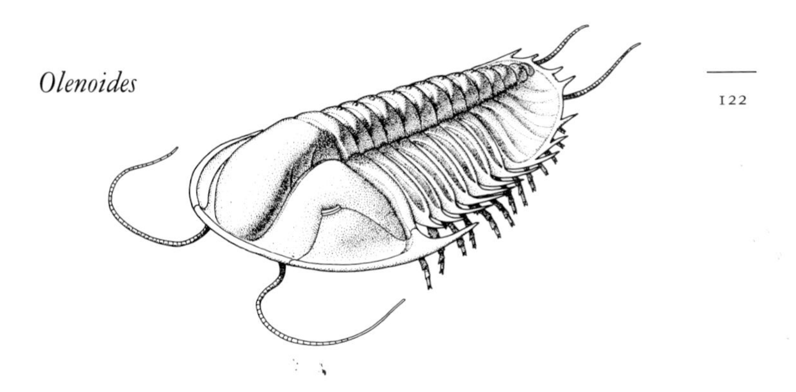

122

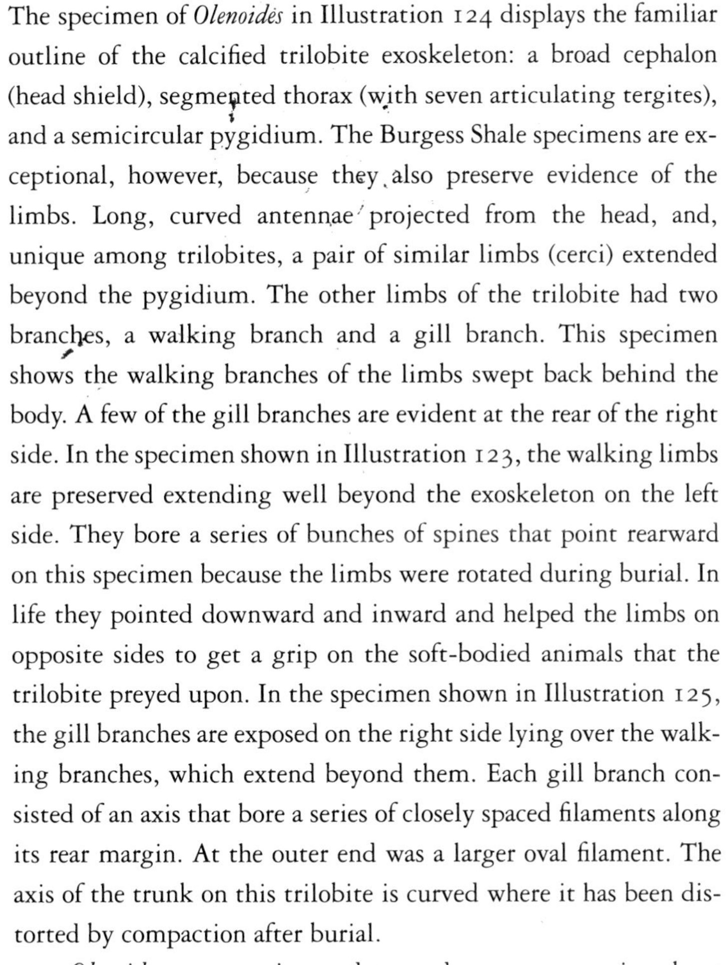

The specimen of *Olenoides* in Illustration 124 displays the familiar outline of the calcified trilobite exoskeleton: a broad cephalon (head shield), segmented thorax (with seven articulating tergites), and a semicircular pygidium. The Burgess Shale specimens are exceptional, however, because they also preserve evidence of the limbs. Long, curved antennae projected from the head, and, unique among trilobites, a pair of similar limbs (cerci) extended beyond the pygidium. The other limbs of the trilobite had two branches, a walking branch and a gill branch. This specimen shows the walking branches of the limbs swept back behind the body. A few of the gill branches are evident at the rear of the right side. In the specimen shown in Illustration 123, the walking limbs are preserved extending well beyond the exoskeleton on the left side. They bore a series of bunches of spines that point rearward on this specimen because the limbs were rotated during burial. In life they pointed downward and inward and helped the limbs on opposite sides to get a grip on the soft-bodied animals that the trilobite preyed upon. In the specimen shown in Illustration 125, the gill branches are exposed on the right side lying over the walking branches, which extend beyond them. Each gill branch consisted of an axis that bore a series of closely spaced filaments along its rear margin. At the outer end was a larger oval filament. The axis of the trunk on this trilobite is curved where it has been distorted by compaction after burial.

123 (×0.5)

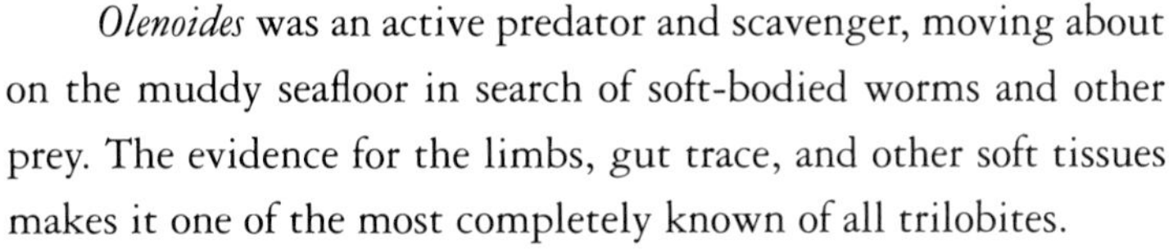

Olenoides was an active predator and scavenger, moving about on the muddy seafloor in search of soft-bodied worms and other prey. The evidence for the limbs, gut trace, and other soft tissues makes it one of the most completely known of all trilobites.

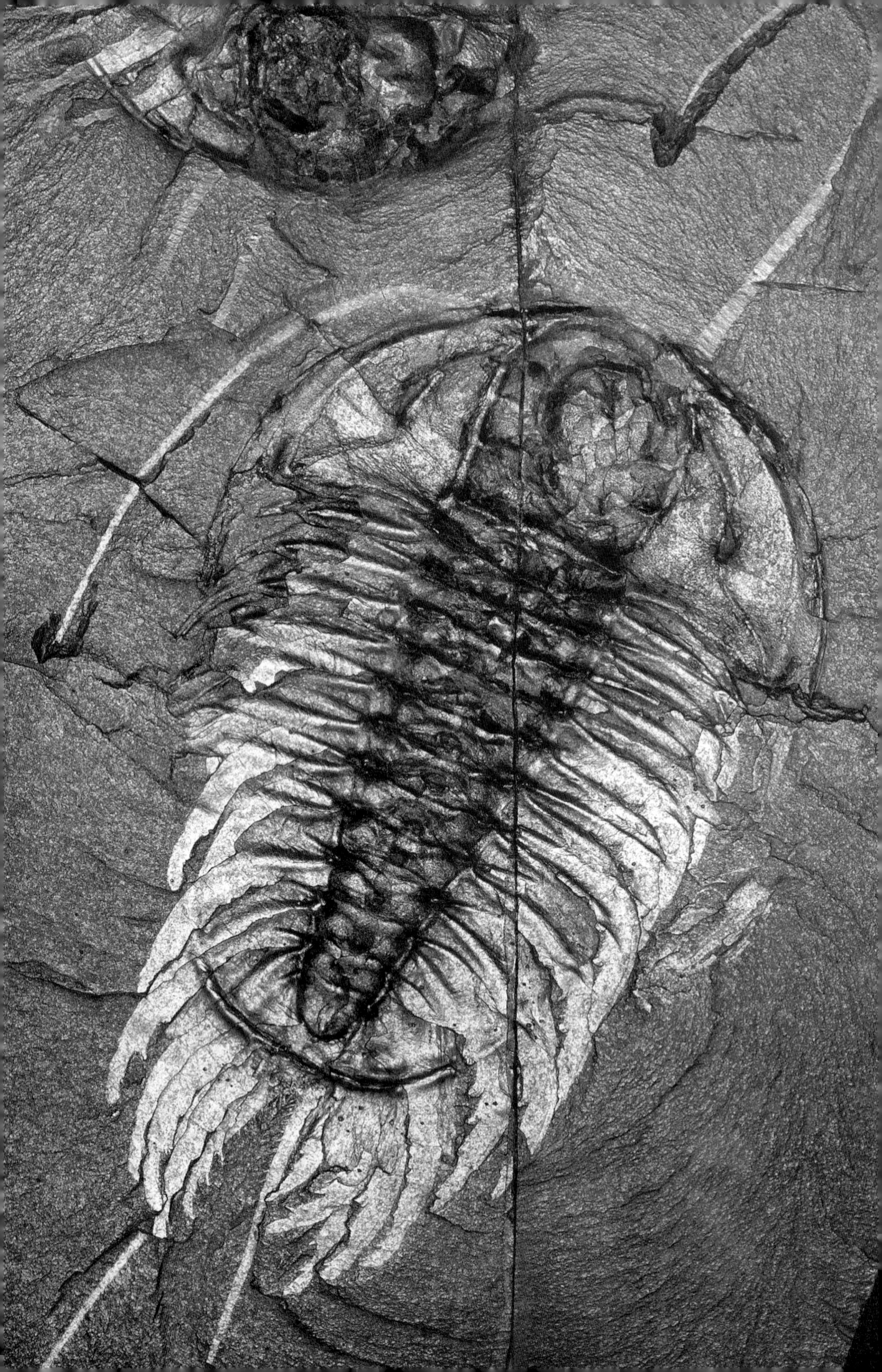

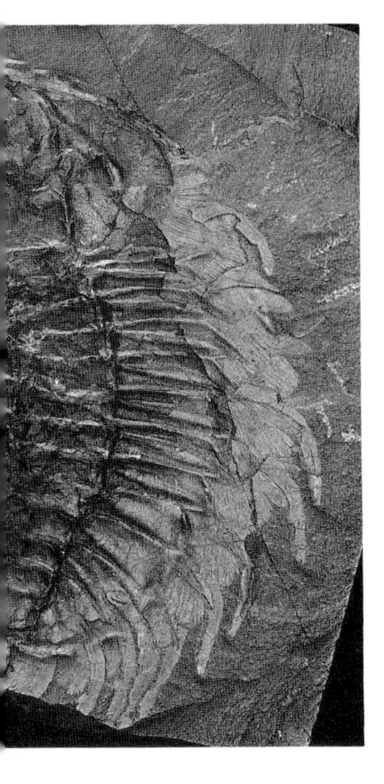

Olenoides serratus (Rominger, 1887) (Corynexochida). USNM 58589, 58588, 65521. Size range: about 50 to 85 mm. Isham reconstruction. Proportion of total Burgess Shale assemblage in terms of numbers of individuals: 0.21%. Occurrence: Middle Cambrian Stephen Formation Burgess Shale and *Ogygopsis* Shale (see Whittington [1975b]). Description: Whittington (1975b, 1980a).

125 (×1)

Oryctocephalus burgessensis Resser, 1938 (Corynexochida). USNM 116220b. Size range: about 16 mm. Occurrence: Middle Cambrian Stephen Formation Burgess Shale. Description: Rasetti (1951).

126 (×4)

124 (×1.9)

Oryctocephalus matthewi Rasetti, 1951 (Corynexochida). USNM 116222a. Size range: up to 16 mm. Occurrence: Middle Cambrian Stephen Formation Burgess Shale and *Ogygopsis* Shale. Description: Rasetti (1951).

127 (×4.5)

Pagetia bootes Walcott, 1916b (Eodiscina, Family Pagetiidae). USNM 356886. Size range: up to about 8 mm. Occurrence: Middle Cambrian Stephen Formation Burgess Shale and a number of adjacent localities (see Rasetti [1951], Collins et al. [1983]). Description: Rasetti (1951).

128 (×8)

Parkaspis decamera Rasetti, 1951 (Corynexochida). USNM 116231. Size range: 20 mm. Occurrence: Middle Cambrian Stephen Formation Burgess Shale. Description: Rasetti (1951). Very rare. Note that the free cheeks are displaced backward, suggesting that this is a molt.

129 (×3)

Ptychagnostus praecurrens (Westergaard, 1936) (= *Triplagnostus burgessensis* Rasetti, 1951) (Agnostina). USNM 112213. Size range: up to 8 mm. Occurrence: Middle Cambrian Stephen Formation Burgess Shale. Description: Rasetti (1951).

130 (×5)

(Chelicerates—Scorpions, Spiders, and their allies)

Sanctacaris

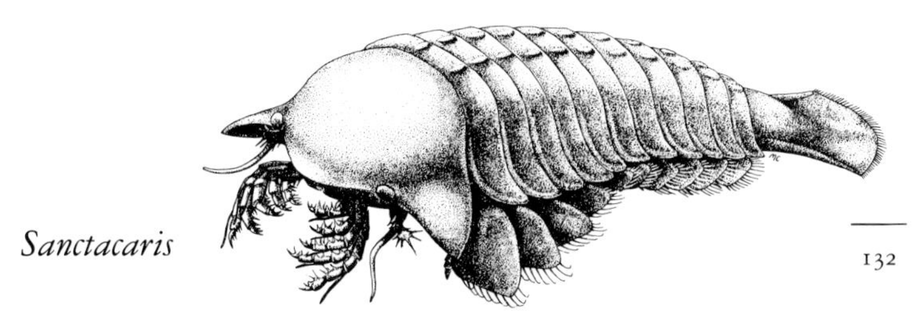

132

The spectacular arthropod *Sanctacaris* is one of the most important discoveries from the new localities found in 1981 and 1982 by Royal Ontario Museum parties under the leadership of Desmond Collins. The Burgess Shale itself had yielded well-preserved trilobites and, in *Canadaspis,* a form that could clearly be related to modern crustaceans. *Sanctacaris* provided the earliest chelicerate (the group including the scorpions and spiders). It completed representation of the three major groups of aquatic arthropods in the Stephen Formation. These critical fossils provided a basis for interpreting the origins of the living arthropods within the Cambrian radiation. *Sanctacaris* had a wide head shield. In the illustrated specimen the six pairs of biramous head appendages are evident projecting forward. The first five carried an array of spines that helped in prey capture. There were 11 divisions of the trunk, which terminated in a wide, flat telson. *Sanctacaris* was a predator, living on and just above the sediment. The lateral projections of the head shield and tergites, and the paddlelike telson, would have functioned in stabilizing and steering.

Sanctacaris is the oldest arthropod that shows the combination of characters that identify it as a chelicerate. The number and type of head appendages, and the divisions of the body, are found in a modified form in later aquatic chelicerates, the eurypterids and horseshoe crabs.

Sanctacaris uncata Briggs and Collins, 1988. ROM 43502. Size range: length from 46 to 93 mm. Marianne Collins reconstruction. Five specimens known. Occurrence: Middle Cambrian Stephen Formation, Mount Stephen, locality 9 of Collins et al. (1983). Description: Briggs and Collins (1988).

131 (×2.7)

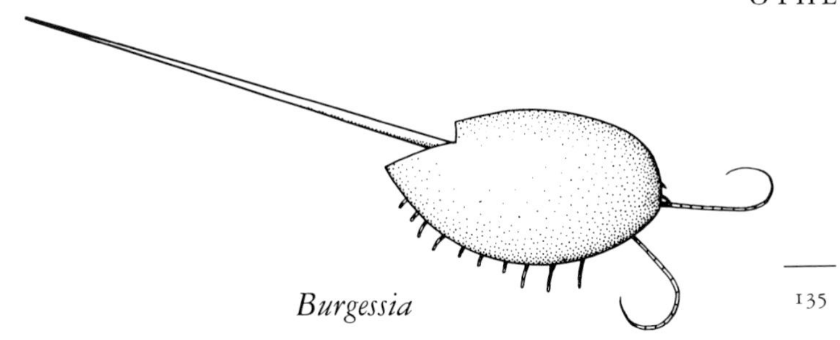

Burgessia

135

The carapace of *Burgessia* was circular, with a wide angular notch at the posterior end. Beyond it, to the rear, extended a long telson spine (Illustration 133). The gut of *Burgessia* extended into a pair of lobes at its anterior extremity. It was connected, on each side, to a complex branching system of canals (diverticula), which was presumably some kind of digestive organ (Illustration 134). A pair of long, flexible antennae projected beyond the front of the carapace; the right one has been exposed in the specimen shown in Illustration 133 by removing some of the rock matrix that concealed it. The rest of the appendages consisted of two branches (they were biramous). Those of the head, which extend beyond the carapace of the specimen in Illustration 133, consisted of a slender, segmented walking branch and a long, whiplike outer branch. The limbs of the trunk, which may be concealed by the carapace or extend posteriorly beyond it, had a similar walking branch, but the outer branch was a small oval gill. *Burgessia* probably moved about on the muddy bottom in search of food. The fossils provide little evidence of how or on what it fed. This arthropod was blind, but the antennae presumably served a sensory function. It most likely fed on small animals and organic particles in the sediment.

Burgessia falls within the arachnomorphs, a large group of arthropods including the chelicerates and trilobites.

133 (×7)

134 (×3)

Burgessia bella Walcott, 1912a. USNM 155624, 57676. Size range: width of carapace from 4 to 16.5 mm. Isham reconstruction. Proportion of total Burgess Shale assemblage in terms of numbers of individuals: 5.35%. Occurrence: Middle Cambrian Stephen Formation Burgess Shale. Description: Hughes (1975).

138

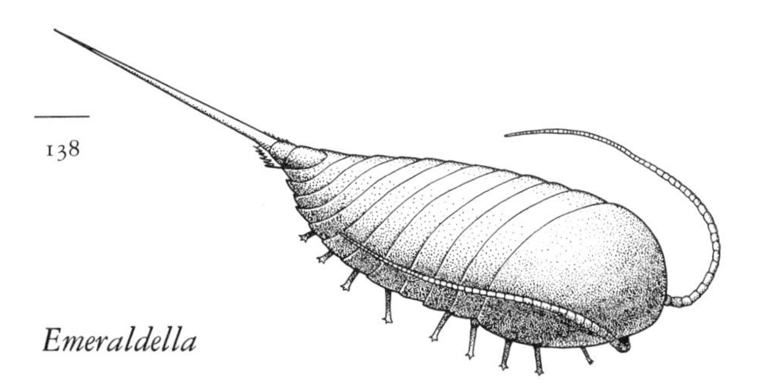

Emeraldella

136 (×4)

137 (×1)

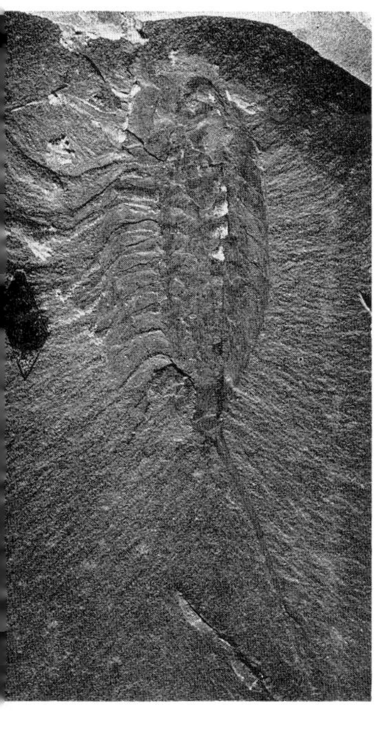

The specimen in Illustration 136 provides a dorsal view of *Emeraldella.* The specimen in Illustration 137 is flattened as if we were looking down on it just slightly from the left side, so that the left limbs project beyond the carapace. The head shield of *Emeraldella* was semicircular. The trunk consisted of 11 broad tergites narrowing toward the rear, followed by two cylindrical segments terminating in a long tail spine or telson. The head carried a pair of long antennae. The rest of the appendages were biramous, with a lobed outer branch and a segmented inner branch. The tips of the long segmented branches, which were used in walking, may be seen extending beyond the overlapping gill flaps. An array of spines along the segmented branch can be seen on the anteriormost appendages of the specimen in Illustration 136. These spines, and others at the base of the limbs, were used to capture and process food. The size of the spines suggests that *Emeraldella* was a predator and scavenger, feeding on soft-bodied organisms in the muddy sediment.

Emeraldella falls within the arachnomorphs, a large group of arthropods including the chelicerates and trilobites.

Emeraldella brocki Walcott, 1912a. USNM 136441, 57702. Size range: length 11 to 65 mm excluding the posterior spine. Isham reconstruction. Proportion of total Burgess Shale assemblage in terms of numbers of individuals: <0.2%. Occurrence: Middle Cambrian Stephen Formation Burgess Shale; equivocal occurrence in the Marjum Formation, Utah. Description: Bruton and Whittington (1983). Other important reference: Briggs and Robison (1984).

139 (×5)

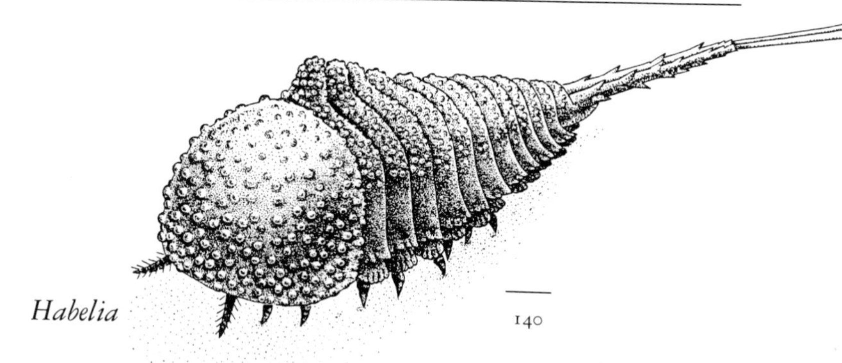

Habelia

This specimen provides a view of the left side of one of the rarer Burgess Shale arthropods. *Habelia* is unusual because the carapace was covered in tubercles, particularly on the head shield and on the axis of the trunk. The 12 tergites of the trunk were followed by a long tail spine. On this specimen the end of the spine is not seen. Other examples show a joint about two-thirds of the way along the length of the tail spine, indicating that the tip could be flexed at an angle relative to the rest. Unusual zig-zag trace fossils from the Middle Cambrian of the Grand Canyon may have been produced by a similar arthropod. The head limbs are poorly known. The first appears to have been an antenna. The remaining limbs were biramous, with a long, stout segmented walking branch, several of which are clearly displayed at the front of this specimen. *Habelia* lived on the muddy bottom and was well armored against predators. The limbs are too poorly known to allow the feeding strategy to be deduced in detail. This arthropod was probably a scavenger, feeding on carcasses and other organic material in the sediment.

Habelia falls within the arachnomorphs, a large group of arthropods including the chelicerates and trilobites.

Habelia optata Walcott, 1912a. USNM 139209. Size range: length ranges from 8 to 25.5 mm excluding the posterior spine. Marianne Collins reconstruction. Proportion of total Burgess Shale assemblage in terms of numbers of individuals: <0.1%. Occurrence: Middle Cambrian Stephen Formation Burgess Shale. Description: Whittington (1981b). Other important reference: Elliott and Martin (1987) described a possible trackway.

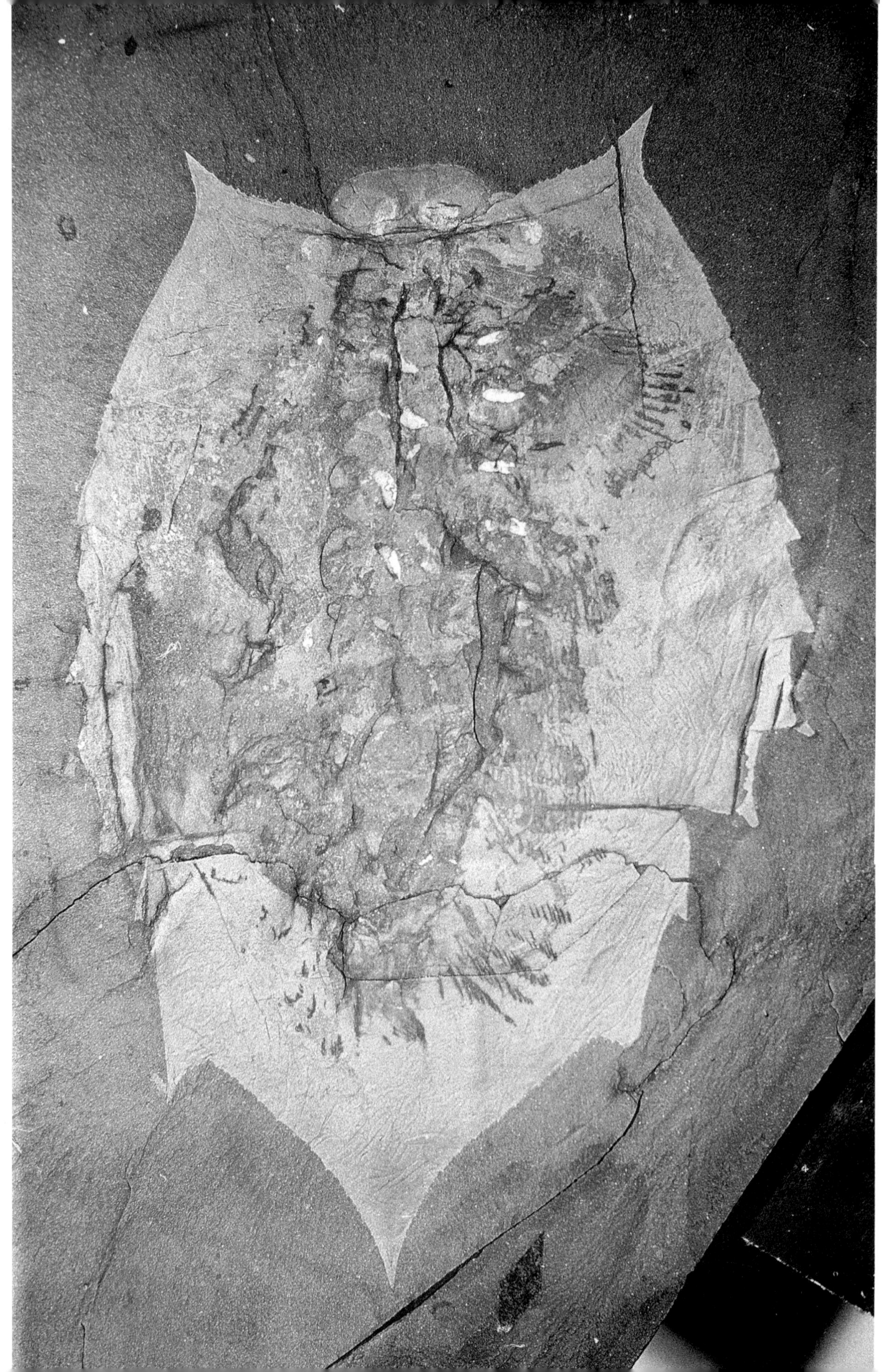

Helmetia

Helmetia is one of the rarer Burgess Shale arthropods; only 12 specimens are known. It had a wide, flat carapace with a very thin cuticle. The carapace was divided into a head shield, six thoracic divisions, and a large tail shield. The anterior margin of the head shield extended into a spine at each corner. An oval structure projected beyond the head shield in the midline. Two large spots are evident near the rear margin of this oval, but its nature is unknown. A pair of circular reflective spots lying behind and on either side of the oval are interpreted as eyes. There are also paired reflective structures along the trunk axis, which may be sites of muscle attachment. The limbs of *Helmetia* are poorly preserved. They are evident as rows of filaments down the right-hand side of this specimen. The wide, thin, flat carapace and filamentous appendages suggest that *Helmetia* was a swimming form. There is no evidence of a branch of the limbs that might have been used in walking. *Helmetia* does not appear streamlined or otherwise adapted to pursue other swimming prey. It was probably a filter feeder.

Helmetia falls within the arachnomorphs, a large group of arthropods including the chelicerates and trilobites.

141 (×1.2)

Helmetia expansa Walcott, 1918a. USNM 83952. Size range: over 20 cm. Proportion of total Burgess Shale assemblage in terms of numbers of individuals: 0.03%. Occurrence: Middle Cambrian Stephen Formation Burgess Shale. Description: Briggs in Conway Morris et al. (1982).

142 (×1.5)

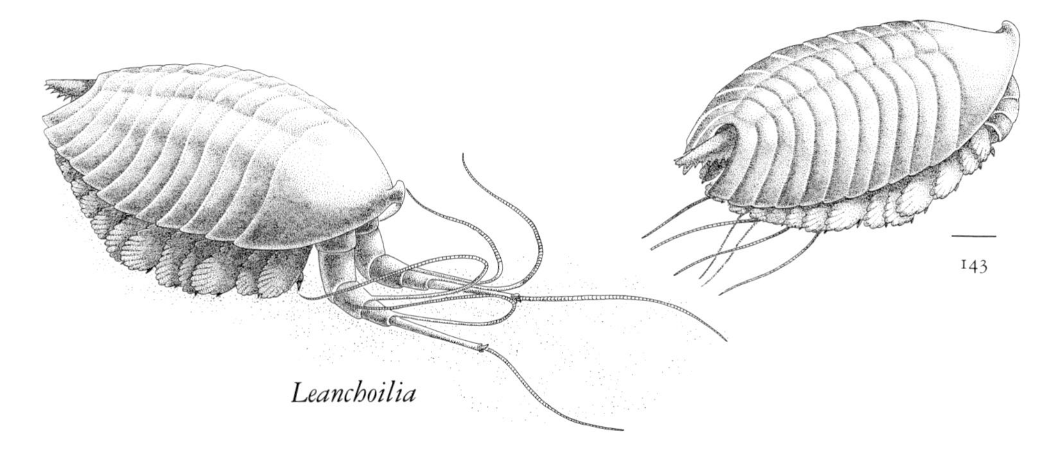

Leanchoilia

Leanchoilia is very common in the Raymond Quarry. This specimen affords a view looking down from above the left side. The most striking feature of *Leanchoilia* is the pair of great appendages. Each of the three branches of this appendage ended in a long whiplike extension, one of which is evident on the right side of this specimen. The anterior of the head shield ended in an upwardly curved "snout," which has broken off where it was compacted overlying the base of the right great appendage of this specimen. The trunk consisted of 11 tergites and ended in a pointed triangular telson with spines along the margin. The outer gill flaps of the biramous appendages, which were fringed with long filaments, can be seen at the front; the segmented walking branches are concealed beneath. The gut is picked out by a reflective trace and is filled in places with dark blobs of the mineral apatite. *Leanchoilia* was blind and presumably used the whiplike extensions of the great appendages for sensing the environment. It lacked well-developed spines on the biramous limbs and probably fed on particles of organic matter in the sediment.

Leanchoilia falls within the arachnomorphs, a large group of arthropods including the chelicerates and trilobites.

Leanchoilia superlata Walcott, 1912a. USNM 83943b. Size range: length averages about 5.0 cm, reaches up to 6.8 cm excluding the tail spine. Marianne Collins reconstruction. Proportion of total Burgess Shale assemblage in terms of numbers of individuals: 0.2%. Occurrence: Middle Cambrian Stephen Formation Burgess Shale; equivocal records in the Spence Shale, Utah, and in the Lower Cambrian Buen Formation of Greenland (see Conway Morris [1989b]). Description: Bruton and Whittington (1983). Other important reference: Briggs and Robison (1984).

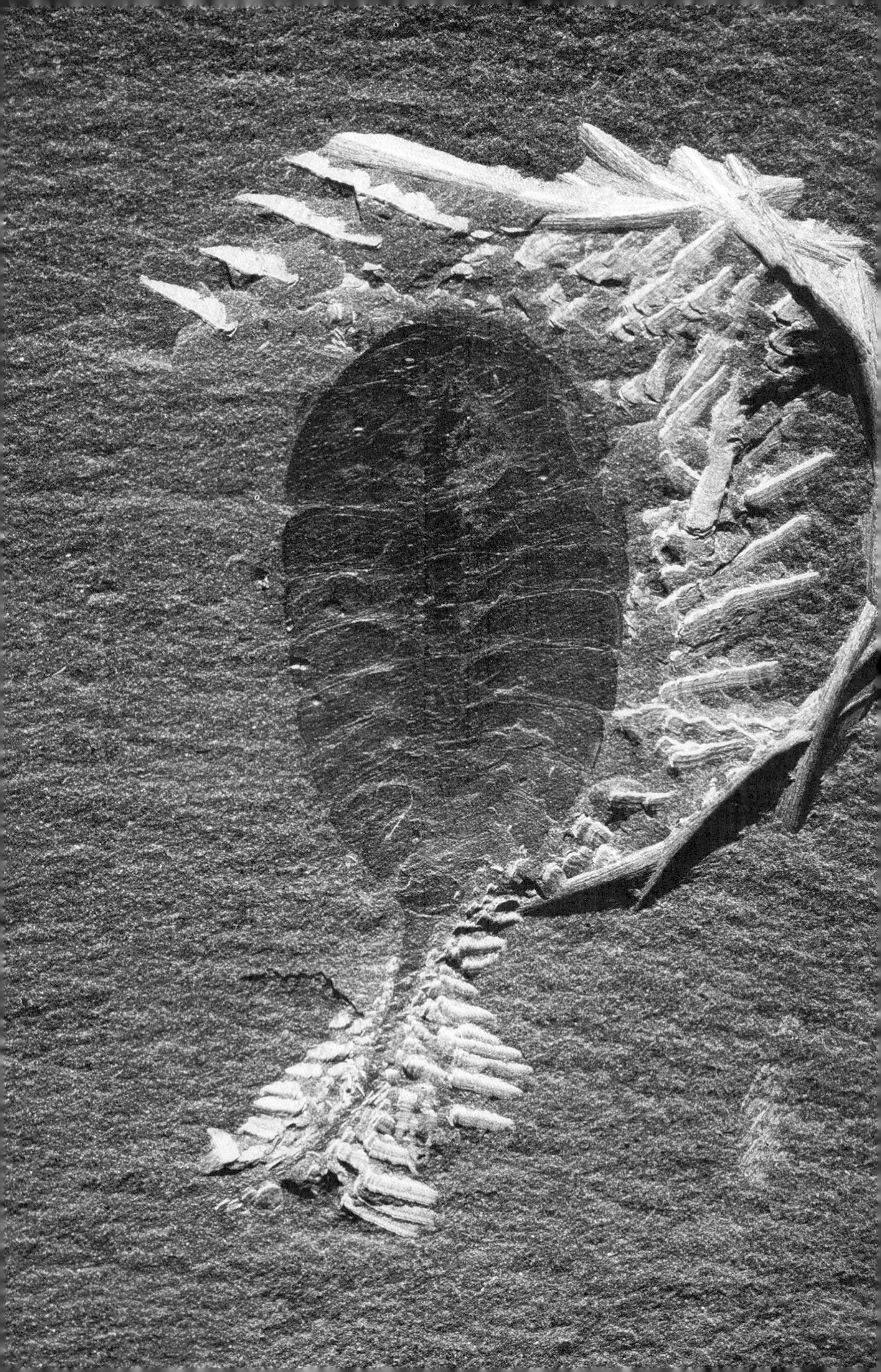

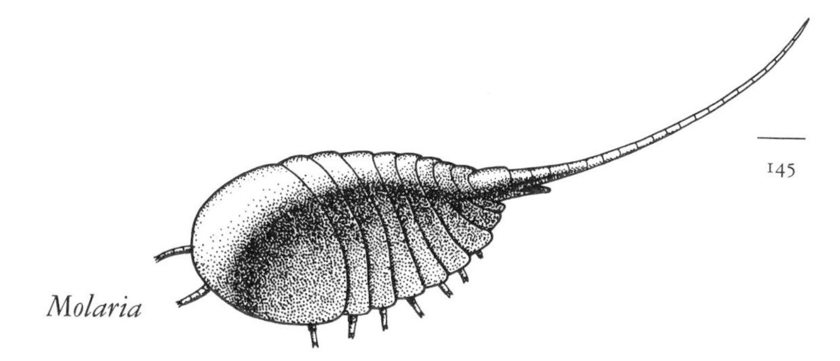

145

These two specimens illustrate *Molaria* in dorsal (Illustration 144) and left lateral (Illustration 146) views. The head shield was semicircular in outline. The trunk exoskeleton consisted of eight tergites. The telson was long and tapering and was divided into a series of articulated segments, which gave it a degree of flexibility. The lateral specimen (Illustration 146) shows a trace of the gut extending through most of the body. The limbs are also evident, although the details are not clear. The inner branch was a segmented walking limb; the outer branch was flaplike and surrounded by a fringe of setae. *Molaria* walked about on the muddy substrate and may have plowed into the sediment using the margin of the head shield. It presumably scavenged for food or fed on detritus in the mud.

Molaria falls within the arachnomorphs, a large group of arthropods including the chelicerates and trilobites.

Molaria spinifera Walcott, 1912a. USNM 272105, 57688. Size range: 7–26 mm. Isham reconstruction. Proportion of total Burgess Shale assemblage in terms of numbers of individuals: 0.3%. Occurrence: Middle Cambrian Stephen Formation Burgess Shale. Description: Whittington (1981b).

146 (×3)

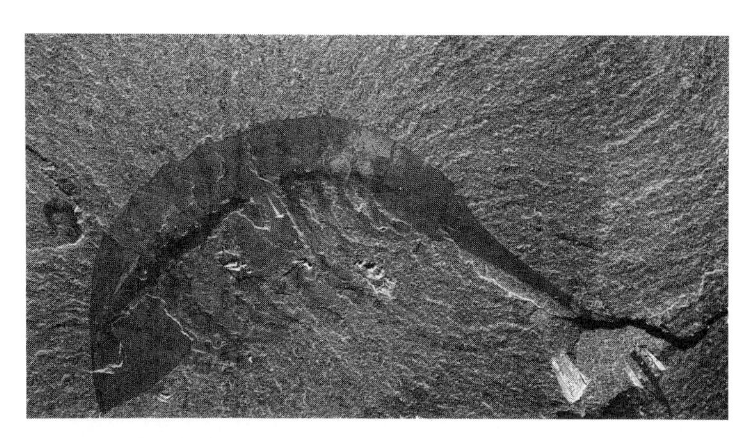

144 (×10)

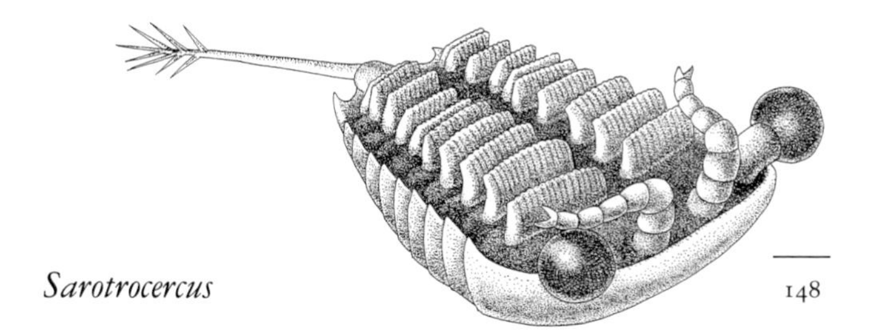

Sarotrocercus 148

Sarotrocercus is one of the rarer and smallest of the Burgess Shale arthropods. A pair of large eyes projects beyond the margin of the semicircular head shield. The nine trunk tergites are separated by dark bands, which presumably represent the articulations between them. The long posterior spine ends in a bunch of smaller spines. The limbs are not evident on this specimen, but consisted of a large jointed head appendage and a series of lobelike trunk limbs, each with a fringe of lamellae. There is little evidence for the mode of life of *Sarotrocercus.* It is likely that it lived in the water column rather than on the muddy substrate. It is reconstructed swimming on its back using the trunk limbs to propel it through the water.

Sarotrocercus falls within the arachnomorphs, a large group of arthropods including the chelicerates and trilobites.

Sarotrocercus oblita Whittington, 1981b. USNM 272171. Size range: length ranges from 8.5 to 11 mm excluding the posterior spine. Marianne Collins reconstruction. Proportion of total Burgess Shale assemblage in terms of numbers of individuals: <0.1%. Occurrence: Middle Cambrian Stephen Formation Burgess Shale. Description: Whittington (1981b).

147 (×9)

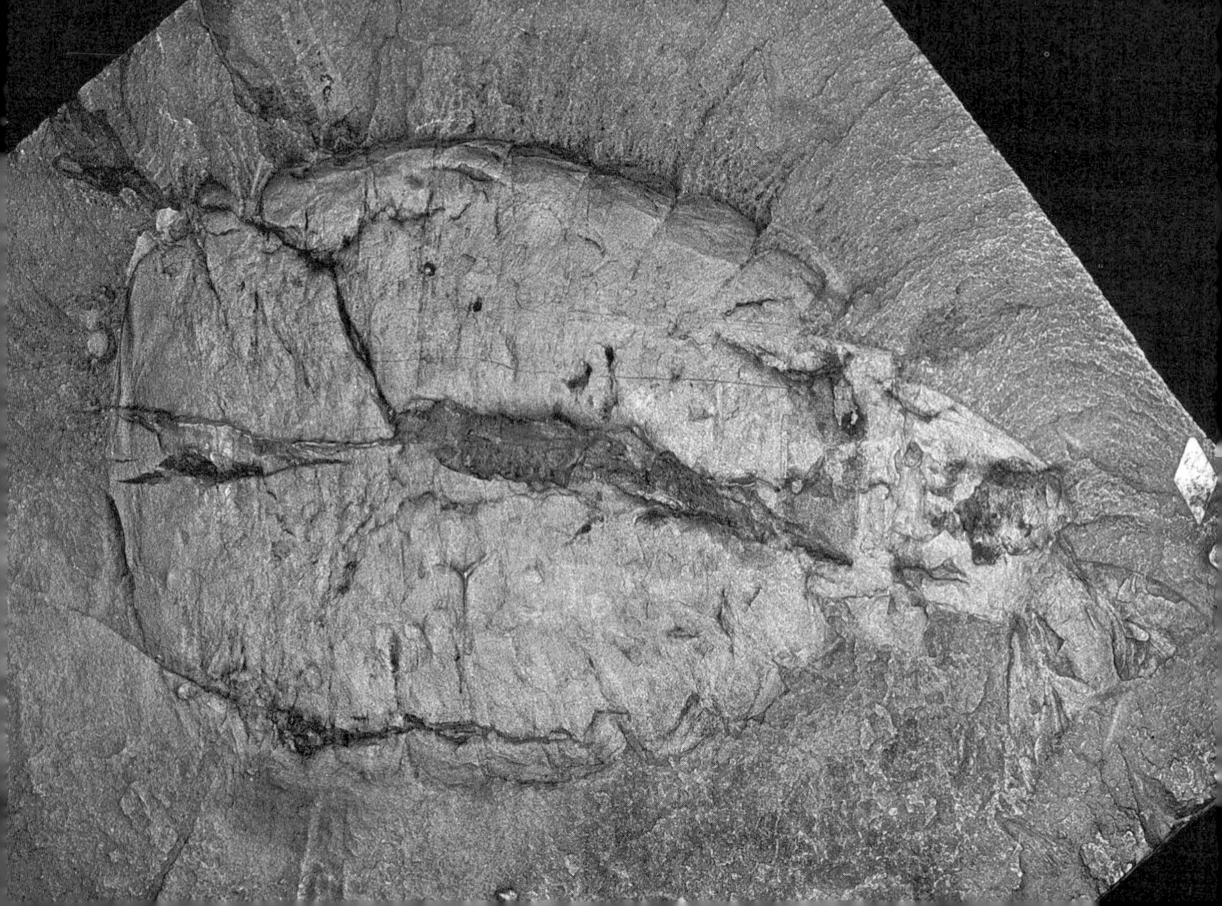

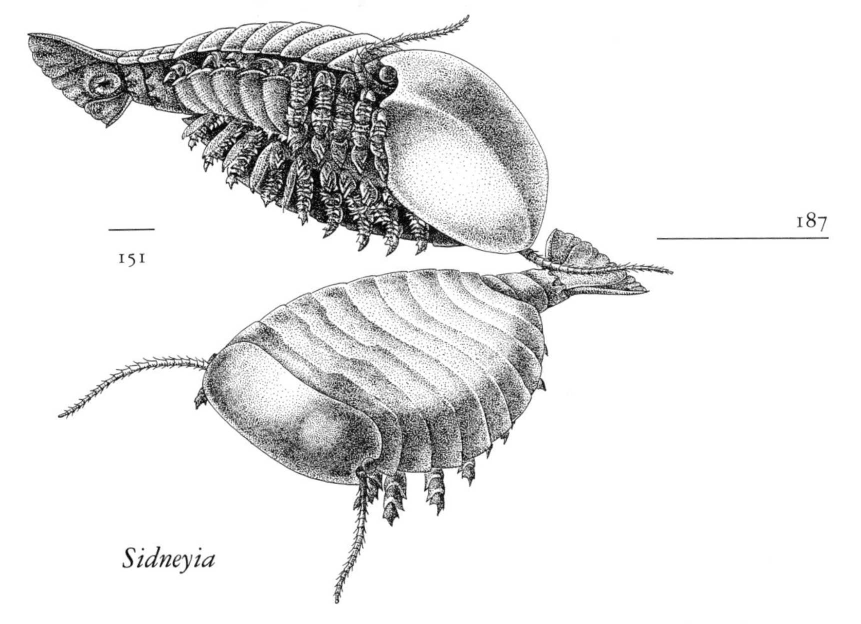

151

Sidneyia

Sidneyia is one of the larger Burgess Shale arthropods and was the first to be described by Charles Walcott. He named it after his second son, Sidney, who apparently discovered the first specimen. The species name *inexpectans* suggests that Sidney was a little surprised at his success! Both these specimens show the short, wide cephalon, from either side of which projected a single antenna. The trunk was divided into a wide thorax with nine articulating tergites, followed by an abdomen of three cylindrical somites. The last abdominal somite bore flaplike appendages that, together with the telson, formed a tail fan. The trunk limbs are not evident on either of these specimens, but they are shown on the reconstruction. The first four limbs consisted only of a large walking leg. The last five also had a flaplike gill. The spines along the length of the walking branch of the legs and on the segment that attaches it to it to the body (the coxa) indicate that *Sidneyia* was a predator. This is supported by the gut contents of the specimen shown in Illustration 149, which include recognizable shelly fragments of hyolithids. Other specimens indicate that the diet also included ostracods (small bivalved crustaceans) and trilobites. *Sidneyia* is the only Burgess Shale arthropod with recognizable shelly debris in the gut, indicating that it could prey on hard-shelled organisms.

Sidneyia falls within the arachnomorphs, a large group of arthropods including the chelicerates and trilobites.

149 (×2)

Sidneyia inexpectans Walcott, 1911a. USNM 57487, 57489. Size range: 5 to 13 cm. Marianne Collins reconstruction. Proportion of total Burgess Shale assemblage in terms of numbers of individuals: 0.44%. Occurrence: Middle Cambrian Stephen Formation Burgess Shale and other localities (see Conway Morris [1989b]). Description: Bruton (1981). Note: Sidney Walcott reminisced about his discovery in Walcott (1971).

150 (×1)

152 (×5)

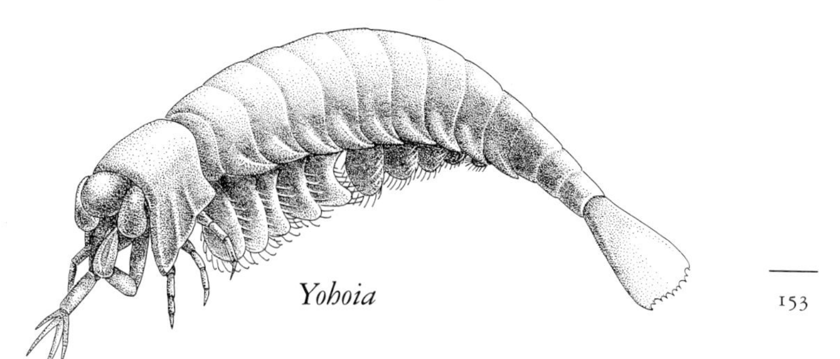

This specimen provides a view of *Yohoia* from the right side. The head shield was followed by 13 trunk tergites. The first 10 tergites extended downward on each side into triangular projections or pleurae. The last three were complete tubes. At the end of the trunk was a flat paddlelike telson. The most striking feature of *Yohoia* is the pair of so-called great appendages at the front of the head shield. They bent at a pronounced "elbow" and ended in four long spines, rather like the fingers of a hand. The limbs behind the great appendages are not so clearly seen. Those of the head were long and segmented and presumably used to support the arthropod on the substrate. The limbs of the trunk were flaplike and fringed with setae. They were used for swimming and oxygen exchange. *Yohoia* presumably lived near the sea bottom, swimming above the mud and using its great appendages for scavenging or capturing prey.

Yohoia falls within the arachnomorphs, a large group of arthropods including the chelicerates and trilobites.

Yohoia tenuis Walcott, 1912a. USNM 179012. Size range: 7 to 23 mm. Marianne Collins reconstruction. Proportion of total Burgess Shale assemblage in terms of numbers of individuals: 0.96%. Occurrence: Middle Cambrian Stephen Formation Burgess Shale. Description: Whittington (1974).

Phylum Echinodermata

CLASS CYSTOIDEA (Cystoids)

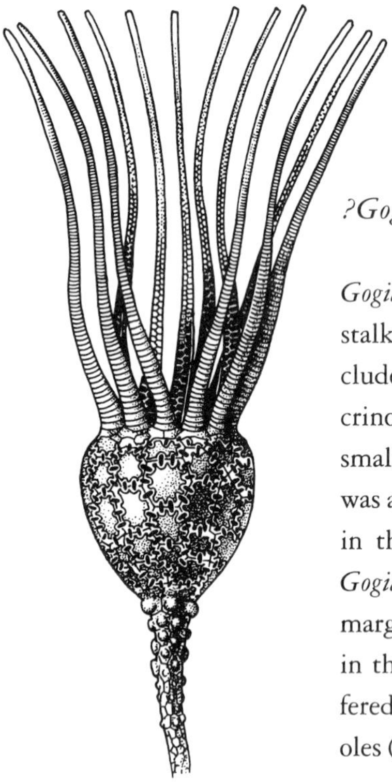

154

?Gogia

Gogia is a representative of one of the most primitive groups of stalked echinoderms, formerly known as the eocrinoids, now included within the cystoids. Like *Echmatocrinus,* the earliest known crinoid, *Gogia* lived attached to the seafloor by a stalk covered in small plates; like other cystoids, it lacked a stem. Atop the stalk was an inflated, irregularly plated spherical calyx (partly concealed in this specimen) with three to five primitive ambulacra. But *Gogia* differed from crinoids in the presence of pores along the margins (sutures) separating the plates. These sutures are evident in the reconstruction as lines between the plates. *Gogia* also differed from crinoids in the presence of short, food-gathering brachioles (armlike structures) situated along the ambulacra. Thus *Gogia* was an attached epifaunal, sessile suspension feeder. *Gogia* is a widely distributed genus in the Middle Cambrian of western North America, but only a few fragmentary specimens have been found in the Burgess Shale. The specimen illustrated here is one of the best recovered from the Burgess Shale, but far more complete specimens of other species have been found elsewhere in western North America, often in large populations.

Gogia lies at the base of the radiation of cystoids, a suite of fascinating Paleozoic echinoderms. Three distinct cystoid lineages appear to have been derived from different species of *Gogia,* each emphasizing a different aspect of the morphology of the genus.

155 (×4)

?Gogia radiata Sprinkle, 1973. USNM 165399. Size: calyx 16–29 mm long. Isham reconstruction. Proportion of total Burgess Shale assemblage in terms of numbers of individuals: none buried alive. Occurrence: Middle Cambrian Stephen Formation Burgess Shale. Description: Sprinkle (1973). Other important references: Paul and Smith (1984), Paul (1988). Note: Smith (1984) demonstrated that the eocrinoids belong to the cystoids.

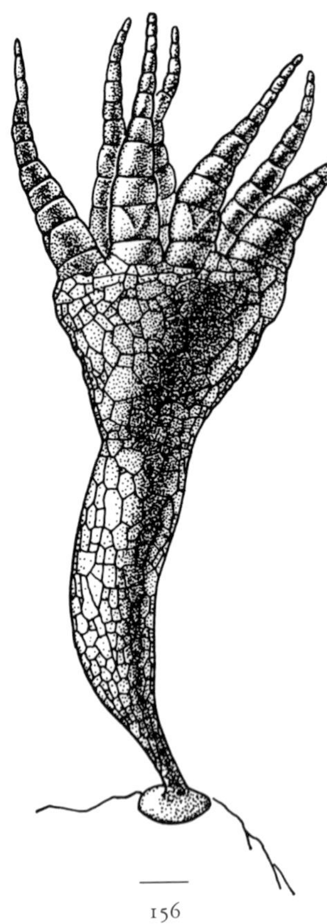

156

Echmatocrinus

Echmatocrinus is the earliest crinoid known, and thus provides some idea of what the ancestor of one of the most diverse classes of Paleozoic invertebrates must have looked like. The five known specimens differ in many ways from later crinoids, which do not appear in the fossil record until the Early Ordovician. Only the exceptional preservation of the tube feet and other structures (particularly the uniserial arms) revealed that the animals belonged within the Class Crinoidea. As it is, their morphology is so unusual that *Echmatocrinus* is placed in the Family Echmatocrinidae and the Subclass Echmatocrinea. As with *Gogia, Echmatocrinus* appears to hold many of the clues to the subsequent history of the class to which it belongs. Curiously, Walcott collected four of the five known specimens of *Echmatocrinus* (although he never described them), but the best specimen was not discovered until 1967 when the Geological Survey of Canada reopened the Walcott Quarry. This specimen came from a layer low in Walcott's original quarry that contains many of the magnificently preserved arthropods, worms, and other animals.

The calyx of *Echmatocrinus* was very primitive in comparison with that of later crinoids and was composed of many irregularly arranged plates. At least eight arms are evident radiating from the calyx and they appear to preserve soft tube feet. The calyx was attached to the seafloor by means of a holdfast covered by numerous irregular plates, unlike later crinoids, which had a stem composed of a series of columnals. One of the specimens is attached to the tube of the priapulid worm *Selkirkia;* an isolated holdfast is attached to a hyolithid shell. *Echmatocrinus* lived as a suspension feeder, filtering food particles out of the seawater, much like later crinoids.

157 (×3)

Echmatocrinus brachiatus Sprinkle, 1973. USNM 165405. Size: up to 8 cm. Isham reconstruction. Proportion of total Burgess Shale assemblage in terms of numbers of individuals: <0.012%. Occurrence: Middle Cambrian Stephen Formation Burgess Shale. Description: Sprinkle (1973). Other important references: Sprinkle and Moore (1978), Paul and Smith (1984), Donovan (1988).

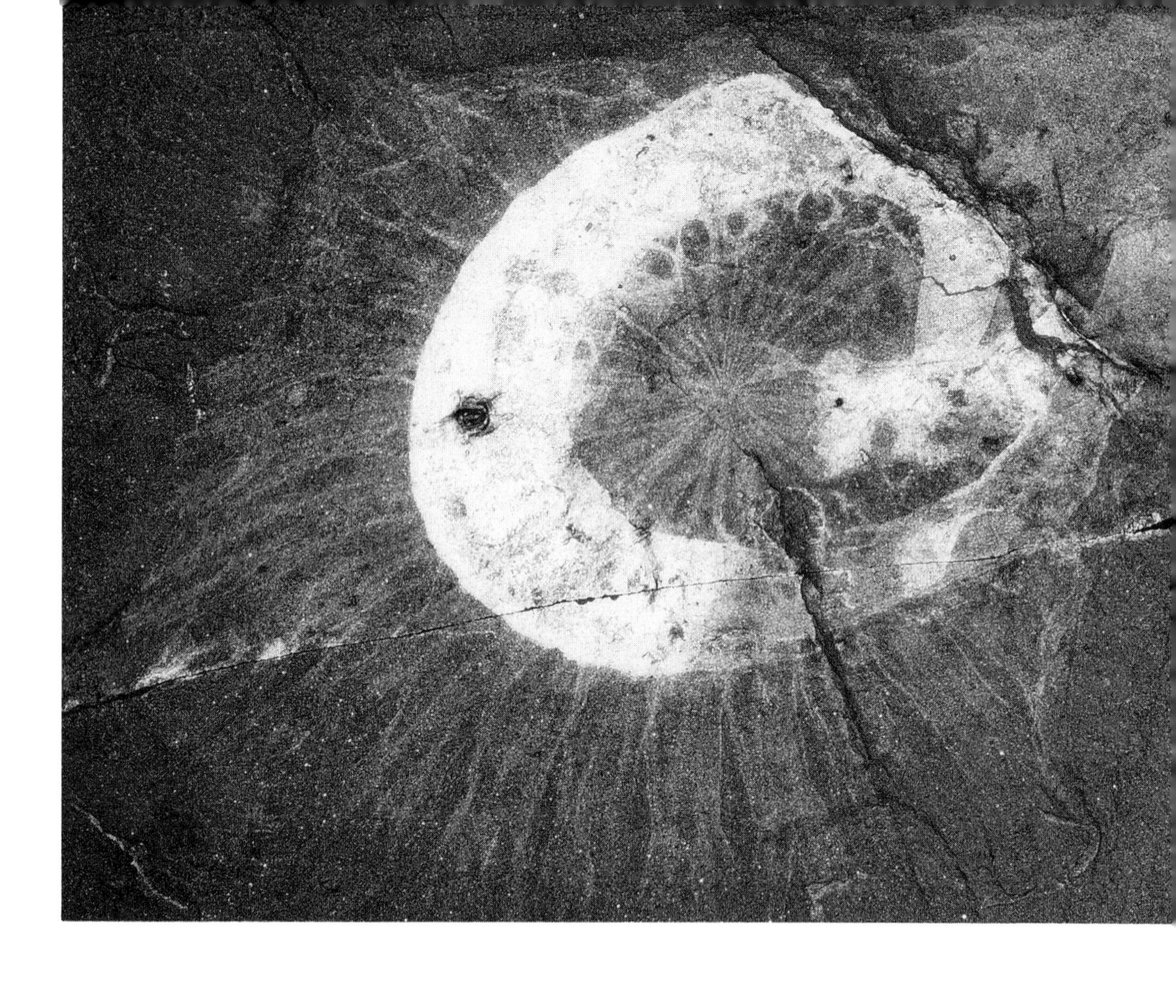

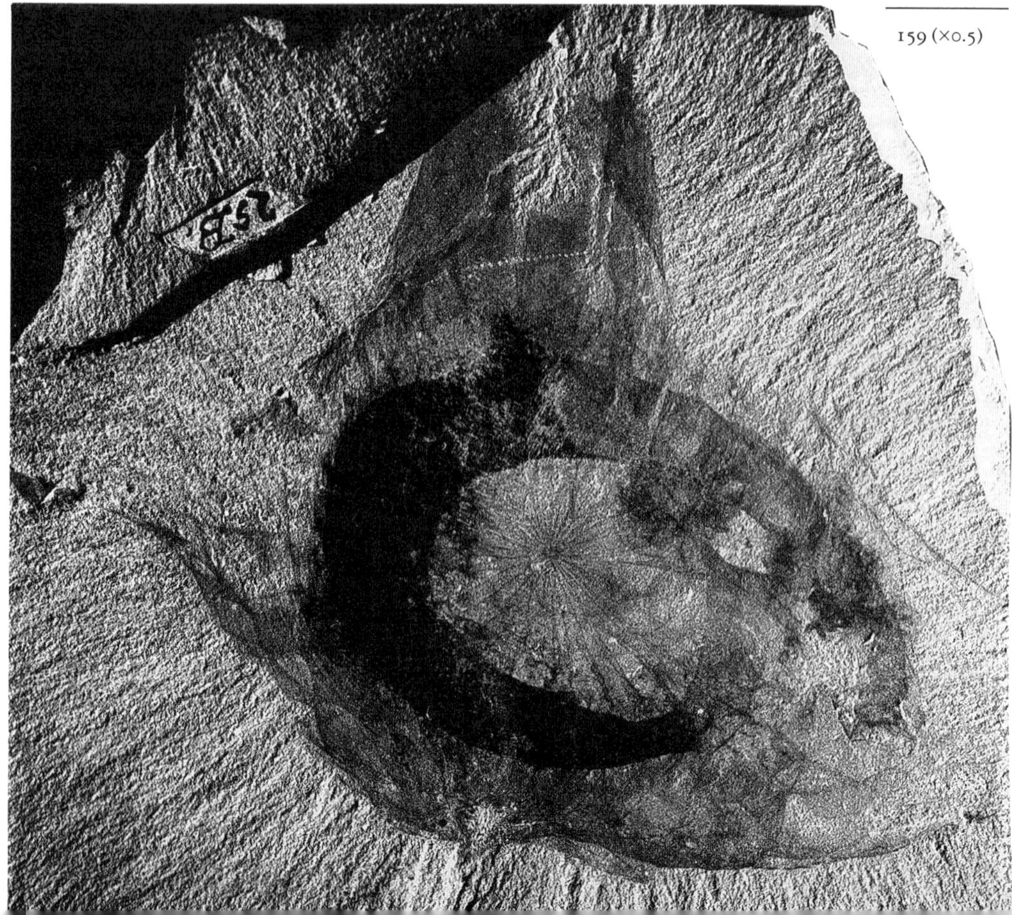

159 (×0.5)

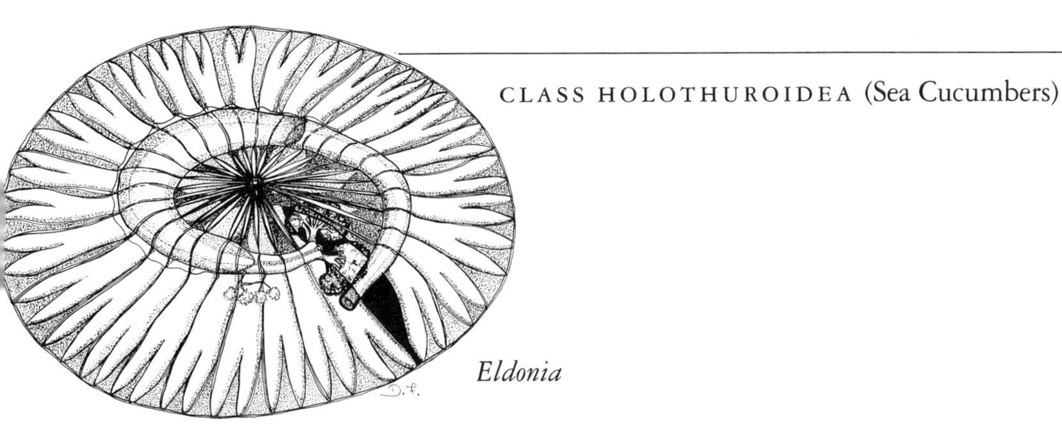

CLASS HOLOTHUROIDEA (Sea Cucumbers)

Eldonia

160

Eldonia looks superficially like a jellyfish, with a large disklike body that enveloped the coiled gut. Thin filamentous strands radiated from the center of the animal and provided much of the support for the body. Adjacent to the mouth are grapelike clusters, which are the oral tentacles. What appear to be the gonads lie beneath the front end of the gut.

158 (×2)

The affinities of *Eldonia* have been the subject of considerable controversy since Walcott first described it in 1911. Walcott believed that it was a pelagic holothurian, a view shared by many other authors, but some paleontologists have argued that it is a siphonophore, within the Phylum Cnidaria. Preliminary results of a new investigation of *Eldonia* suggest that Walcott's original conclusion was correct.

Eldonia ludwigi Walcott, 1911c. USNM 57540, 57537. Size range: 6.7 to 12+ cm. Duncan Friend reconstruction. Proportion of total Burgess Shale assemblage in terms of numbers of individuals: <2%. Occurrence: Middle Cambrian Stephen Formation Burgess Shale. Description: Friend (in preparation). Note: Madsen (1962) argued for a cnidarian affinity.

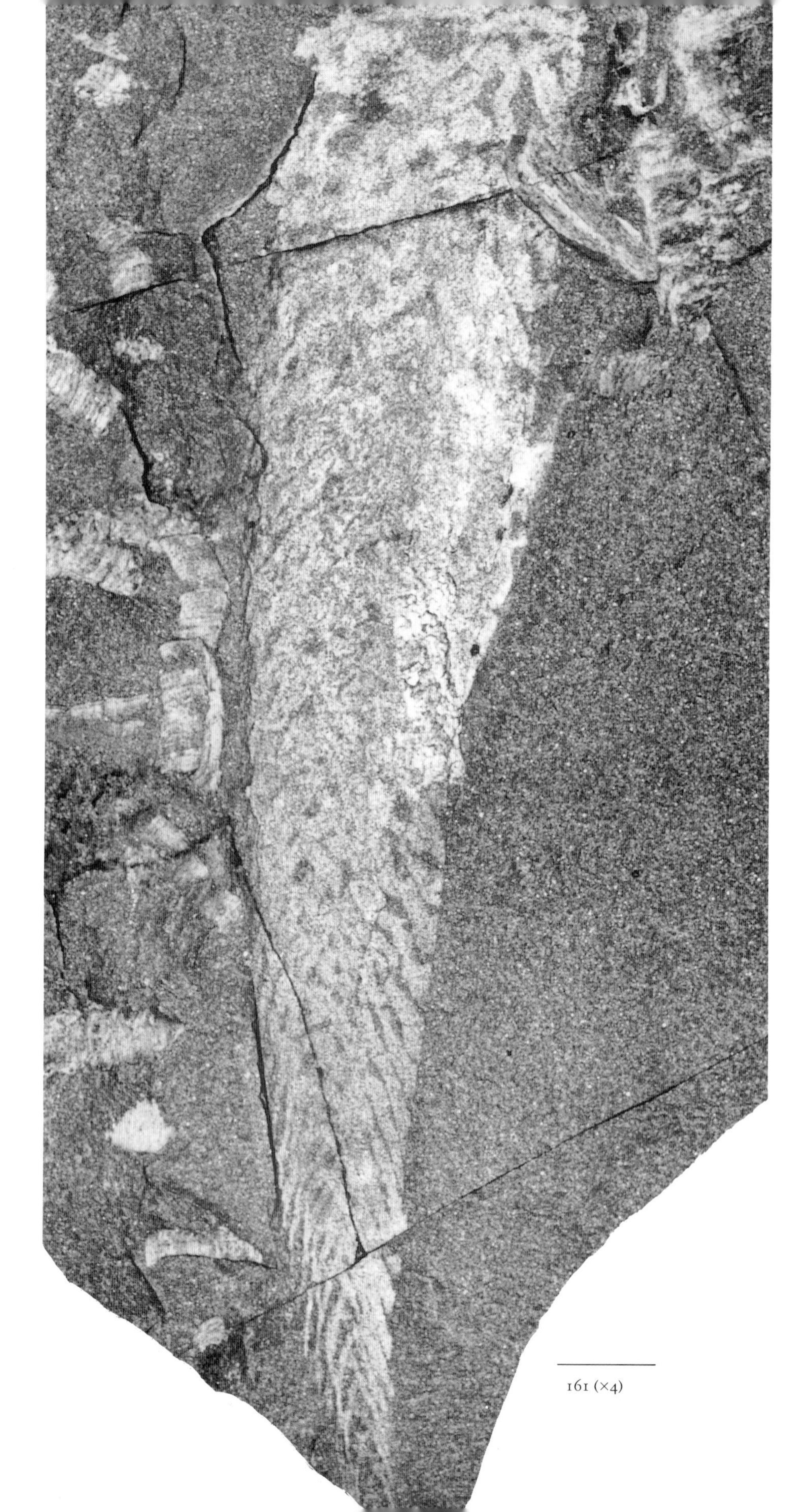

161 (×4)

Phylum Chordata (Chordates)

Metaspriggina

This, the only specimen presently assigned to *Metaspriggina,* is blunt anteriorly and tapers posteriorly presumably to a point. No obvious head is preserved. The trunk appears to consist of a series of anteriorly pointing V-like structures that are offset on opposite sides of the body. A reflective area on the right of the specimen may represent the gut. If so, the anus appears to be positioned on the right side of the specimen about halfway along its length. The flattened body suggests that *Metaspriggina* was an active swimmer. This is supported by its rarity. Animals living in the water column were much less likely to be caught up and transported in the mud flows than organisms that lived on the seabed.

Simonetta and Insom named this fossil *Metaspriggina* on the basis of a fancied resemblance to the Ediacaran animal *Spriggina,* a segmented wormlike form from the Ediacaran Fauna of Australia. Alternatively, the Vs represent the muscle blocks of a chordate, shrunken slightly by decay and offset on either side of the body. The specimen might then be interpreted as the posterior part of a relatively large chordate. In that case, the affinities of *Metaspriggina* lie closer to *Pikaia,* the more completely known Burgess Shale representative of this group.

Metaspriggina walcotti Simonetta and Insom, 1993. USNM 198611. Size 60 mm. Proportion of total Burgess Shale assemblage in terms of numbers of individuals: <0.01%. Occurrence: Middle Cambrian Stephen Formation Burgess Shale. Description: Simonetta and Insom (1993). Other important reference: Briggs and Kear (in press).

162 (×3.5)

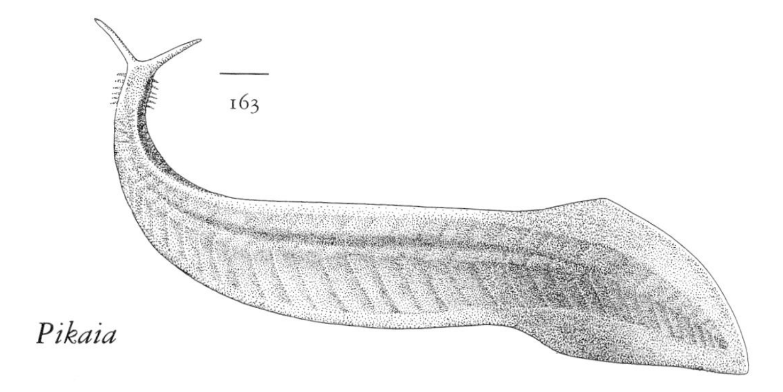

Pikaia

Pikaia was first described (by Walcott) as a polychaete worm. It is now recognized, however, as a primitive chordate and, as such, the earliest known representative of the phylum to which we ourselves belong. The narrow anterior end bore a pair of short tentacles, which are not visible on this specimen. The trunk clearly preserves reflective traces of the curved sigmoidal muscle blocks and, along the dorsal margin, the notochord or stiffening rod. The tail expanded into a fin. *Pikaia* swam above the seafloor, probably close to the bottom. It propelled itself by undulating the body, using the muscles. It may have been a filter feeder, but this is not certain.

Pikaia is not a vertebrate, but it is similar to more primitive chordates like the living cephalochordate *Branchiostoma,* commonly known as the lancelet.

Pikaia gracilens Walcott, 1911d. USNM 83940b. Size: averages about 4 cm. Marianne Collins reconstruction. Proportion of total Burgess Shale assemblage in terms of numbers of individuals: 0.15%. Occurrence: Middle Cambrian Stephen Formation Burgess Shale. Description: yet to be redescribed (see Conway Morris and Whittington [1979] and Briggs and Kear [1994]).

164 (×0.5)

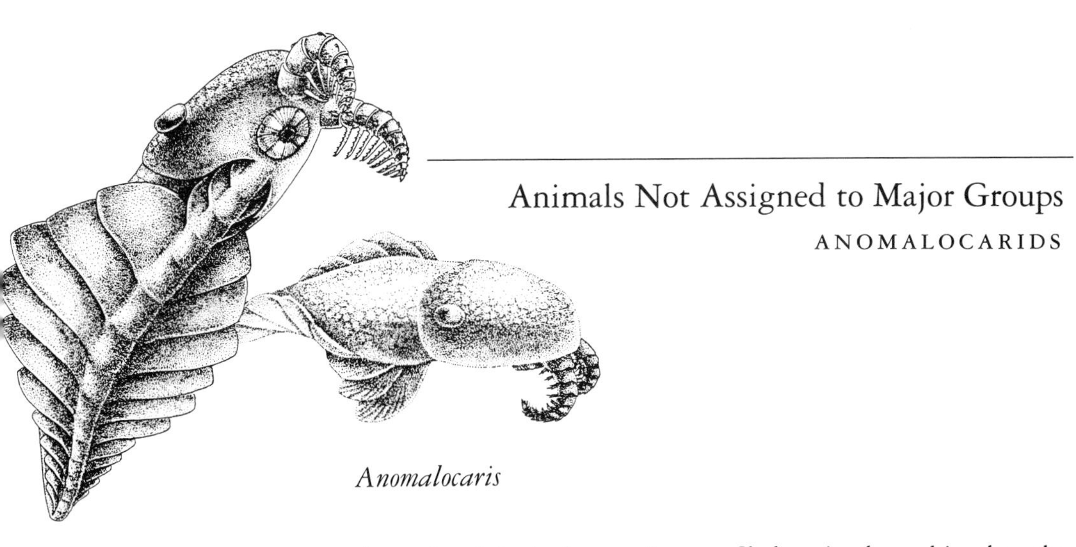

165

Animals Not Assigned to Major Groups

ANOMALOCARIDS

Anomalocaris

Anomalocaris is the largest Burgess Shale animal, reaching lengths approaching 0.5 meters. As the animal decayed, bits of the carcass tended to fall off, and complete specimens are rare. Indeed, the first descriptions of *Anomalocaris* were of some of the parts. In 1892, Whiteaves described isolated limbs, like those shown here (Illustration 164), from the *Ogygopsis* Shale on Mount Stephen (he thought that they were the bodies of a shrimplike arthropod). Walcott found similar limbs in the Burgess Shale, together with a second type that are assumed to belong to a different species. Walcott also discovered circlets of plates that he called *Peytoia* and interpreted as some kind of floating jellyfish. The discovery of complete specimens of *Anomalocaris* among the collections finally showed that the limbs and so-called jellyfish are elements of one kind of animal (Illustration 165). The giant limbs were attached at the front of the head and used to capture prey. The disclike "jelly-fish" had teeth and represents a jaw. Illustration 164 shows the largest known appendages of *Anomalocaris,* which are over 20 centimeters in length. Both limbs belonged to the same individual, but they have become separated from the body. The cuticle of the limbs, and of the circular jaw, must have been more robust and resistant to decay than the other tissues, which explains why they are much more commonly preserved. The isolated jaw shown in Illustration 166 shows the array of teeth on the inner margin of the plates. The aperture itself was rectangular, not circular. It could not be closed; the teeth did not meet in the middle. The jaw could be opened, however, to admit prey, and the plates could then be pulled together to draw the prey into the mouth. This would have had the effect of cracking or breaking the exoskeleton of an arthropod. Indeed, trilobites are known with healed bites in the edge of the exoskeleton that may have been made by the jaw of *Anomalocaris.* Some specimens of the jaw preserve additional teeth inside those preserved here, which lined the wall of the mouth and further processed the food. The body of *Anomalocaris* was flanked by a series of lobes that were used in swimming. With the large spiny limbs at the front, this Cambrian giant must have been a formidable predator.

Recent discoveries have shown *Anomalocaris* to be one of the most widely distributed of the Burgess Shale animals. It is now known not only from North America, but also from China, Australia, and Greenland. In addition, a number of new specimens collected by Desmond Collins (Royal Ontario Museum) from localities near the Walcott Quarry show that there are still other kinds waiting to be described.

Anomalocaris canadensis Whiteaves, 1892. GSC 75535, part and counterpart, and USNM 213483, 213484, 57538. Size: the largest isolated appendages (USNM 213483) are over 20 cm long, indicating a total body length of at least twice that figure. Marianne Collins reconstruction. Proportion of total Burgess Shale assemblage in terms of numbers of individuals: <0.1%. Occurrence: the genus occurs in a range of Lower and Middle Cambrian localities (see Conway Morris [1989b]). Description: Whittington and Briggs (1985). Other important reference: Briggs (1979a).

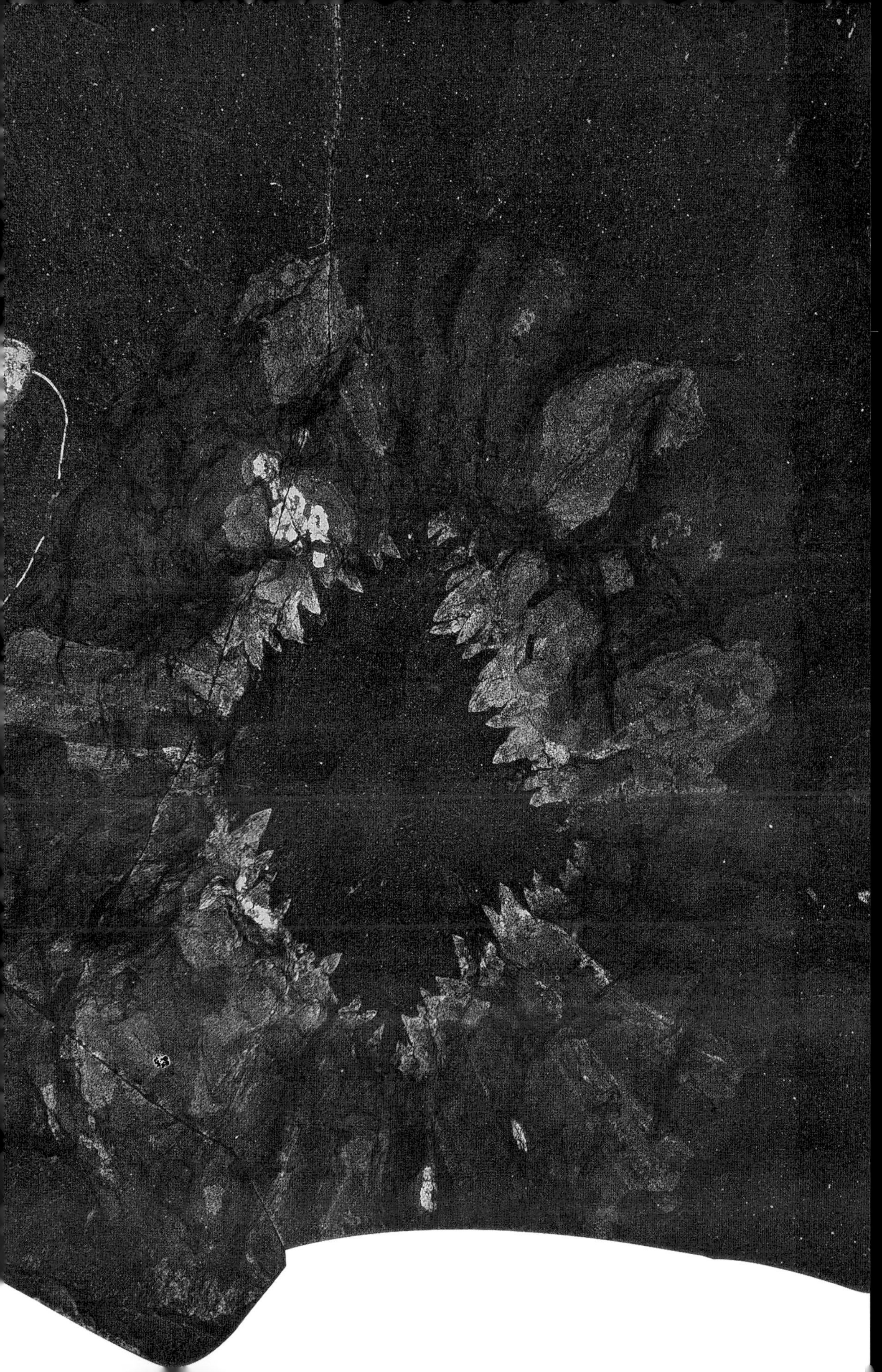

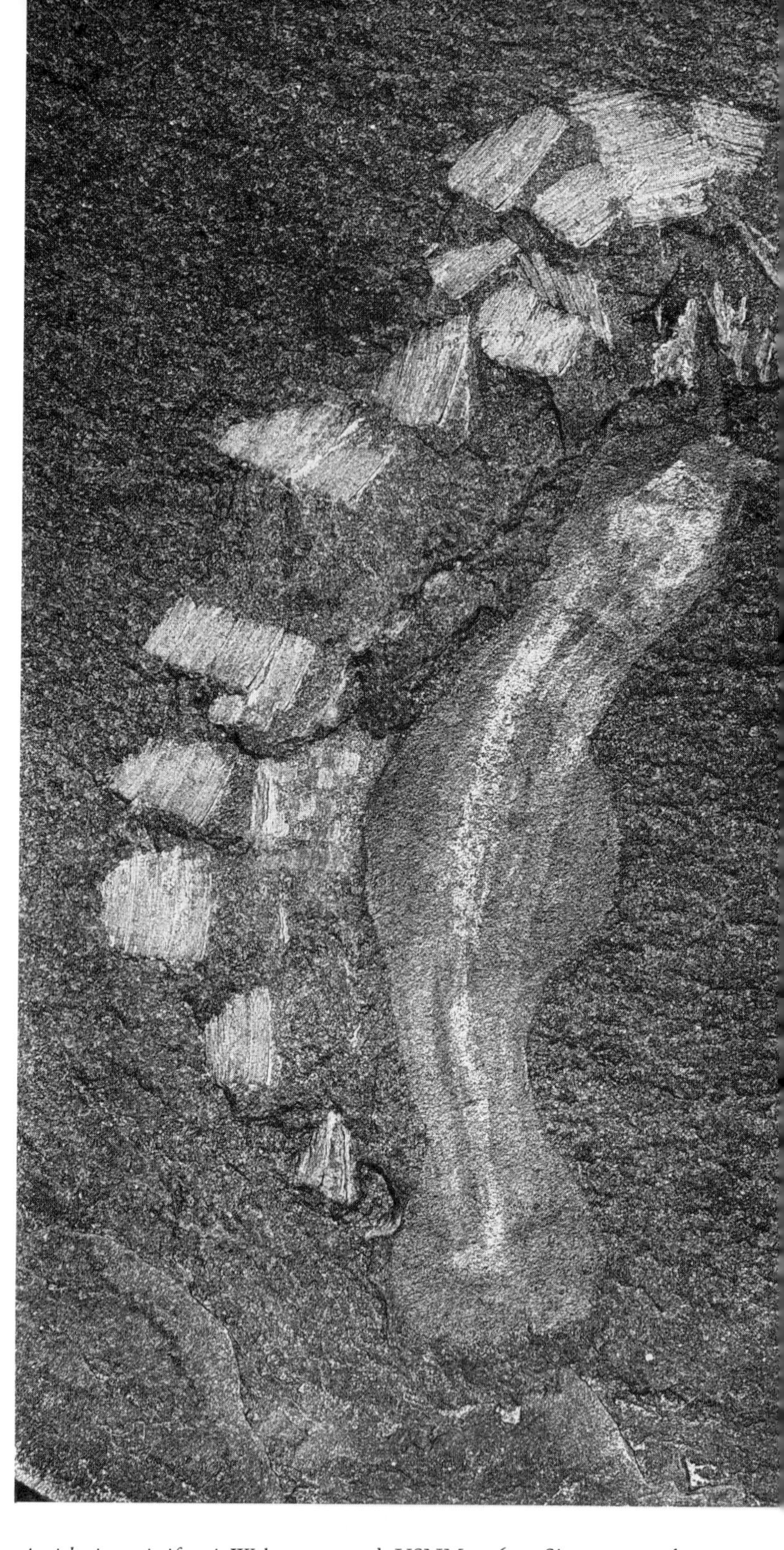

167 (×4.5)

Amiskwia sagittiformis Walcott, 1911d. USNM 57644. Size: 11 to at least 23 mm. Marianne Collins reconstruction. Proportion of total Burgess Shale assemblage in terms of numbers of individuals: <0.01%. Occurrence: Middle Cambrian Stephen Formation Burgess Shale. Description: Conway Morris (1977c).

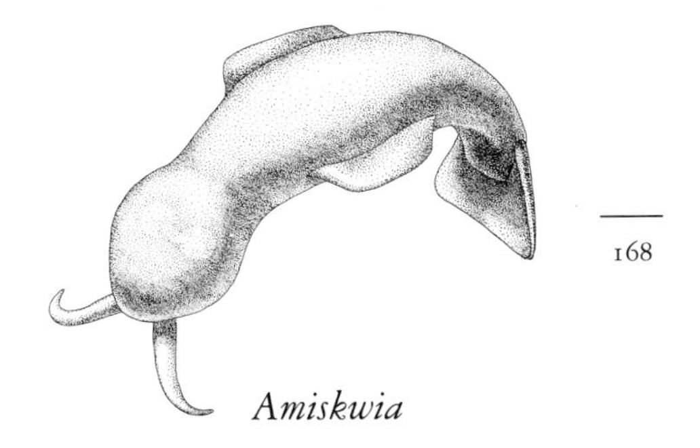

168

Amiskwia

The body of *Amiskwia* was divided into a head and trunk and dorsoventrally flattened in life. A pair of prominent tentacles projected from the head. There is a highly reflective area in the head of this specimen that may include traces of cerebral ganglia. The trunk was unsegmented. The broad reflective area that is evident running along the length of the trunk is the gut. Narrow linear structures in the trunk may be traces of blood vessels and the nerve cord. Extensions of the trunk epidermis formed a pair of gently rounded lateral fins and a tail fin. The flattened body and projecting fins suggest that *Amiskwia* was an active swimmer. This is supported by its rarity in the Burgess Shale fauna. Swimming animals were much less likely to be caught up and transported in the mud flows that buried the fauna than those forms that lived on and in the sediment.

Walcott considered *Amiskwia* to be a chaetognath (arrow-worm). Chaetognaths, however, use a complex arrangement of grasping spines and teeth to capture and comminute food, and these are not evident in the specimens of *Amiskwia.* In contrast, grasping spines are preserved in an undescribed chaetognath from the Stephen Formation. The position of the anus at the posterior of the trunk in *Amiskwia* is not typical of chaetognaths, in which the anus is located farther anteriorly and the trunk is divided from the tail by a transverse septum. *Amiskwia* has also been compared with the ribbon worms (Nemertea), but there are a number of critical differences such as the absence of a proboscis, lack of characteristically positioned reproductive organs, insertion of the tentacles, straight gut without diverticula, and the position of the anus. The affinities of this rare nektonic member of the Burgess Shale fauna remain uncertain.

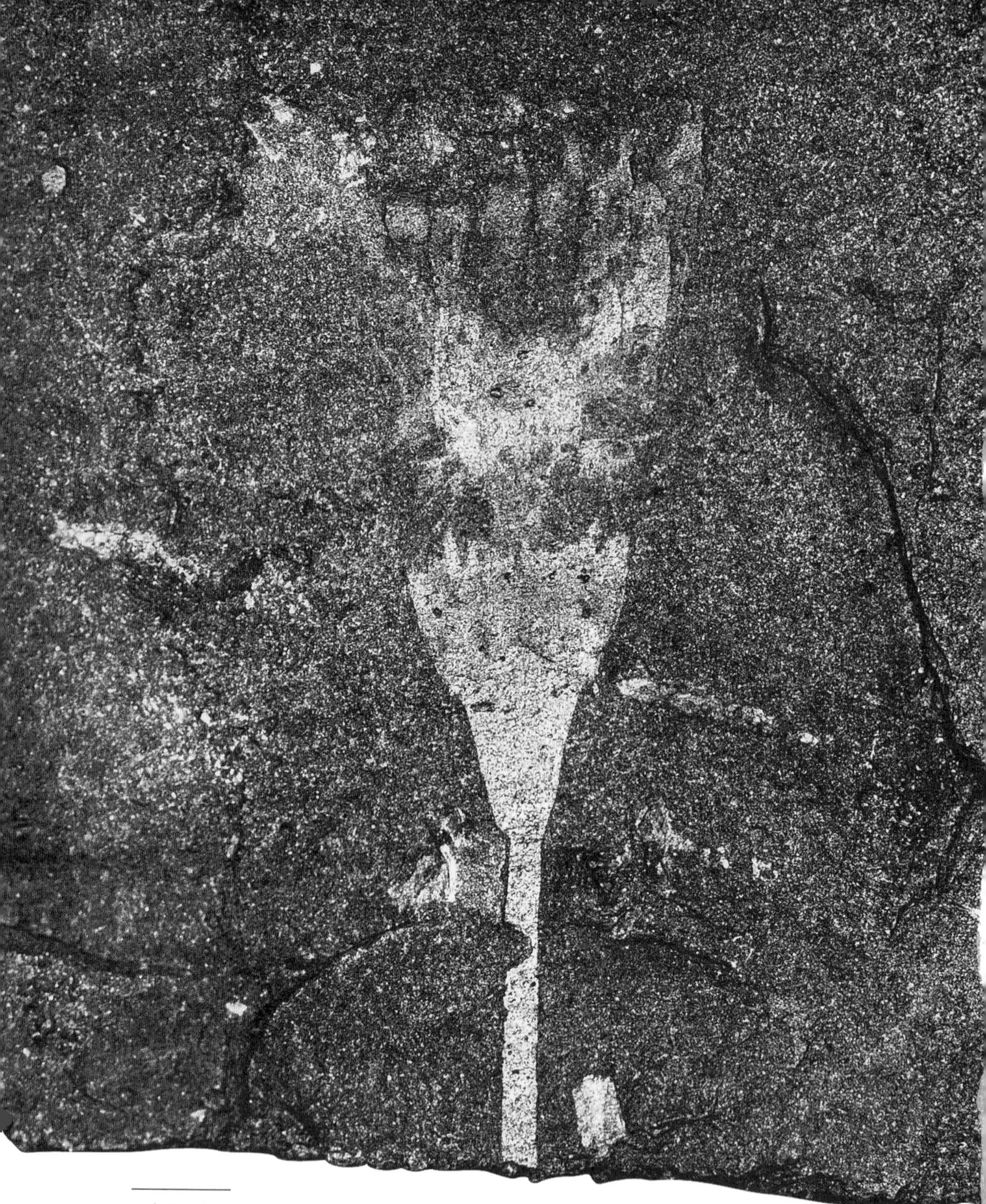

169 (×12)

Dinomischus isolatus Conway Morris, 1977b. USNM 198735. Size: 10 mm from base of calyx to tip of bracts. Marianne Collins reconstruction. Proportion of total Burgess Shale assemblage in terms of numbers of individuals: <0.01%. Occurrence: Lower Cambrian Chengjiang Fauna of China; Middle Cambrian Stephen Formation Burgess Shale. Description: Conway Morris (1977b). Other important reference: Chen et al. (1989).

170

Dinomischus

Dinomischus is one of the rarest of the Burgess Shale animals. The body consisted of a calyx supported by an elongate stem. The calyx was shaped like a cone, with the upper margin surrounded by a series of long platelike structures, which are termed bracts. The reflective area in this specimen represents a U-shaped gut. The central saclike portion is interpreted as the stomach. It appears to be suspended by reflective muscle strands. Both the mouth and anus opened on the upper surface of the calyx. The termination of the stem is not preserved on this specimen. A more complete specimen, however, shows that it ended in a bulbous swelling. This presumably anchored *Dinomischus* in the sediment. *Dinomischus* lived on the seabed, with the calyx held clear of the sediment by the stem. The animal presumably fed by filtering suspended particles out of the water. Another specimen shows the bracts spread out a little (rather than projecting straight upward) as if to increase the surface area for feeding. It is difficult to explain why an animal that lived attached to the seafloor should be so rarely preserved. Presumably it was not abundant where the Burgess Shale biota lived. Specimens of *Dinomischus* have also been discovered in the Lower Cambrian Chengjiang Fauna from China.

A variety of modern groups including sponges, cnidarians, tunicates, echinoderms, ectoprocts, and entoprocts have some members with a morphology similar to that of *Dinomischus* with its cuplike calyx and long stem. In most cases the similarity is superficial, but *Dinomischus* shares a number of features, including a calyx, stem, and recurved gut, with the entoprocts, a minor phylum of small, sessile, and almost exclusively marine animals. It lacks true tentacles, however, and although *Dinomischus* may be distantly related to the entoprocts, its affinities remain unresolved.

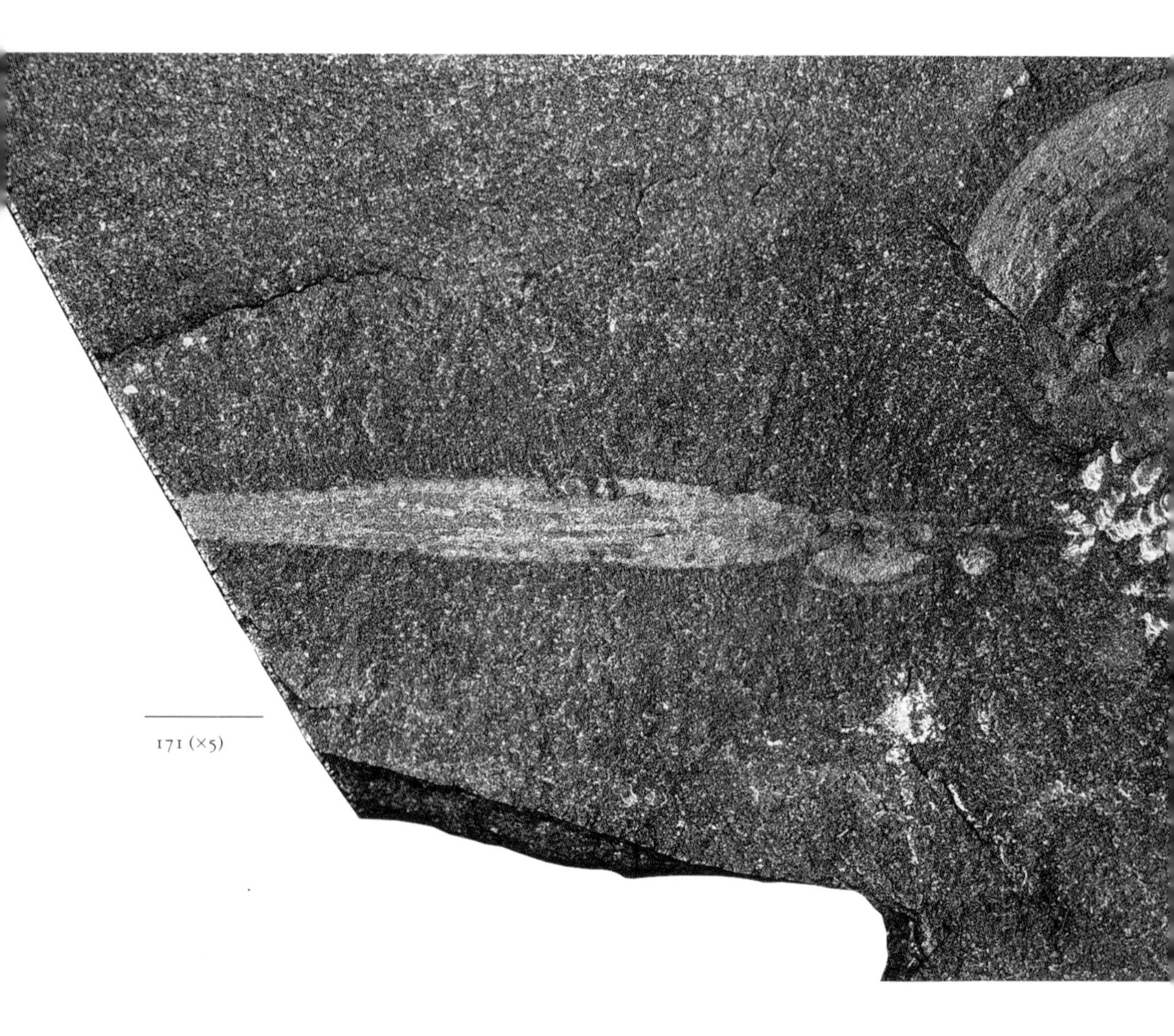

171 (×5)

Nectocaris pteryx Conway Morris, 1976b. USNM 198667. Size: about 2 cm long. Marianne Collins reconstruction. Proportion of total Burgess Shale assemblage in terms of numbers of individuals: <0.01%. Occurrence: Middle Cambrian Stephen Formation Burgess Shale. Description: Conway Morris (1976b). Other important reference: Simonetta (1988).

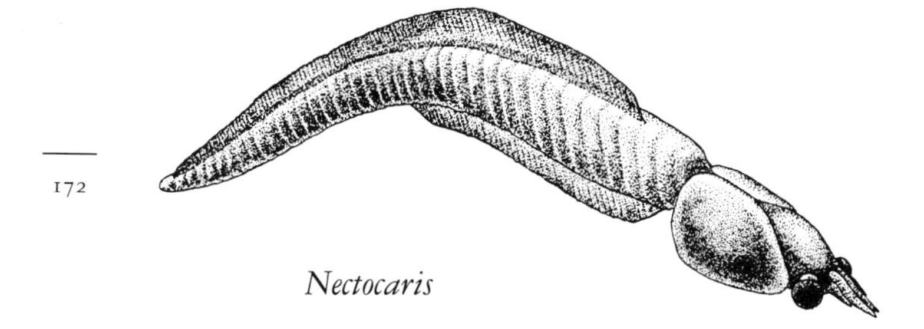

172

Nectocaris

Nectocaris is one of the rarest of the Burgess Shale animals; only a single specimen is known. Most of the head was enclosed in an oval shield. At least one pair of appendages projected forward beyond this head shield, and below them a large reflective eye can be seen. The long, segmented trunk carried a series of dorsal and ventral rays that presumably supported fins. The dorsal fin was more extensive than the ventral. A narrow reflective strip that is evident running through much of the trunk probably represents the gut. The flattened body and dorsal and ventral fins of *Nectocaris* suggest that it was an active swimmer. This is supported by its rarity in the Burgess Shale fauna. Swimming forms were much less likely to be caught up and transported in the mud flows that buried the fauna than animals that lived on and in the sediment. The large eyes suggest that *Nectocaris* may have actively pursued prey.

Some features of the head of *Nectocaris* are reminiscent of crustaceans: the appendages, eye, and the carapacelike shield. The trunk of the animal, however, is quite unlike that of any arthropod. In his original description of *Nectocaris,* Conway Morris declared that its affinities were enigmatic. Simonetta subsequently placed it within the chordates. This interpretation is certainly more plausible than a relationship to the arthropods, but certain features of the animal are not chordatelike. The affinities of *Nectocaris* remain problematic and are only likely to be resolved with the discovery of more specimens.

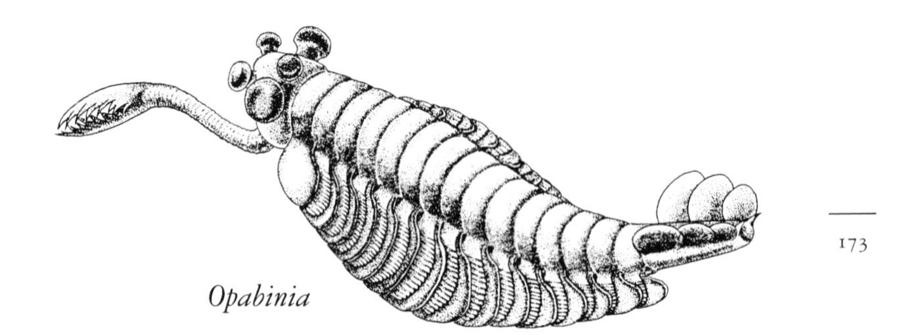

Opabinia

173

Opabinia had five eyes at the front of the head and a long, flexible proboscis that ended in an array of grasping spines. In the specimen shown in Illustration 174, the proboscis projects forward and up; in the other it is curved back beneath the head (Illustration 175). The trunk was divided into 15 segments, each bearing a pair of downward-directed lateral lobes. Overlying each lobe was a lamellate gill. Three pairs of upward-directed flaps formed a tail fan. *Opabinia* was the first Burgess Shale fossil redescribed as part of the investigation initiated in the 1960s that did not fit easily into any known major group of animals. When Harry Whittington showed his new reconstruction to an audience of paleontologists in Oxford in 1972 it was greeted with loud laughter! *Opabinia* is thought to have lived in the soft sediment on the seabed. It swam in pursuit of prey using the lateral lobes. The tail functioned as a stabilizer. The long proboscis was presumably used to grasp prey and transfer it to the mouth beneath the head. It may even have been plunged into burrows to extract worms.

Walcott regarded *Opabinia* as a branchiopod crustacean, but it lacks the characters that identify members of this group. Most subsequent authors compared *Opabinia* with the trilobites. This idea was based on a misinterpretation of the lobes as extensions of a dorsal carapace, equivalent to the pleurae of trilobites, which covered the gill branches. Whittington regarded *Opabinia* as an offshoot of the ancestral stock that gave rise to both annelids and arthropods. A number of authors have compared *Opabinia* with *Anomalocaris* and even with the Carboniferous *Tullimonstrum,* from the Mazon Creek biota of Illinois, but it is not clear whether the similarities are true homologies or merely superficial.

174 (×1.8)

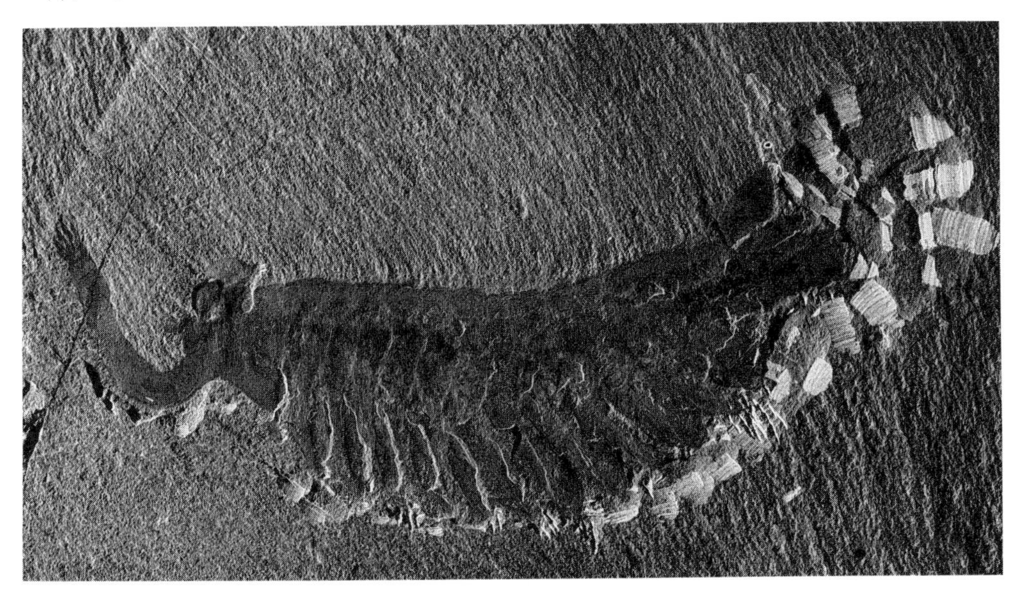

175 (×2)

Opabinia regalis Walcott, 1912a. USNM 57683, 155600. Size range: 4.3–7.0 cm long, excluding proboscis. Marianne Collins reconstruction. Proportion of total Burgess Shale assemblage in terms of numbers of individuals: 0.07%. Occurrence: Middle Cambrian Stephen Formation Burgess Shale. Description: Whittington (1975a). Other important references: Bergström (1986, 1987), Briggs and Whittington (1987). Note: Beall (1991) compared *Opabinia* with *Tullimonstrum*.

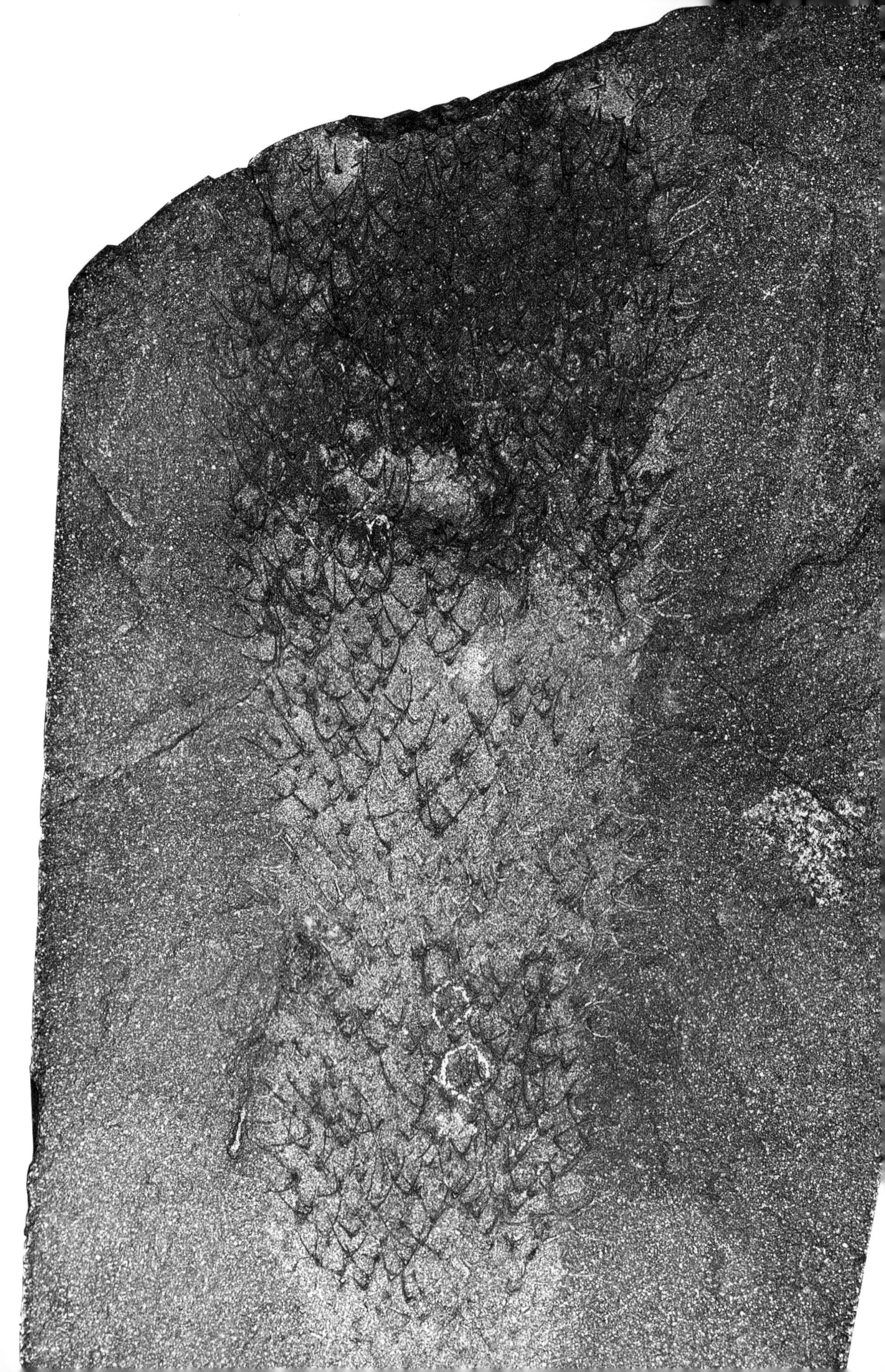

Chancelloria

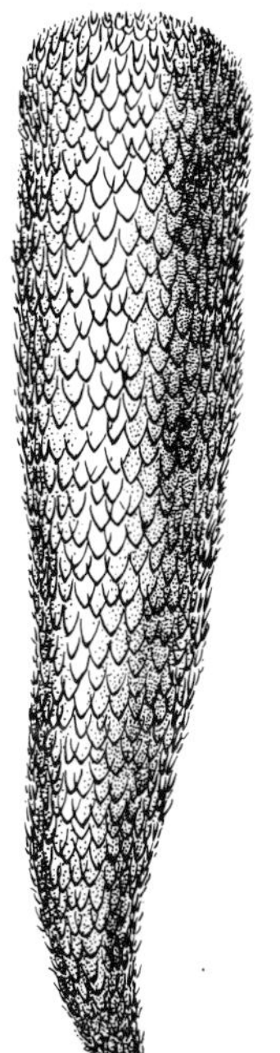

177

176 (×12)

Chancelloria eros was an elongate saclike animal, up to 10 cm long, with characteristic closely spaced calcareous sclerites in the wall. The sclerites have a central disk and six rays, all in the same plane. They are not united into a fused skeleton. *Chancelloria* lived a sessile existence on the seafloor, presumably extracting food particles from the water by filter feeding.

Walcott based the genus *Chancelloria* on specimens from the Burgess Shale and interpreted it as a heteractinellid sponge. This identification was followed by most authors until 1981, when Bengtson and Missarzhevsky noted that the so-called spicules of *Chancelloria* were hollow sclerites and must have been secreted from the inside, rather than by a covering of tissue, as are sponge spicules. Indeed, unlike sponge spicules, the sclerites of *Chancelloria* appear to have been external and protective in function. Bengtson and Missarzhevsky proposed a new class, the Coeloscleritophora, to include the Chancelloridae, as well as the Wiwaxiidae and other Lower Cambrian sclerite-bearing animals, the Siphogonuchitidae. These animals with a covering of sclerites (a scleritome) were particularly important in the Lower Cambrian. They represent a type of skeleton that evolved in early metazoans but disappeared later.

Chancelloria eros Walcott, 1920. USNM 66526. Size: 88 mm. Isham reconstruction. Proportion of total Burgess Shale assemblage in terms of numbers of individuals: <1%. Occurrence: Middle Cambrian Stephen Formation Burgess Shale and other localities (see Collins et al. [1983]). Description: Walcott (1920). Other important reference: Bengtson and Missarzhevsky (1981).

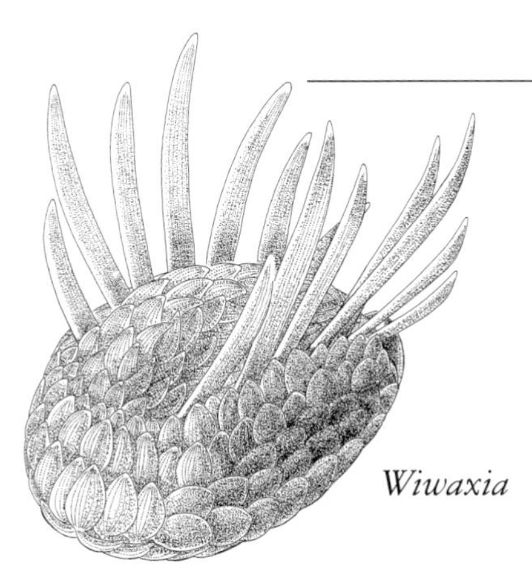

Wiwaxia

179

Wiwaxia was originally described in 1899 by G. F. Matthew on the basis of an isolated spine from the Middle Cambrian *Ogygopsis* Shale on Mount Stephen. The locality lies across the valley of the Kicking Horse River from the ridge where Walcott later discovered the Burgess Shale. Complete specimens of *Wiwaxia* from the Burgess Shale showed that the dorsal surface of the animal was covered by flattened scalelike sclerites in addition to spines like that described by Matthew. The ventral surface was naked. The covering of sclerites tends to obscure details of the internal morphology. The jaw is occasionally evident near the anterior, where it is marked by two rows of teeth. The sclerites differed in shape and size on different parts of the body of *Wiwaxia.* Longer spine-like sclerites projected upward in two rows, providing protection from predators. Their appearance varies depending on the orientation of the specimen to bedding. Where the specimen is preserved in an attitude approaching head on (Illustration 180), the two rows of spines are obvious; where it is flattened dorsally (Illustration 178) they may project sideways or be concealed in the rock. Some specimens of *Wiwaxia* have broken spines, possibly as a result of unsuccessful attacks by predators. The body was protected by regularly arranged rows of shorter flat-lying sclerites, each with a rootlike base by which it was attached. *Wiwaxia* may have grown by molting the sclerites. It is assumed to have lived on the sediment, crawling along the surface by muscular contractions. The jaws were used for feeding, possibly on organic material on the substrate.

Although *Wiwaxia* was sluglike, the armor of sclerites ("scleritome") shows that it does not belong to the molluscs. Wal-

178 (×6)

180 (×2.5)

cott considered *Wiwaxia* to be a bristle worm (a polychaete annelid), a view recently reasserted by Butterfield, who disputed the evidence for molting. Conway Morris, on the other hand, argued that the structure and arrangement of wiwaxiid sclerites is unlike that in any polychaete, and he grouped *Wiwaxia* with other Cambrian scleritome-bearing animals. Its affinities remain controversial.

Wiwaxia corrugata (Matthew, 1899). USNM 57635, 83938, 198669. Size: 3.5–55 mm long. Marianne Collins reconstruction. Proportion of total Burgess Shale assemblage in terms of numbers of individuals: 0.34%. Occurrence: Middle Cambrian Spence Shale, Utah; Stephen Formation Burgess Shale, *Ogygopsis* Shale (see Conway Morris [1989b]). Description: Conway Morris (1985a). Other important references: Butterfield (1990a), Conway Morris (1992).

Species Recorded from the Burgess Shale

This listing is based on sources cited in the Bibliography of the Burgess Shale, particularly the compilation by Whittington (1985b). Taxa with an asterisk (*) are illustrated in this volume. By convention, the author and date following each taxon refer to the original published description where the taxon was first named. If the author and date are in parentheses, this indicates that the species has since been transferred to a new or different genus than the one to which it was originally assigned. Where one or more additional taxa follow the first, prefixed by an equals sign, this shows that they are now considered to be the same and that only the first name is valid. The grouping of species into higher taxa is still a subject of active research and is an important key to understanding the nature of the Cambrian radiation.

Cyanobacteria-Hormogonales
(Filamentous Cyanobacteria)

**Marpolia spissa* Walcott, 1919
Morania confluens Walcott, 1919
Morania elongata Walcott, 1919
Morania fragmenta Walcott, 1919
Morania? frondosa Walcott, 1919
Morania? globosa Walcott, 1919
Morania parasitica Walcott, 1919
Morania? reticulata Walcott, 1919

Algae

CHLOROPHYTA (Green Algae)
**Margaretia dorus* Walcott, 1931

?CHLOROPHYTA (Green Algae)
**Yuknessia simplex* Walcott, 1919

RHODOPHYTA (Red Algae)
Bosworthia gyges Walcott, 1919
Bosworthia simulans Walcott, 1919
Dalyia nitens Walcott, 1919
**Dalyia racemata* Walcott, 1919
Wahpia mimica Walcott, 1919
Wahpia virgata Walcott, 1919
**Waputikia ramosa* Walcott, 1919

RHODOPHYTA (Calcareous Algae)
Sphaerocodium? cambria Walcott, 1919
Sphaerocodium? praecursor Walcott, 1919

Possible Algae

**Dictyophycus gracilis* Ruedemann, 1931

Phylum Porifera

CLASS DEMOSPONGIA (Demosponges)

Capsospongia undulata (Walcott, 1920)
Choia carteri Walcott, 1920
Choia ridleyi Walcott, 1920
Crumillospongia biporosa Rigby, 1986
Crumillospongia frondosa (Walcott, 1920)
Falospongia falata Rigby, 1986
Fieldospongia bellilineata (Walcott, 1920)
Halichondrites elissa Walcott, 1920
Hamptonia bowerbanki Walcott, 1920
Hazelia conferta Walcott, 1920
Hazelia crateria Rigby, 1986
Hazelia delicatula Walcott, 1920
Hazelia dignata (Walcott, 1920)
Hazelia grandis Walcott, 1920
Hazelia luteria Rigby, 1986
Hazelia nodulifera Walcott, 1920
Hazelia obscura Walcott, 1920
Hazelia palmata Walcott, 1920
Leptomitus lineatus (Walcott, 1920)
Moleculopina mammillata (Walcott, 1920)
Pirania muricata Walcott, 1920
Sentinelia draco Walcott, 1920
Takakkawia lineata Walcott, 1920
Vauxia bellula Walcott, 1920
Vauxia densa Walcott, 1920
Vauxia gracilenta Walcott, 1920
Vauxia venata Walcott, 1920
Wapkia grandis Walcott, 1920

CLASS HEXACTINELLIDA (Glass Sponges)

Diagoniella hindei Walcott, 1920
Protospongia hicksi Hinde, 1887
Stephanospongia magnipora Rigby, 1986

CLASS CALCAREA (Calcareous Sponges)

Canistrumella alternata Rigby, 1986
Eiffelia globosa Walcott, 1920

Phylum Cnidaria

?CLASS ANTHOZOA

?Order Pennatulacea (Sea Pens and Sea Pansies)

Thaumaptilon walcotti Conway Morris, 1993

?Order Actiniaria (Sea Anemones)

Mackenzia costalis Walcott, 1911c

?CLASS HYDROZOA

?Suborder Chondrophorina (By-the-wind Sailors)

Gelenoptron tentaculatum Conway Morris, 1993

?Phylum Cnidaria

Cambrorhytium fragilis (Walcott, 1911d)
Cambrorhytium major (Walcott, 1908a)

Phylum Ctenophora (Comb Jellies)

Fasciculus vesanus Simonetta and Delle Cave, 1978a

?Superphylum Lophophorata

Odontogriphus omalus Conway Morris, 1976a

Superphylum Lophophorata

Phylum Brachiopoda (Lamp Shells)

CLASS INARTICULATA (Inarticulates)

Acrothyra gregaria Walcott, 1924a
Lingulella waptaensis Walcott, 1924a
Micromitra burgessensis Resser, 1938
Paterina zenobia (Walcott, 1924a)

CLASS ARTICULATA (Articulates)

Diraphora bellicostata (Walcott, 1924a)
Nisusia burgessensis Walcott, 1924a

?Phylum Mollusca (Molluscs)
CLASS HELCIONELLOIDA (Monoplacophora)
Scenella amii (Matthew, 1902)

Phylum Hyolitha (Hyoliths)
Haplophrentis carinatus (Matthew, 1899)

Phylum Priapulida (Priapulids)
Ancalagon minor (Walcott, 1911d)
Fieldia lanceolata Walcott, 1912a
Louisella pedunculata Walcott, 1911d (=*Miskoia preciosa* Walcott, 1911d)
Ottoia prolifica Walcott, 1911d (=*Miskoia placida* Walcott, 1931)
Selkirkia columbia Conway Morris, 1977d (=*S. major* Walcott, 1911d)

Probable Priapulids
Lecythioscopa simplex (Walcott, 1931)
Scolecofurca rara Conway Morris, 1977d

Phylum Annelida
CLASS POLYCHAETA (Bristle Worms and their allies)
Burgessochaeta setigera (Walcott, 1911d)
Canadia spinosa Walcott, 1911d (=*C. regularis* Walcott, 1911d and *C. grandis* Walcott, 1931)
Insolicorypha psygma Conway Morris, 1979a
Peronochaeta dubia (Walcott, 1911d)
Stephenoscolex argutus Conway Morris, 1979a

Phylum Onychophora (Velvet Worms)
Aysheaia pedunculata Walcott, 1911d
Hallucigenia sparsa (Walcott, 1911d)

Phylum Arthropoda
Primitive
Branchiocaris pretiosa (Resser, 1929)
Marrella splendens Walcott, 1912a
Subphylum Crustacea and Crustaceanomorphs (Crabs and their allies)
Canadaspis ovalis (Walcott, 1912a)
Canadaspis perfecta (Walcott, 1912a) (=*Hymenocaris obliqua* Walcott, 1912a and *Canadaspis obesa* Simonetta and Delle Cave, 1975)
Carnarvonia venosa Walcott, 1912a
Isoxys acutangulus (Walcott, 1908a)
Isoxys longissimus Simonetta and Delle Cave, 1975
Odaraia alata Walcott, 1912a (=*Eurysaces pielus* Simonetta and Delle Cave, 1975)
Perspicaris dictynna (Simonetta and Delle Cave, 1975)
Perspicaris recondita Briggs, 1977
Plenocaris plena (Walcott, 1912a)
Tuzoia burgessensis Resser, 1929
Tuzoia canadensis Resser, 1929
Tuzoia? parva (Walcott, 1912a)
Tuzoia praemorsa Resser, 1929
Tuzoia retifera Walcott, 1912a
Waptia fieldensis Walcott, 1912a
CLASS OSTRACODA (Ostracods)
Aluta? sp. indet.
CLASS CIRRIPEDIA? (Barnacles)
Priscansermarinus barnetti Collins and Rudkin, 1981
Subphylum Arachnomorpha
CLASS TRILOBITA (Trilobites)
Chancia palliseri (Walcott, 1908b)
Ehmaniella burgessensis Rasetti, 1951
Ehmaniella waptaensis Rasetti, 1951

**Elrathia permulta* (Walcott, 1918b)
cf. *Elrathina brevifrons* Rasetti, 1951
**Elrathina cordillerae* (Rominger, 1887)
Hanburia gloriosa Walcott, 1916b
**Kootenia burgessensis* Resser, 1942
**Naraoia compacta* Walcott, 1912a (= *N. pammon* Simonetta and Delle Cave, 1975 and *N. halia* Simonetta and Delle Cave, 1975)
Naraoia spinifer Walcott, 1931
**Olenoides serratus* (Rominger, 1887) (=*Nathorstia transitans* Walcott, 1912a)
**Oryctocephalus burgessensis* Resser, 1938
**Oryctocephalus matthewi* Rasetti, 1951
Oryctocephalus reynoldsi Reed, 1899
Oryctocephalus sp. indet.
**Pagetia bootes* Walcott, 1916b
**Parkaspis decamera* Rasetti, 1951
Peronopsis montis (Matthew, 1899)
**Ptychagnostus praecurrens* (Westergaard, 1936) (=*Triplagnostus burgessensis* Rasetti, 1951)
Spencella sp. indet. 1 (Rasetti, 1951)
Spencella sp. indet. 2 (Rasetti, 1951)
Tegopelte gigas Simonetta and Delle Cave, 1975

CLASS CHELICERATA
(Chelicerates—Scorpions, Spiders, and their allies)
**Sanctacaris uncata* Briggs and Collins, 1988

OTHER ARTHROPODS
Actaeus armatus Simonetta, 1970
Alalcomenaeus cambricus Simonetta, 1970
**Burgessia bella* Walcott, 1912a (=*Hymenocaris? circularis* Walcott, 1912a)
**Emeraldella brocki* Walcott, 1912a (=*Emeraldoides problematicus* Simonetta, 1964)
Habelia? brevicauda Simonetta, 1964
**Habelia optata* Walcott, 1912a
**Helmetia expansa* Walcott, 1918a
Houghtonites gracilis (Walcott, 1912a)
**Leanchoilia superlata* Walcott, 1912a (=*Bidentia difficilis* Walcott, 1912a; *Emeraldella micrura* Walcott, 1912a; *Leanchoilia major* Walcott, 1931; *Leanchoilia amphiction* Simonetta, 1970; *Leanchoilia persephone* Simonetta, 1970; *Leanchoilia protogonia* Simonetta, 1970)
**Molaria spinifera* Walcott, 1912a
Mollisonia rara Walcott, 1912a (=*Parahabelia rara* Simonetta, 1964)
Mollisonia symmetrica Walcott, 1912a
**Sarotrocercus oblita* Whittington, 1981b
**Sidneyia inexpectans* Walcott, 1911a
Skania fragilis Walcott, 1931
Thelxiope palaeothallasia Simonetta and Delle Cave, 1975
**Yohoia tenuis* Walcott, 1912a

Phylum Echinodermata

CLASS CYSTOIDEA (Cystoids)

*?*Gogia radiata* Sprinkle, 1973

CLASS CRINOIDEA (Sea Lilies)

**Echmatocrinus brachiatus* Sprinkle, 1973

CLASS EDRIOASTEROIDEA (Edrioasteroids)

Walcottidiscus magister Bassler, 1936

Walcottidiscus typicalis Bassler, 1935

CLASS HOLOTHUROIDEA (Sea Cucumbers)

**Eldonia ludwigi* Walcott, 1911c

Phylum Hemichordata

CLASS ENTEROPNEUSTA? (Acorn Worms)

"Ottoia" tenuis Walcott, 1911d

CLASS GRAPTOLITHINA? (Graptolites)

Chaunograptus scandens Ruedemann, 1931

Phylum Chordata (Chordates)

**Metaspriggina walcotti* Simonetta and Insom, 1993

**Pikaia gracilens* Walcott, 1911d

Animals Not Assigned to Major Groups

ANOMALOCARIDS

Amiella ornata Walcott, 1911d

**Anomalocaris canadensis* Whiteaves, 1892

Anomalocaris nathorsti (Walcott, 1911a) (=*Laggania cambria* Walcott, 1911a and *Peytoia nathorsti* Walcott, 1911a)

Hurdia dentata Simonetta and Delle Cave, 1975

Hurdia triangulata Walcott, 1912a

Hurdia victoria Walcott, 1912a

Proboscicaris agnosta Rolfe, 1962

Proboscicaris ingens Rolfe, 1962

Proboscicaris obtusa Simonetta and Delle Cave, 1975

OTHERS

**Amiskwia sagittiformis* Walcott, 1911d

Banffia constricta Walcott, 1911d

**Dinomischus isolatus* Conway Morris, 1977b

**Nectocaris pteryx* Conway Morris, 1976b

Oesia disjuncta Walcott, 1911d

**Opabinia regalis* Walcott, 1912a

"Platydendron ovale" Simonetta and Delle Cave, 1978a

Pollingeria grandis Walcott, 1911d

**Portalia mira* Walcott, 1918a

Worthenella cambria Walcott, 1911d

Scleritome-bearing Animals

**Chancelloria eros* Walcott, 1920

**Wiwaxia corrugata* (Matthew, 1899)

References

This list includes references to papers other than those on the Burgess Shale. References to the Burgess Shale are included in the Bibliography of the Burgess Shale, which follows this section.

Aldridge, R. J., D. E. G. Briggs, E. N. K. Clarkson, and M. P. Smith. 1986. The affinities of conodonts—new evidence from the Carboniferous of Edinburgh, Scotland. *Lethaia* 19:279–291.

Aldridge, R. J., D. E. G. Briggs, M. P. Smith, E. N. K. Clarkson, and N. D. L. Clark. 1993. The anatomy of conodonts. *Philosophical Transactions of the Royal Society of London Series B* 340:405–421.

Allison, P. A., and D. E. G. Briggs. 1993a. Exceptional fossil record: Distribution of soft-tissue preservation through the Phanerozoic. *Geology* 21:527–530.

Ballard, J. W. O., G. J. Olsen, D. P. Faith, W. A. Odgers, D. M. Rowell, and P. W. Atkinson. 1992. Evidence from 12s ribosomal RNA sequences that onycophorans are modified arthropods. *Science* 258:1345–1348.

Bengtson, S. and V. V. Missarzhevsky. 1981. Coeloscleritophora—A major group of enigmatic Cambrian metazoans, pp. 19–21. In M. E. Taylor (ed.), *Short Papers for the Second International Symposium on the Cambrian System.* U.S. Geological Survey Open-file Report 81-743.

Bowring, S. A., J. P. Grotzinger, C. E. Isachsen, A. H. Knoll, S. M. Pelechaty, and P. Kolosov. 1993. Calibrating rates of Early Cambrian evolution. *Science* 261:1293–1298.

Briggs, D. E. G., E. N. K. Clarkson, and R. J. Aldridge. 1983. The conodont animal. *Lethaia* 16:1–14.

Conway Morris, S. 1993. The fossil record and the early evolution of the Metazoa. *Nature* 361:219–225.

Elliott, D. K., and D. L. Martin. 1987. A new trace fossil from the Cambrian Bright Angel Shale, Grand Canyon, Arizona. *Journal of Paleontology* 61:641–648.

Erwin, D. H. 1991. Metazoan phylogeny and the Cambrian radiation. *Trends in Ecology and Evolution* 6:131–134.

Foote, M., and S. J. Gould. 1992. Cambrian and Recent morphologic disparity. *Science* 258:1816.

Glaessner, G. F. 1984. *The Dawn of Animal Life.* Cambridge: Cambridge University Press.

Hou, X.-G., L. Ramskold, and J. Bergström. 1991. Composition and preservation of the Chengjiang fauna—a Lower Cambrian soft-bodied biota. *Zoologica Scripta* 20:395–411.

Knight, J. B. 1941. *Paleozoic Gastropod Genotypes.* Geological Society of America Special Paper No. 32.

Knoll, A. H. 1992. Latest Proterozoic stratigraphy and earth history. *Nature* 356:673–678.

Lipps, J. H., and P. W. Signor (eds.). 1992. *Origin and Early Evolution of the Metazoa.* New York: Plenum Press.

McMenamin, M. A. S., and D. L. Schulte-McMenamin. 1990. *The Emergence of Animals.* New York: Columbia University Press.

Marek, L., and E. L. Yochelson. 1976. Aspects of the biology of the Hyolitha (Mollusca). *Lethaia* 9:65–82.

Paul, C. R. C. 1988. The phylogeny of the cystoids, pp. 199–213. In C. R. C. Paul and A. B. Smith (eds.), *Echinoderm Phylogeny and Evolutionary Biology.* Oxford: Clarendon Press.

Peel, J. S. 1991. The Classes Tergomya and Helcionelloida, and early molluscan evolution. *Bulletin Gronlands Geologiske Undersokelse* 161:11–65.

Qian Yi and S. Bengtson. 1989. Paleontology and biostratigraphy of the Early Cambrian Meichucunian Stage in Yunnan Province, South China. *Fossils and Strata* 24:156 p.

Runnegar, B. 1980. Hyolitha: Status of the phylum. *Lethaia* 13:21–25.

Schopf, J. W., and C. Klein (eds.). 1992. *The Proterozoic Biosphere.* Cambridge: Cambridge University Press.

Seilacher, A. 1992. Vendobionta and Psammocorralia: Lost constructions of Precambrian evolution. *Journal of the Geological Society of London* 149:607–613.

Simonetta, A. M., and S. Conway Morris (eds.). 1991. *The Early Evolution of Metazoa and the Significance of Problematic Taxa.* Cambridge: Cambridge University Press.

Valentine, J. W., S. M. Awramik, P. W. Signor, and P. M. Sadler. 1991. The biological explosion and the Precambrian-Cambrian boundary. In M. K. Hecht, B. Wallace, and R. J. MacIntyre (eds.), *Evolutionary Biology* 25:279–356.

Valentine, J. W., and D. H. Erwin. 1987. Interpreting great developmental experiments: The fossil record, pp. 71–107. In R. A. Raff and E. C. Raff (eds.), *Development as an Evolutionary Process.* New York: Liss.

Yochelson, E. L., and M. D. Gil Cid. 1984. Reevaluation of the systematic position of *Scenella. Lethaia* 17:331–340.

Zhang, W.-T., and X.-G. Hou. 1985. Preliminary notes on the occurrence of the unusual trilobite *Naraoia* in Asia. *Acta Palaeontologica Sinica* 24:591–595.

Bibliography of the Burgess Shale

This list includes the main publications on the fossils, sedimentology, and stratigraphy of the Burgess Shale; abstracts are excluded.

Aitken, J. D., and W. H. Fritz. 1968. Burgess Shale project, British Columbia (82H/8 (West Half)). *Canadian Geological Survey Paper* 68-1A: 190–192.

Aitken, J. D., W. H. Fritz, and H. B. Whittington. 1967. Stratigraphy, palaeontology and palaeoecology of the Burgess Shale. *Canadian Geological Survey Paper* 67-1A: 52.

Aitken, J. D., and I. A. McIlreath. 1984. The Cathedral Reef escarpment, a Cambrian great wall with humble origins. *Geos: Energy Mines and Resources, Canada* 13(1): 17–19.

———. 1990. Comment on "The Burgess Shale: Not in the shadow of the Cathedral Escarpment." *Geoscience Canada* 17:111–116.

Allison, P. A., and D. E. G. Briggs. 1991a. The taphonomy of soft-bodied animals, pp. 120–140. In S. K. Donovan (ed.), *Fossilization: The Process of Taphonomy.* London: Belhaven Press.

———. 1991b. Taphonomy of non-mineralized tissues, pp. 25–70. In P. A. Allison and D. E. G. Briggs (eds.), *Taphonomy: Releasing the Data Locked in the Fossil Record.* New York: Plenum Press.

———. 1993b. Burgess Shale-type biotas burrowed away? *Lethaia* 26:184–185.

Aronson, R. B. 1992. Decline of the Burgess Shale fauna: Ecologic or taphonomic restriction. *Lethaia* 25:225–229.

———. 1993. Burgess Shale-type biotas were not just burrowed away: Reply. *Lethaia* 26:185.

Babcock, L. E., and R. A. Robison. 1988. Taxonomy and paleobiology of some Middle Cambrian *Scenella* (Cnidaria) and hyolithids (Mollusca) from western North America. *University of Kansas Paleontological Contributions* 121.

Baird, D. M. 1962. Yoho National Park—the mountains, the rocks, the scenery. *Geological Survey of Canada Miscellaneous Report* 4:1–107.

Banta, W. C., and M. E. Rice. 1970. A restudy of the Middle Cambrian Burgess Shale fossil worm *Ottoia prolifica.* In M. E. Rice (ed.), *Proceedings of the International Symposium on the Biology of the Sipuncula and Echiura.* Vol. 2: 79–90. Belgrade, Yugoslavia.

Bassler, R. S. 1935. The classification of Edrioasteroidea. *Smithsonian Miscellaneous Collections* 93:1–11.

———. 1936. New species of American Edrioasteroidea. *Smithsonian Miscellaneous Collections* 95:1–33.

Beall, B. S. 1991. The Tully Monster and a new approach to analyzing problematica, pp. 271–285. In A. M. Simonetta and S. Conway Morris (eds.), *The Early Evolution of Metazoa and the Significance of Problematic Taxa.* Cambridge: Cambridge University Press.

Behrensmeyer, A. K. 1984. Taphonomy and the fossil record. *American Scientist* 72:558–566.

Bengtson, S., and S. Conway Morris. 1984. A comparative study of Lower Cambrian *Halkieria* and Middle Cambrian *Wiwaxia. Lethaia* 17:307–329.

———. 1986. Fjälliga djur från det kambriska havet. *Fauna och Flora* 81:27–34.

Bergström, J. 1986. *Opabinia* and *Anomalocaris*, unique Cambrian 'arthropods.' *Lethaia* 19:242–246.

———. 1987. The Cambrian *Opabinia* and *Anomalocaris. Lethaia* 20:187–188.

———. 1992. The oldest arthropods and the origin of the Crustacea. *Acta Zoologica* (Stockholm) 73:287–291.

Briggs, D. E. G. 1976. The arthropod *Branchiocaris* n. gen., Middle Cambrian, Burgess Shale, British Columbia. *Geological Survey of Canada Bulletin* 264:1–29.

———. 1977. Bivalved arthropods from the Cambrian Burgess Shale of British Columbia. *Palaeontology* 20:595–621.

———. 1978. The morphology, mode of life, and affinities of *Canadaspis perfecta* (Crustacea: Phyllocarida), Middle Cambrian, Burgess Shale, British Columbia. *Philosophical Transactions of the Royal Society of London Series B* 281:439–487.

———. 1979a. *Anomalocaris*, the largest known Cambrian arthropod. *Palaeontology* 22:631–664.

———. 1979b. Crustacea, pp. 144–146. *McGraw-Hill Yearbook of Science and Technology.*

———. 1981a. The arthropod *Odaraia alata* Walcott, Middle Cambrian, Burgess Shale, British Columbia. *Philosophical Transactions of the Royal Society of London Series B* 291:541–585.

———. 1981b. The Burgess Shale project, pp. 34–37. In M. E. Taylor (ed.), *Short Papers for the Second International Symposium on the Cambrian System.* U.S. Geological Survey Open-file Report 81-743.

———. 1983. Affinities and early evolution of the Crustacea: The evidence of the Cambrian fossils, pp. 1–22. In F. R. Schram (ed.), *Crustacean Phylogeny.* Rotterdam: Balkema.

———. 1985. Les premiers arthropodes. *La Recherche* 16(164): 340–349.

———. 1990a. Flattening, pp. 244–247. In D. E. G. Briggs and P. R. Crowther (eds.), *Palaeobiology — A Synthesis.* Oxford: Blackwell Scientific Publications.

———. 1990b. Early arthropods: Dampening the Cambrian explosion. *Short Courses in Paleontology* 3:24–43. Paleontological Society.

———. 1991. Extraordinary fossils. *American Scientist* 79:130–141.

———. 1992. Phylogenetic significance of the Burgess Shale crustacean *Canadaspis. Acta Zoologica* (Stockholm) 73:293–300.

Briggs, D. E. G., and D. Collins. 1988. A Middle Cambrian chelicerate from Mount Stephen, British Columbia. *Palaeontology* 31:779–798.

Briggs, D. E. G., and S. Conway Morris. 1986. Problematica from the Middle Cambrian Burgess Shale of British Columbia, pp. 167–183. In A. Hoffman and M. H. Nitecki (eds.), *Problematic Fossil Taxa.* New York: Oxford University Press.

Briggs, D. E. G., and R. A. Fortey. 1989. The early radiation and relationships of the major arthropod groups. *Science* 246:241–243.

Briggs, D. E. G., R. A. Fortey, and M. A. Wills. 1992a. Morphologic disparity in the Cambrian. *Science* 256:1670–1673.

———. 1992b. Reply to Foote and Gould, and Lee. *Science* 258:1817–1818.

———. 1993. How big was the Cambrian explosion? A taxonomic and morphological comparison of Cambrian and Recent arthropods, pp. 33–44. In D. Edwards and D. Lees (eds.), *Evolutionary Patterns and Processes.* Linnean Society Symposium Series No. 14. London: Academic Press.

Briggs, D. E. G., and A. J. Kear. 1994. Decay of the lancelet *Branchiostoma lanceolatum* (Cephalochordata); implications for the interpretation of soft-tissue preservation in conodonts and other primitive chordates. *Lethaia* 26:275–287.

Briggs, D. E. G., and J. D. Mount. 1982. The occurrence of the giant arthropod *Anomalocaris* in the Lower Cambrian of Southern California and the overall distribution of the genus. *Journal of Paleontology* 56(5): 1112–1118.

Briggs, D. E. G., and R. A. Robison. 1984. Exceptionally preserved nontrilobite arthropods and *Anomalocaris* from the Middle Cambrian of Utah. *University of Kansas Paleontological Contributions* 111.

Briggs, D. E. G., and H. B. Whittington. 1981. Relationships of arthropods from the Burgess Shale and other Cambrian sequences, pp. 38–41. In M. E. Taylor (ed.), *Short Papers for the Second International Symposium on the Cambrian System.* U.S. Geological Survey Open-file Report 81-743.

———. 1985a. Modes of life of arthropods from the Burgess Shale, British Columbia. *Transactions of the Royal Society of Edinburgh* 76:149–160.

———. 1985b. Terror of the trilobites. *Natural History* 1985/12: 34–39.

———. 1987. The affinities of the Cambrian animals *Anomalocaris* and *Opabinia. Lethaia* 20:185–186.

Briggs, D. E. G., and S. H. Williams. 1981. The restoration of flattened fossils. *Lethaia* 14:157–164.

Bruton, D. L. 1981. The arthropod *Sidneyia inexpectans,* Middle Cambrian, Burgess Shale, British Columbia. *Philosophical Transactions of the Royal Society of London Series B* 295:619–656.

Bruton, D. L., and H. B. Whittington. 1983. *Emeraldella* and *Leanchoilia,* two arthropods from the Burgess Shale, British Columbia. *Philosophical Transactions of the Royal Society of London Series B* 300:553–585.

Burling, L. D. 1915. Shallow water deposition in the Cambrian of the Canadian Cordillera. *The Ottawa Naturalist* 29 November 1915: 87–88.

Butterfield, N. J. 1990a. Organic preservation of non-mineralizing organisms and the taphonomy of the Burgess Shale. *Paleobiology* 16(3): 272–286.

———. 1990b. A reassessment of the enigmatic Burgess Shale fossil *Wiwaxia corrugata* (Matthew) and its relationship to the polychaete *Canadia spinosa* Walcott. *Paleobiology* 16(3): 287–303.

Calman, W. T. 1919. Dr. Walcott's researches on the appendages of trilobites. *Geological Magazine,* n.s. 6:359–363.

Chen, J.-Y., X.-G. Hou, and H.-Z. Lu. 1989. Early Cambrian hock glass-like rare animal *Dinomischus* and its ecological features. *Acta Palaeontologica Sinica* 28:58–71.

Clark, A. H. 1912. Restoration of the genus *Eldonia,* a genus of free-swimming Holothurians from the middle Cambrian. *Sonderabdruck aus dem Zoologischen Anzeiger* 39:723–725.

———. 1913. Cambrian holothurians. *American Naturalist* 48:488–507.

———. 1915. The present distribution of the Onychophora, a group of terrestrial invertebrates. *Smithsonian Miscellaneous Collections* 65:1–25.

Clark, H. L. 1912. Fossil holothurians. *Science,* n.s. 35(894): 274–278.

Collier, F. J. 1983. The Burgess Shale, an incredible window on the Cambrian period. *Rocks and Minerals* 58(6): 257–264.

Collins, D. H. 1978. A palaeontologist's paradise. *Rotunda* (Royal Ontario Museum) 11(4): 12–19.

———. 1986a. Paradise revisited. *Rotunda* (Royal Ontario Museum) 19(1): 30–39.

———. 1986b. The great *Anomalocaris* mystery. How a shrimp became the world's first monster. *Rotunda* (Royal Ontario Museum) 19(3): 51–57.

———. 1987. Life in the Cambrian seas. *Nature* 326:127.

———. 1993. *Geology and Paleontology of the Mt. Stephen trilobite beds and the Burgess Shale in the Stephen Formation, Yoho National Park, British Columbia.* SEPM (Society of Economic Paleontologists and Mineralogists) Annual Meeting Field Trip Guidebook, Trip no. 22.

Collins, D. H., D. E. G. Briggs, and S. Conway Morris. 1983. New Burgess Shale fossil sites reveal Middle Cambrian faunal complex. *Science* 222:163–167.

Collins, D., and D. M. Rudkin. 1981. *Priscansermarinus barnetti,* a probable lepadomorph barnacle from the Middle Cambrian Burgess Shale of British Columbia. *Journal of Paleontology* 55:1006–1015.

Collins, D., and W. D. Stewart. 1991. The Burgess Shale and its environmental setting, Fossil Ridge, Yoho National Park, pp. 105–118. In P. L. Smith (ed.), *A Field Guide to the Paleontology of Southwestern Canada.* Victoria: University of British Columbia.

Conway Morris, S. 1976a. A new Cambrian lophophorate from the Burgess Shale of British Columbia. *Palaeontology* 19:199–222.

———. 1976b. *Nectocaris pteryx,* a new organism from the Middle Cambrian Burgess Shale of British Columbia. *Neues Jahrbuch für Geologie und Paläontologie, Monatshefte* 12:705–713.

———. 1977a. A new metazoan from the Cambrian Burgess Shale, British Columbia. *Palaeontology* 20:623–640.

———. 1977b. A new entoproct-like organism from the Burgess Shale of British Columbia. *Palaeontology* 20:833–845.

———. 1977c. A redescription of the Middle Cambrian worm *Amiskwia sagittiformis* Walcott from the Burgess Shale of British Columbia. *Paläontologische Zeitschrift* 51:271–287.

———. 1977d. Fossil priapulid worms. *Special Papers in Palaeontology* 20.

———. 1978. *Laggania cambria* Walcott: A composite fossil. *Journal of Paleontology* 52:126–131.

———. 1979a. Middle Cambrian polychaetes from the Burgess Shale of British Columbia. *Philosophical Transactions of the Royal Society of London Series B* 285:227–274.

———. 1979b. The Burgess Shale (Middle Cambrian) fauna. *Annual Review of Ecology and Systematics* 10:327–349.

———. 1979c. Burgess Shale, pp. 153–160. In R. W. Fairbridge and D. Jablonski (eds.), *Encyclopedia of Paleontology.* Stroudsburg, Pennsylvania: Dowden, Hutchinson, and Ross.

———. 1981a. The Burgess Shale fauna as a mid-Cambrian community, pp. 47–49. In M. E. Taylor (ed.), *Short Papers for the Second International Symposium on the Cambrian System.* U.S. Geological Survey Open-file Report 81-743.

———. 1981b. Parasites and the fossil record. *Parasitology* 82:489–509.

———. 1982a. *Wiwaxia corrugata* (Matthew). A problematical Middle Cambrian animal from the Burgess Shale of British Columbia, pp. 93–98. In B. Mamet and M. J. Copeland (eds.), *Proceedings of the Third North American Paleontological Convention, Montreal,* vol. 1.

———. 1982b. Burgess Shale. *McGraw-Hill Encyclopedia of Science and Technology,* 5th ed. 2:488–489.

———. 1985a. The Middle Cambrian metazoan *Wiwaxia corrugata* (Matthew) from the Burgess Shale and *Ogygopsis* Shale, British Columbia, Canada. *Philosophical Transactions of the Royal Society of London Series B* 307:507–582.

———. 1985b. Cambrian Lagerstätten: Their distribution and significance. *Philosophical Transactions of the Royal Society of London Series B* 311:49–65.

———. 1986. The community structure of the Middle Cambrian phyllopod bed (Burgess Shale). *Palaeontology* 29:423–467.

———. 1989a. Burgess Shale faunas and the Cambrian explosion. *Science* 246:339–346.

———. 1989b. The persistence of Burgess Shale-type faunas: Implications for the evolution of deep-water faunas. *Transactions of the Royal Society of Edinburgh* 80:271–283.

———. 1989c. Early metazoans. *Science Progress* (Oxford) 73:81–99.

———. 1990a. Late Precambrian and Cambrian soft-bodied faunas. *Annual Review of Earth and Planetary Sciences* 18:101–122.

———. 1990b. Burgess Shale, pp. 270–274. In D. E. G. Briggs and P. R. Crowther (eds.), *Palaeobiology — A Synthesis.* Oxford: Blackwell Scientific Publications.

———. 1990c. Palaeontology's hidden agenda. *New Scientist,* pp. 38–42.

———. 1992. Burgess Shale-type faunas in the context of the 'Cambrian explosion': A review. *Journal of the Geological Society, London* 149:631–636.

———. 1993. Ediacaran-like fossils in Cambrian Burgess Shale-type faunas of North America. *Palaeontology* 36(3): 539–635.

Conway Morris, S., and D. L. Bruton. 1981. Fossiler fra Burgess skiferen—innblick i en kambrisk dyreverden. *Naturen* 1981(2): 51–55.

Conway Morris, S., and D. W. T. Crompton. 1982. The origin and evolution of the *Acanthocephala. Biological Review* 56:85–115.

Conway Morris, S., and J. S. Peel. 1990. Articulated halkieriids from the Lower Cambrian of north Greenland. *Nature* 345:802–805.

Conway Morris, S., J. S. Peel, A. K. Higgins, N. J. Soper, and N. C. Davis. 1987. A Burgess Shale-like fauna from the Lower Cambrian of north Greenland. *Nature* 326:181–183.

Conway Morris, S., and R. A. Robison. 1982. The enigmatic medusoid *Peytoia* and a comparison of some Cambrian biotas. *Journal of Paleontology* 56:116–122.

———. 1986. Middle Cambrian priapulids and other soft-bodied fossils from Utah and Spain. *University of Kansas Paleontological Contributions* 117.

———. 1988. More soft-bodied animals and algae from the Middle Cambrian of Utah and British Columbia. *University of Kansas Paleontological Contributions* 122.

Conway Morris, S., and H. B. Whittington. 1979. The animals of the Burgess Shale. *Scientific American* 241:122–133.

———. 1985. Fossils of the Burgess Shale. A national treasure in Yoho National Park, British Columbia. *Geological Survey of Canada, Miscellaneous Reports* 43:1–31.

———. 1986. The Burgess Shale—A world heritage site in Canada's Rockies yields the richest Cambrian fossil record. *Geos* 1986/1: 6–9.

Conway Morris, S., H. B. Whittington, D. E. G. Briggs, C. P. Hughes, and D. L. Bruton. 1982. *Atlas of the Burgess Shale.* London: Palaeontological Association.

Dahl, E. 1983. Phylogenetic systematics and the Crustacea Malacostraca—A problem of prerequisites. *Verhandlungen des naturwissenschaftlichen Vereins in Hamburg* 26:355–371.

———. 1984. The subclass Phyllocarida (Crustacea) and the status of some early fossils; a neontologist's view. *Videnskabelige Meddelelser fra Dansk naturhistorisk Forening* 145:61–76.

Deiss, C. 1939. Cambrian formations of southwestern Alberta and southeastern British Columbia. *Bulletin of the Geological Society of America* 50:951–1026.

———. 1940. Lower and Middle Cambrian stratigraphy of southwestern Alberta and southeastern British Columbia. *Bulletin of the Geological Society of America* 51:731–794.

de Laubenfels, M. W. 1955. Porifera, pp. E21–E112. In R. C. Moore (ed.), *Treatise on Invertebrate Paleontology, Part E. Archaeocyatha and Porifera.* Lawrence, Kansas: Geological Society of America and University of Kansas Press.

Delle Cave, L., and A. M. Simonetta. 1975. Notes on the morphology and taxonomic position of *Aysheaia* (Onychophora?) and of *Skania* (undetermined phylum). *Monitore Zoologico Italiano,* n.s. 9:67–81.

———. 1991. Early Paleozoic arthropods and problems of arthropod phylogeny; with notes on taxa of doubtful affinities, pp. 189–244. In A. M. Simonetta and S. Conway Morris (eds.), *The Early Evolution of Metazoa and the Significance of Problematic Taxa.* Cambridge: Cambridge University Press.

Donovan, S. K. 1988. The early evolution of the Crinoidea, pp. 235–244. In C. R. C. Paul and A. B. Smith (eds.), *Echinoderm Phylogeny and Evolutionary Biology.* Oxford: Clarendon Press.

Durham, J. W. 1974. Systematic position of *Eldonia ludwigi* Walcott. *Journal of Paleontology* 48:750–755.

Fedotov, D. 1925. On the relations between the Crustacea, Trilobita, Merostomata and Arachnida. *Bulletin de l'Académie des Sciences de Russie,* pp. 383–408.

Fortey, R. A. 1983. The Burgess Shale. Strange animals from the Cambrian seas. *Nature* 302:570.

Fritz, W. H. 1968. Middle Cambrian trilobite studies near Field, British Columbia. *Canadian Geological Survey Paper* 68-1A: 102.

———. 1971. Geological setting of the Burgess Shale, pp. 1155–1170. In *Proceedings of the North American Paleontological Convention, Chicago, 1969,* vol. 1. Lawrence, Kansas: Allen Press.

———. 1990. In defense of the escarpment near the Burgess Shale fossil locality. *Geoscience Canada* 17:106–110.

Gore, R. 1993. Explosion of life: The Cambrian Period. *National Geographic* 184:120–136.

Gould, S. J. 1985. Treasures in a taxonomic wastebasket. *Natural History* 1985/12: 22–33.

———. 1986a. A short way to big ends. *Natural History* 1986/1: 18–28.

———. 1986b. Play it again, life. *Natural History* 1986/2: 18–26.

———. 1988. A web of tales. *Natural History* 1988/10: 16–23.

———. 1989. *Wonderful Life: The Burgess Shale and the Nature of History.* New York: W. W. Norton & Co.

———. 1990. In touch with Walcott. *Natural History* 1990/7: 10–19.

———. 1991a. The disparity of the Burgess Shale arthropod fauna and the limits of cladistic analysis: Why we must strive to quantify morphospace. *Paleobiology* 17:411–423.

———. 1991b. Origines de l'homme. L'animal qui change tout. Un entretien avec le Pr. Stephen Jay Gould. *L'Express* July 1991, pp. 52–60.

Gunther, L. F., and V. G. Gunther. 1981. Some Middle Cambrian fossils of Utah. *Brigham Young University Geology Studies* 28:1–87.

Henriksen, K. L. 1928. Critical notes upon some Cambrian arthropods described by Charles D. Walcott. *Videnskabelige Meddelelser fra Dansk Naturhistorisk Forening: Khobenhavn* 86:1–20.

Hinde, G. J. 1887. A monograph of the British fossil sponges, Part 1, pp. 1–92. *Palaeontographical Society Monographs.* London.

Hou, X.-G. 1987. Early Cambrian large bivalved arthropods from Chengjiang, eastern Yunnan. *Acta Palaeontologica Sinica* 26:286–298.

Hou, X.-G., and W.-G. Sun. 1988. Discovery of Chengjiang fauna at Meichucun, Jinning, Yunnan. *Acta Palaeontologica Sinica* 27:1–12.

Hughes, C. P. 1975. Redescription of *Burgessia bella* from the Middle Cambrian Burgess Shale, British Columbia. *Fossils and Strata* 4:415–436.

Hutchinson, G. E. 1931. Restudy of some Burgess Shale fossils. *Proceedings of the United States National Museum* 78(11):1–24.

———. 1969. *Aysheaia* and the general morphology of the Onychophora. *American Journal of Science* 267:1062–1066.

Knight, C. R. 1942. Parade of life through the ages. *National Geographic Magazine* 81:141–184.

Lessem, D. 1993. 'Weird wonders' fuel a battle over evolution's path. *Smithsonian* (January): 107–115.

Lohmann, H. 1921. *Oesia disjuncta* Walcott, eine Appendicularie aus dem Kambrium. *Mitteilungen aus dem Zoologischen Staatsinstitut und Zoologischen Museum in Hamburg, Beiheft zum Jahrbuch der Hamburgischen Wissenschaftlichen Anstalten* 38:69–75.

Ludvigsen, R. 1989. The Burgess Shale: Not in the shadow of the Cathedral escarpment. *Geoscience Canada* 16(2): 51–59.

———. 1990. Reply to comments by Fritz and Aitken and McIlreath. *Geoscience Canada* 17:116–118.

McIlreath, I. A. 1977. Accumulation of a Middle Cambrian, deep-water limestone debris apron adjacent to a vertical, submarine carbonate escarpment, southern Rocky Mountains, Canada. *Society of Economic Paleontologists and Mineralogists, Special Publication* 25:113–124.

Madsen, F. J. 1956. *Eldonia* a Cambrian siphonophore—formerly interpreted as a holothurian. *Meddelelser Dansk Naturhistorisk Forening* 118:7–14.

———. 1957. On Walcott's supposed Cambrian holothurians. *Journal of Paleontology* 31:281–282.

———. 1962. The systematic position of the Middle Cambrian fossil *Eldonia*. *Meddelelser Dansk Geologisk Forening* 15:87–89.

Massa, W. R., Jr. 1984. Guide to the Charles D. Walcott Collection, 1851–1940. *Guides to Collections*. Archives and Special Collections of the Smithsonian Institution, Washington.

Matthew, G. F. 1899. Studies on Cambrian faunas, no. 3: Upper Cambrian fauna of Mt. Stephen, British Columbia. *Transactions of the Royal Society of Canada*, Series 2, 5:39–66.

———. 1902. Notes on Cambrian faunas. *Transactions of the Royal Society of Canada* 8(4): 93–112.

Montastersky, R. 1993. Mysteries of the Orient. *Discover* 14 (April): 38–48.

Owre, H. B., and F. M. Bayer. 1962. The systematic position of the Middle Cambrian fossil *Amiskwia* Walcott. *Paleontological Notes* 36(6): 1361–1393.

Paul, C. R. C., and A. B. Smith. 1984. The early radiation and phylogeny of echinoderms. *Biological Review* 59:443–481.

Piper, D. J. W. 1972. Sediments of the Middle Cambrian Burgess Shale, Canada. *Lethaia* 5:169–175.

Pringle, H. 1989. Stone bestiary. *Equinox* (May/June): 47–57.

Ramsköld, L. 1992. The second leg row of *Hallucigenia* discovered. *Lethaia* 25:221–224.

———. 1992. Homologies in Cambrian Onychophora. *Lethaia* 25:443–460.

Ramsköld, L., and X.-G. Hou. 1991. New early Cambrian animal and onychophoran affinities of enigmatic metazoans. *Nature* 351:225–228.

Rasetti, F. 1951. Middle Cambrian stratigraphy and faunas of the Canadian Rocky Mountains. *Smithsonian Miscellaneous Collections* 116:1–277.

———. 1954. Internal shell structures in the Middle Cambrian gastropod *Scenella* and the problematic genus *Stenothecoides*. *Journal of Paleontology* 28:59–66.

———. 1963. Middle Cambrian ptychoparioid trilobites from the conglomerates of Quebec. *Journal of Paleontology* 37:575–594.

Raymond, P. E. 1913. Chapter on Trilobites (revised by Dr. Percy E. Raymond), pp. 691–730. In K. A. von Zittel, *Paleontology* (translation by C. R. Eastman [ed.]). London: MacMillan.

———. 1920a. The appendages, anatomy and relationships of trilobites. *Memoirs of the Connecticut Academy of Arts and Sciences* 7:1–169.

———. 1920b. Phylogeny of the Arthropoda with especial reference to the trilobites. *American Naturalist* 54:398–413.

———. 1931. Notes on invertebrate fossils, with descriptions of new species. *Bulletin of the Museum of Comparative Zoology, Harvard University* 55(6): 165–213.

———. 1935. *Leanchoilia* and other Mid-Cambrian Arthropoda. *Bulletin of the Museum of Comparative Zoology, Harvard University* 76(6): 205–230.

Raymond, P. E., and B. Willard. 1931. A structure section across the Canadian Rockies. *Journal of Geology* 39(2): 97–116.

Reed, F. R. C. 1899. A new trilobite from Mount Stephen, Field, B. C. *Geological Magazine,* n.s., dec. 4 6:358–361.

Resser, C. E. 1929. New Lower and Middle Cambrian Crustacea. *Proceedings of the United States National Museum* 76:1–18.

———. 1935. Nomenclature of some Cambrian trilobites. *Smithsonian Miscellaneous Collections* 93(5): 1–46.

———. 1936. Second contribution to nomenclature of Cambrian fossils. *Smithsonian Miscellaneous Collections* 95(4): 1–29.

———. 1937. Third contribution to nomenclature of Cambrian fossils. *Smithsonian Miscellaneous Collections* 95(22): 1–29.

———. 1938. Fourth contribution to nomenclature of Cambrian fossils. *Smithsonian Miscellaneous Collections* 97(10): 1–43.

———. 1942. Fifth contribution to nomenclature of Cambrian fossils. *Smithsonian Miscellaneous Collections* 101(15): 1–58.

Rigby, J. K. 1986. Sponges of the Burgess Shale (Middle Cambrian) British Columbia. *Palaeontographica Canada* 2:1–105.

Robison, R. A. 1984. New occurrences of the unusual trilobite *Naraoia* from the Cambrian of Idaho and Utah, pp. 1–8. *University of Kansas Paleontological Contributions* 112.

———. 1985. Affinities of *Aysheaia* (Onychophora) with description of a new Cambrian species. *Journal of Paleontology* 59:226–235.

Rolfe, W. D. I. 1962. Two new arthropod carapaces from the Burgess Shale (Middle Cambrian) of Canada. *Breviora (Museum of Comparative Zoology, Harvard University)* 160:1–9.

Rominger, C. 1887. Description of primordial fossils from Mt. Stephens, N.W. Territory of Canada. *Proceedings of the Academy of Natural Sciences of Philadelphia* 1887:12–19.

Ruedemann, R. 1931. Some new Middle Cambrian fossils from British Columbia. *Proceedings of the United States National Museum* 79:1–18.

Satterthwait, D. F. 1976. Paleobiology and paleoecology of Middle Cambrian algae from western North America. Ph.D. dissertation, University of California, Los Angeles.

Schuchert, C. 1927. Charles Doolittle Walcott, paleontologist, 1850–1927. *Science* 65:455–458.

———. 1928. Charles Doolittle Walcott (1850–1927). *Proceedings of the American Academy of Arts and Sciences* 62:276–285.

Simonetta, A. M. 1962. Note sugli artropodi non trilobiti della Burgess Shale, cambriano medio della Columbia Britannica (Canada). *Monitore Zoologico Italiano* 69:172–185.

———. 1963. Osservazioni sugli artropodi non trilobiti della 'Burgess Shale' (Cambriano medio). *Monitore Zoologico Italiano* 70–71:99–108.

———. 1964. Osservazioni sugli artropodi non trilobiti della 'Burgess Shale' (Cambriano medio). III contributo. *Monitore Zoologico Italiano* 72:215–231.

———. 1970. Studies on non-trilobite arthropods of the Burgess Shale (Middle Cambrian). *Palaeontographica Italica* 66 (n.s. 36): 35–45.

———. 1976. Remarks on the origin of the Arthropoda. *Atti della Società Toscana di Scienze Naturali, Memorie* (1975), B 82:112–134.

———. 1988. Is *Nectocaris pteryx* a chordate? *Bollettino di Zoologia* 55:63–68.

Simonetta, A. M., and L. Delle Cave. 1975. The Cambrian non-trilobite arthropods from the Burgess Shale of British Columbia. A study of their comparative morphology, taxinomy [*sic*] and evolutionary significance. *Palaeontographica Italica* 69 (n.s. 39): 1–37.

———. 1978a. Notes on new and strange Burgess Shale fossils (Middle Cambrian of British Columbia). *Atti della Società Toscana di Scienze Naturali, Memorie,* A 85:45–49.

———. 1978b. Una possibile interpretazioni filogenetica degli artropodi paleozoici. *Bollettino di Zoologia* 45:87–90.

———. 1980. The phylogeny of the Palaeozoic arthropods. *Bollettino di Zoologia* 47(supplement): 1–19.

———. 1981. An essay in the comparative and evolutionary morphology of Palaeozoic arthropods. *Atti dei Convegni Lincei, Roma* 49:389–439.

———. 1982. New fossil animals from the Middle Cambrian. *Bollettino di Zoologia* 49:107–114.

Simonetta, A. M., and E. Insom. 1993. New animals from the Burgess Shale (Middle Cambrian) and their possible significance for the understanding of the Bilateria. *Bollettino di Zoologia* 60:97–107.

Smith, A. B. 1984. Classification of the Echinodermata. *Palaeontology* 27:431–459.

Smith, G. O. 1928. Charles Doolittle Walcott. *Smithsonian Report for 1927,* pp. 555–561.

Sprinkle, J. 1973. Morphology and evolution of blastozoan echinoderms. *Museum of Comparative Zoology, Harvard University, Special Publication.*

Sprinkle, J., and R. C. Moore. 1978. Echmatocrinea, pp. 405–407. In R. C. Moore and C. Teichert (eds.), *Treatise on Invertebrate Paleontology, Part T, Echinodermata 2.* Lawrence, Kansas: Geological Society of America and University of Kansas Press.

Stewart, W. D. 1991. Stratigraphy and sedimentology of the lower and middle Chandellor "Group," Rocky Mountain Ranges, southeastern British Columbia. Ph.D. dissertation, University of Ottawa, Ottawa, Ontario.

Stewart, W. D., O. A. Dixon, and B. R. Rust. 1993. Middle Cambrian Canadian Rocky Mountains. *Geology* 21:687–690.

Stolzenburg, W. 1990. Back when life got hard. *Science News* 138(8): 120–123.

Størmer, L. 1939. Studies on trilobite morphology. Part 1. The thoracic appendages and their phylogenetic significance. *Norsk Geologisk Tidsskrift* 19:143–273.

———. 1944. On the relationships and phylogeny of fossil and recent Arachnomorpha. *Skrifter Utgitt av det Norske Videnskaps-Akademi i Oslo, 1: Matenatisk-naturvidenskapelig Klasse* 5:1–158.

Taft, W. H., J. C. Merriam, J. S. Anes, G. O. Smith, and C. G. Abott. 1928. Charles Doolittle Walcott: Memorial meeting, January 24, 1928. *Smithsonian Miscellaneous Collections* 80(12): 1–37.

Walcott, C. D. 1908a. Mount Stephen rocks and fossils. *Canadian Alpine Journal* 1(2): 232–248.

———. 1908b. Cambrian trilobites. Cambrian Geology and Paleontology. *Smithsonian Miscellaneous Collections* (part of vol. LIII): 13–52.

———. 1910. Abrupt appearance of the Cambrian fauna on the North American continent. Cambrian Geology and Paleontology II. *Smithsonian Miscellaneous Collections* 57:1–16.

———. 1911a. Middle Cambrian Merostomata. Cambrian Geology and Paleontology II. *Smithsonian Miscellaneous Collections* 57:17–40.

———. 1911b. A geologist's paradise. *National Geographic Magazine* 22:509–521.

———. 1911c. Middle Cambrian Holothurians and Medusae. Cambrian Geology and Paleontology II. *Smithsonian Miscellaneous Collections* 57:41–68.

———. 1911d. Middle Cambrian Annelids. Cambrian Geology and Paleontology II. *Smithsonian Miscellaneous Collections* 57:109–144.

———. 1912a. Middle Cambrian Branchiopoda, Malacostraca, Trilobita and Merostomata. Cambrian Geology and Paleontology II. *Smithsonian Miscellaneous Collections* 57:145–228.

———. 1912b. Cambrian of the Kicking Horse Valley, British Columbia. *Summary Report Geological Survey Branch, Department of Mines, Canada, 1911, Sessional Paper* 26:188–191.

———. 1912c. Studies in Cambrian geology and paleontology in the Canadian Rockies. In Expeditions organized or participated in by the Smithsonian Institution in 1910 and 1911. *Smithsonian Miscellaneous Collections* 59:39–45.

———. 1912d. Cambrian Brachiopoda. *United States Geological Survey Monograph* 51: pt. 1, 1–872; pt. 2, 1–363.

———. 1913. Geological exploration in the Canadian Rockies. In Explorations and fieldwork of the Smithsonian Institution in 1912. *Smithsonian Miscellaneous Collections* 60:24–31.

———. 1914. Geological explorations in the Canadian Rockies. In Explorations and fieldwork of the Smithsonian Institution in 1913. *Smithsonian Miscellaneous Collections* 63:2–12.

———. 1916a. Evidence of primitive life. *Annual Report of the Smithsonian Institution for 1915*, pp. 235–255.

———. 1916b. Cambrian trilobites. Cambrian Geology and Paleontology III. *Smithsonian Miscellaneous Collections* 64:303–456.

———. 1918a. Geological explorations in the Canadian Rockies. In Explorations and fieldwork of the Smithsonian Institution in 1917. *Smithsonian Miscellaneous Collections* 68:4–20.

———. 1918b. Appendages of trilobites. Cambrian Geology and Paleontology IV. *Smithsonian Miscellaneous Collections* 67:115–216.

———. 1919. Middle Cambrian Algae. Cambrian Geology and Paleontology IV. *Smithsonian Miscellaneous Collections* 67:217–260.

———. 1920. Middle Cambrian Spongiae. Cambrian Geology and Paleontology IV. *Smithsonian Miscellaneous Collections* 67:261–364.

———. 1921. Notes on structure of *Neolenus*. Cambrian Geology and Paleontology IV. *Smithsonian Miscellaneous Collections* 67:365–456.

———. 1922. Geological explorations in the Canadian Rockies. Explorations and Field-Work of the Smithsonian Institution in 1921. *Smithsonian Miscellaneous Collections* 72:1–22.

———. 1923a. Nomenclature of some Post Cambrian and Cambrian Cordilleran formations (2). Cambrian Geology and Paleontology IV. *Smithsonian Miscellaneous Collections* 67:457–476.

———. 1923b. Geological explorations in the Canadian Rockies. Explorations and Field-Work of the Smithsonian Institutions in 1922. *Smithsonian Miscellaneous Collections* 74:1–24.

———. 1924a. Cambrian and Ozarkian Brachiopoda. Cambrian Geology and Paleontology IV. *Smithsonian Miscellaneous Collections* 67:477–554.

———. 1924b. Geological explorations in the Canadian Rockies. Explorations and Field-Work of the Smithsonian Institutions in 1923. *Smithsonian Miscellaneous Collections* 76:1–8.

———. 1925. Geological explorations in the Canadian Rockies. Explorations and Field-Work of the Smithsonian Institutions in 1924. *Smithsonian Miscellaneous Collections* 77:1–14.

———. 1926. Geological explorations in the Canadian Rockies. Explorations and Field-Work of the Smithsonian Institutions in 1925. *Smithsonian Miscellaneous Collections* 78:1–9.

———. 1928. Pre-Devonian paleozoic formations of the Cordilleran provinces of Canada. Cambrian Geology and Paleontology V. *Smithsonian Miscellaneous Collections* 75:175–368.

———. 1931. Addenda to descriptions of Burgess Shale fossils. *Smithsonian Miscellaneous Collections* 85:1–46 (with explanatory notes by Charles E. Resser).

Walcott, S. S. 1971. How I found my own fossil. *Smithsonian* 1(12): 28–29.

Walton, J. 1923. On the structure of a Middle Cambrian alga from British Columbia (*Marpolia spissa* Walcott). *Proceedings of the Cambridge Philosophical Society, Biological Sciences* 1:59–62.

Westergaard, A. H. 1936. *Paradoxides oelandicus* beds of Ooland, with an account of diamond boring through the Cambrian at Mossberga. *Sveriges Geologiska Undersokning Arsbok Series C,* no. 394, 30 (1936), no. 1.

Whiteaves, J. F. 1892. Description of a new genus and species of phyllocarid crustacea from the Middle Cambrian of Mount Stephen, B.C. *Canadian Record of Science* 5:205–208.

Whittington, H. B. 1971a. The Burgess Shale: History of research and preservation of fossils, pp. 1170–1201. In *Proceedings of the North American Paleontological Convention, Chicago, 1969,* vol. 1. Lawrence, Kansas: Allen Press.

———. 1971b. Redescription of *Marrella splendens* (Trilobitoidea) from the Burgess Shale, Middle Cambrian, British Columbia. *Geological Survey of Canada Bulletin* 209:1–24.

———. 1974. *Yohoia* Walcott and *Plenocaris* n. gen., arthropods from the Burgess Shale, Middle Cambrian, British Columbia. *Geological Survey of Canada Bulletin* 231:1–21 (figs. 1–6 of plate X should be interchanged with figs. 1–5 of plate XII).

———. 1975a. The enigmatic animal *Opabinia regalis,* Middle Cambrian, Burgess Shale, British Columbia. *Philosophical Transactions of the Royal Society of London Series B* 271:1–43.

———. 1975b. Trilobites with appendages from the Middle Cambrian, Burgess Shale, British Columbia. *Fossils and Strata* 4:97–136.

———. 1977. The Middle Cambrian trilobite *Naraoia,* Burgess Shale, British Columbia. *Philosophical Transactions of the Royal Society of London Series B* 280:409–443.

———. 1978. The lobopod animal *Aysheaia pedunculata* Walcott, Middle Cambrian, Burgess Shale, British Columbia. *Philosophical Transactions of the Royal Society of London Series B* 284:165–197.

———. 1979. Early arthropods, their appendages and relationships, pp. 253–268. In M. R. House (ed.), *The Origin of Major Invertebrate Groups.* Systematics Association, Special Volume 12. London: Academic Press.

———. 1980a. Exoskeleton, moult stage, appendage morphology and habits of the Middle Cambrian trilobite *Olenoides serratus. Palaeontology* 23:171–204.

———. 1980b. The significance of the fauna of the Burgess Shale, Middle Cambrian, British Columbia. *Proceedings of the Geologists' Association* 91:127–148.

———. 1981a. Cambrian animals: Their ancestors and descendants. *Proceedings of the Linnean Society, New South Wales* 105:79–87.

———. 1981b. Rare arthropods from the Burgess Shale, Middle Cambrian, British Columbia. *Philosophical Transactions of the Royal Society of London Series B* 292:329–357.

———. 1982. The Burgess Shale fauna and the early evolution of metazoan animals, pp. 11–24. In E. M. Gallitelli (ed.), *Paleontology, Essentials of Historical Geology.* Modena: STEM Mucchi.

———. 1985a. *Tegopelte gigas,* a second soft-bodied trilobite from the Burgess Shale, Middle Cambrian, British Columbia. *Journal of Paleontology* 59:1251–1274.

———. 1985b. *The Burgess Shale.* New Haven: Yale University Press.

Whittington, H. B., and D. E. G. Briggs (eds.). 1982. A new conundrum from the Middle Cambrian Burgess Shale, pp. 573–575. In B. Mamet and M. J. Copeland (eds.), *Proceedings of the Third North American Paleontological Convention, Montreal,* vol. 2. Department of Geology, University of Montreal, Montreal, and Geological Survey of Canada, Ottawa.

———. 1985. The largest Cambrian animal, *Anomalocaris,* Burgess Shale, British Columbia. *Philosophical Transactions of the Royal Society of London Series B* 309:569–609.

Whittington, H. B., and S. Conway Morris (eds.). 1985. Extraordinary fossil biotas: Their ecological and evolutionary significance. London: Royal Society. [Published originally in *Philosophical Transactions of the Royal Society of London Series B* 311:1–192.]

Yochelson, E. L. 1961. The operculum and mode of life of *Hyolithes. Journal of Paleontology* 35:152–161.

———. 1967. Charles Doolittle Walcott, 1850–1927. *Biographical Memoirs, National Academy of Sciences of the United States* 39:471–540.

———. 1987. Walcott in Albany, New York: James Hall's "special assistant." *Earth Sciences History* 6(1): 86–94.

———. 1988. The Bulletin of the Geological Sociey of America and Charles Doolittle Walcott. *Geological Society of America Bulletin* 100:3–11.

Index

Page numbers in italics indicate descriptions of genera